GREEN & SILVER

L.T.C. ROLT

With photographs by Angela Rolt

CANALBOOKSHOP

GREEN & SILVER

L.T.C. ROLT

To Angela
who suggested this
Irish Journey

First edition published by Allen & Unwin 1949; Second impression 1968
Third edition published by the Athlone Branch
of the Inland Waterways Association of Ireland 1993
Fourth edition published in Ireland by Shackleton Publishing (Varsity Press Group) 2011

Fifth edition November 2015
Reprinted March 2016, October 2017, December 2020, April 2023
CanalBookShop
Audlem Mill Limited The Wharf Audlem Cheshire CW3 0DX

ISBN 978-0-9574037-5-8

CONTENTS

ACKNOWLEDGMENTS

I should like to pay tribute to the kindness and unfailing help of all those Irish people (and this includes everyone that we met) who contributed to the success of the journey which is the subject of this book.

I also wish to thank Messrs. The Grand Canal Company and of Coras Iompair Eireann for their courteous assistance when I passed through their respective canals, and also for their subsequent help in checking the Itinerary which appears as an Appendix to this book.

Most of my information relating to the history of the Irish waterways was obtained from contemporary sources, but I would like, in conclusion, to acknowledge my indebtedness to the following recent works to which I have referred:-

Brendan the Navigator, by Doctor George Little.
I Remember Maynooth, by Neil Kevin.
Where the River Shannon Flows, by Richard Hayward.
Narrow Gauge Railways of Ireland, by H. Fayle.
'Are Ye Right There Michael' is inserted by special permission of Pigott & Co., Ltd., Dublin - owners of the Copyright.

L. T. C. R.
1949

FOREWORD TO THE FIFTH EDITION, 2015

When Angela had the idea for this Irish journey, they left behind their narrow boat home *Cressy* at Tooley's boatyard in Banbury. They set off for a land neither of them had visited before, to a waterways system little known and even less well recorded.

The resulting book has a freshness and lightness of touch, and the accompanying photographs are a wonderfully evocative record of that time. It is as much an account of the weather and the changing scenery as it is an account of the canals as they found them. It is also very much the story of the people and the villages, the towns and the landscapes, they encountered on their way. However its chief subject, in common with much my father wrote, is the reciprocal shaping of people and place. My father was clearly charmed by what he found in Ireland. As he states it, the industrial revolution had largely passed Ireland by, so the canal system is an altogether more rural affair than its English counterpart. So this then, is a story of deep pastoral Ireland, a land that time had largely forgotten. From the vantage point of 2015 it seems a very remote and dreamlike place and I wonder just how much has changed?

It is very pleasing to record that their triangular canal journey is now once again navigable. The Royal Canal became impassable soon after their voyage and the canal lay moribund for many years. Thanks to the heroic and persistent efforts of lobbyists and volunteers, the Royal Canal was reopened in 2010. I don't think this is something my father would have ever predicted. In a generous tribute to the part this book played, the triangular passage has now become known as the Green & Silver route. That these tranquil waterways are once again open for exploration and discovery by a new generation is indeed something to celebrate.

As to the book itself, it is a curious mixture of the humdrum everyday requirements of eking out limited petrol supplies, or the difficulties of passing in a small craft through some of the locks, to descriptions of encounters with a very mixed and rich cast of characters; from the piper Michael, the tinker families of the Byrnes and the McGinley's, to Sir Cecil Stafford King-Harman, owner of Rockingham House...to meditations on the catholic church and its effect on people and place... to the history and background to the building of the canals themselves.

Principally Tom and Angela found that in Ireland there was always a sense that there was 'time enough'. Indeed a slowed down pace is something the book itself achieves which perhaps lends the narrative its beguilingly otherworldly quality - remote, yet somehow comforting - taking us into a world of light and weather, a world that moves at a comfortable regulated pace, a world where there is time enough to stop and stare.

As Tom put it:

"…our journey from Athlone to Dublin and back to the Shannon could have been accomplished by car in half a day or by air in an hour or so, but this is mere movement, it is not travel. Travel is not susceptible of measurement. A ten-mile walk can store the mind with memories while a hundred-mile car journey can leave it empty."

This book is a gloriously slow and leisurely store of memories, sights and sounds.

Tim Rolt
November 2015

FOREWORD TO THE SECOND IMPRESSION, 1968

This book describes a voyage through the inland waterways of Ireland in 1946. So little was known about these waterways then, that our journey was undertaken in a spirit of discovery, as a venture into the unknown. In Ireland, as in England, there has since been so great a revival of interest in inland waterways that a reprint of the book was felt to be justified.

Many English people think of Ireland as a country where the wind of change, if it blows at all, is only the gentlest of breezes. This is not so. In the twenty-one years that have elapsed there have been so many changes, some for the better, others saddening, that this book has become a part of history.

As an historical document, in some respects the book gains in interest. For example, the Royal Canal is now little more than a memory. I had no idea when I wrote my account of our voyage through the Royal from Dublin to the Shannon that 1 was writing its epitaph. Admittedly it was very little used even in 1946, but I too readily assumed that, like our own Kennet and Avon Canal, it might linger on for years, or even enjoy a revival as a cruising ground. In the event, however, the Royal became disused in 1951, when the last bye-trader, Leach of Killucan, whose horses took such exception to our boat when we passed him at Moyvalley, ceased to operate. Ten years later the canal was officially closed. So no one any more may follow in our wake through Maynooth and Mullingar to Cloondara on the Shannon, and I feel a kind of mournful satisfaction in having recorded for posterity, at the eleventh hour, what it was really like to voyage through this lost waterway.

On the Grand Canal and the Shannon Navigation the story is similar, though it has had a brighter sequel, thanks largely to the vigour of the campaign launched by the Inland Waterways Association of Ireland, formed in 1954. Only four years after my voyage, the Grand Canal Company ceased to exist when, on the advocacy of an inquiry held in 1948, it was taken over by the national transport authority. Thereafter, Coras Iompair Eireann became responsible for all commercial traffic operating over the Grand Canal and the Shannon. In 1958, however, on the recommendation of the Beddy Commission's Report on Internal Transport, C.I.E. were relieved of their obligation to carry goods by water and by 1960 all commercial traffic on canal and river had ceased. The Grand Canal was threatened with closure, and there were plans for fixed bridges over the Shannon of such restricted headroom that they would have closed the river to all but the smallest craft.

However, the Irish Inland Waterways Association's argument that canal and river were a potential asset to Ireland's tourist trade saved the day and both were reprieved. More than this, the Irish Tourist Board has since decided to invest £140,000 in waterway development.

In 1959, only seventy boats passed through Albert Lock at Jamestown on the Shannon, but by 1964 this number had grown to 1,672. This is a measure of the rate at which pleasure traffic is expanding. It is pleasant to know that these waterways will remain open so that others can enjoy what we enjoyed so many years ago: the broad sky-reflecting reaches of the Shannon and the sound of the wind in the reeds; the lonely levels of the Grand Canal, slicing across the Midland bogs. Nevertheless, I am glad I experienced these waterways when I did. For no canal or river can ever be quite the same when their commercial life is dead, when the low-laden craft are seen no more and once busy wharves grow silent.

Ireland, like England, has become a sad country for the railway enthusiast, particularly one who, like myself, has a particular affection for the narrow gauge. The little lines of Ireland are all gone now and our journeys over the Cavan and Leitrim and the West Clare Railways, described in this book, have, like our voyage through the Royal Canal, become a part of history. When I revisited it recently, Drumshambo station on the Cavan & Leitrim presented such a scene of desolation that recollections of my journey took on the quality of a dream. Could I ever have stepped into a train from that platform? If so, surely it must have been fifty, not twenty years ago. Beside Ennis station, once the junction for the West Clare line, a locomotive, salvaged from the wreck, stands upon a plinth, sole witness now to that slow, unrepeatable journey along the storm-swept western rim of Europe.

But if these changes, though inevitable, are saddening, others are to be welcomed as wholly for the good. There has been a vast improvement in social conditions in Ireland in the last twenty years and today you would never find a cabin such as we photographed at Abbeysrule. Again, the little town of Banagher, which I described in such unflattering terms, has been utterly changed until its appearance is as bright and seemly as that of its neighbour Portumna.

Above all, I am delighted to retract all the derogatory remarks I made in this book about the condition of that outstanding monument beside the Shannon - the Seven Churches of Clonmacnoise. I am happy to assure readers who have never visited Clonmacnoise that its appearance has been completely transformed, with smooth green lawns where once were weeds and rank untended grass. I have been told that my strictures have given some offence in Ireland, and for this I am sorry, yet if this provocation has helped in any way to bring about such a transformation, then it has served a useful purpose.

If I rejoice in Clonmacnoise, I mourn for Rockingham. For that masterpiece by John Nash has been completely destroyed by fire, caused, it is believed, by a defect in the central heating system while the family were away in England. Now this great house stands a gaunt ruin above the lake with its wooded islets and I have only the memory of its splendid circular drawing room. So, as the years pass, we count our gains and losses, but who can assess fairly the final score?

Although this book contains some historical background information about the Irish Waterways, it is primarily a personal account of a voyage of discovery. Historical information was hard to come by in 1946 but now, thanks to a great revival of interest in the subject, there is no such excuse. Any reader of this book who may be inspired by it to cruise on the Irish waterways will find the answers to all his historical questions in V.T.H. and D. R. Delany's book *The Canals of the South of Ireland*. I only wish I could have had it in my cabin on *Le Coq* in 1946, for a thorough knowledge of the past can add immeasurably to our appreciation of the present. But now *Green and Silver*, in a very different way, speaks also of things past. Some may derive added pleasure from the fact that it has become a tale of far away and long ago. Others may be tempted to see for themselves and venture out on the great lakes of Ree and Derg. To them I wish good sailing. They will find their channel better buoyed than we did.

1968
L. T. C. ROLT

THE IRISH CABIN AT ITS BEST. Cottage at Moghermore, near Clonmacnoise.

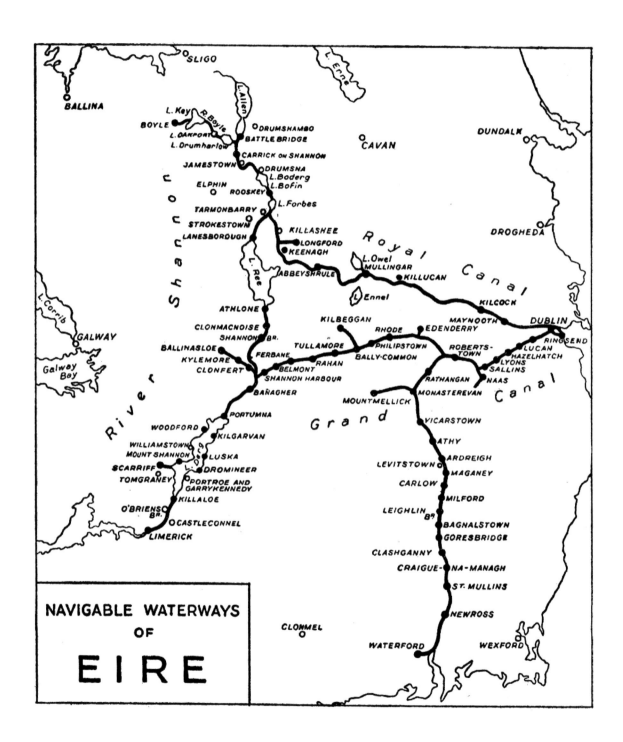

NAVIGABLE WATERWAYS
OF
EIRE

CHAPTER ONE

THE JOURNEY IS PLANNED

It was Samuel Smiles of 'Self Help' fame who really began it all. One winter's evening on board my own boat *Cressy* I was reading his *Life of John Rennie* when I came upon the following paragraph which amused me so much that I read it aloud to Angela.

'In 1802 Mr. Rennie was requested to examine the works of the Royal Canal of Ireland. The origin of this project was curious. The Grand Canal had already been formed to connect the navigation of the Liffey with that of the Shannon near Banagher; and though enormous blunders had marred its construction, and its cost had consequently been excessive, the traffic upon it was so great as nevertheless to render it exceedingly profitable to its proprietors. The managing committee consisted for the most part of persons of high rank, but amongst them was a retired shoemaker, who had invested a very large sum of money in the undertaking and made himself exceedingly busy in its concerns. Offence seems to have been taken at this person, and his meddling in various matters without authority caused a rupture between him and the other members of the committee. They thwarted him at every turn, outvoted him, snubbed him, and "sent him to Coventry". Vowing revenge, the shoemaker threw up his seat at the board, and, on parting with his colleagues, said to them, "You may think me a very insignificant person, but I will soon show you the contrary. I will sell out forthwith, start a rival canal, and carry all the traffic". The threat was, of course, treated with contempt, and the shoemaker was laughed out of the board-room. But the indignant man set to work with energy, got up a company, laid down a line of navigation from Dublin to the Shannon near Longford, passing by Mullingar, secured the support of the landed proprietors through whose property the line passed, and succeeded in obtaining an Act of Parliament authorizing the construction of the Royal Canal of Ireland, in an unusually short space of time. The works were commenced with great *éclat*, but, before they had proceeded far, it was found that the levels were entirely wrong, and there were numerous difficulties to be overcome for which no provision had been made. Then it was that Mr. Rennie was called in, and found the whole concern in confusion; the works at a standstill in many places, in bogs, in cuttings, in embankments, and in limestone rocks, and the proprietors involved in almost endless claims for compensation. He found it necessary to resurvey the whole line and to alter the plans in many essential respects; after which the works proceeded. It proved to be a work of an extraordinary character as, regarded the difficulties, mostly unnecessary, which had been encountered in its construction; but as respected the beneficial results to the proprietors, it proved an almost total failure. The shoemaker, no doubt, had his revenge upon his former associates, inflicting great injury upon the Grand Canal by the diversion of much of its traffic; but he accomplished this at a terrible sacrifice to many, and at the almost total loss of his own fortune'.

'Why shouldn't we explore the Irish canals?' asked Angela, when I had finished reading this. 'You know we've always wanted to go to Ireland. Don't you think that's a marvellous idea?' I agreed. It was a marvellous idea, but having an idea and putting it into execution were two very different things. In the first place, though my knowledge of the English canals was fairly extensive, I knew no more of the Irish waterways than was contained in the paragraph I had just read. I thought that the Grand Canal might still be navigable, but that if Smiles, writing in 1862, could describe the Royal Canal as 'an almost total failure', it was highly probable that it had become no more than a dry ditch like our Wey and Arun or Wilts and Berks Canals. Again *Cressy*, an English canal 'narrow boat' seventy feet long but only seven feet beam, could not make the necessary sea passage, while even if she could, she would probably be too long for the Irish Canal locks. We should have to charter a boat in Ireland.

We knew of no friends in Ireland who could give us any information about the canals or who could help us to hire a boat, while the only advice which an Irish friend in England could offer was the suggestion that we should write to the Irish Tourist Association in Dublin. I did so, but, knowing how difficult it is for the layman to obtain information about the canals in this country, I did not feel very sanguine of success. I was wrong, for I received a helpful and prompt reply giving me the addresses of the companies responsible. and informing me that: 'Both canals are still used for trade purposes having a 4 ft. navigation capable of taking a barge 61 ft. long with a beam of 12 ft. 11 in. and a headroom of 9 ft. The smallest lock would be capable of taking a barge of these dimensions.' Enclosed was a map of the Grand Canal system on which the line of the Royal Canal had been drawn in pencil, and a typed list of names and addresses of boat owners together with particulars of the craft available. This was very encouraging but, alas, the replies I received from the four owners whom I selected from the list were disappointing. One no longer had any craft available while two were even more discouraging. No fuel had been allowed for pleasure craft during the 'emergency' in Ireland, and to enforce compliance with this rule the Government had ordered the propellers of all pleasure craft to be removed. There was little likelihood of petrol being issued for this purpose during the coming year, and consequently their boats were laid up. But the fourth, a Mr. John Beahan of Athlone, sounded a little more hopeful. He had heard rumours of a petrol allowance next season, and had made application to the Department of Supplies. He owned *Le Coq*, a twenty-six feet by eight feet converted ship's lifeboat which was lying at moorings on the Shannon. She had been out of commission during the war, but he promised to have her refitted by the spring and supplied with all equipment including 'delph'. He also undertook to provide a fourteen feet boat to serve as a dinghy, while the proposed terms of charter were very reasonable. He enclosed a photograph of the boat, which showed that she had two cabins fore and aft of a central wheelhouse. As a rule I prefer an open aft cockpit on small craft of this type, but from what I had heard of the Irish climate I felt we might be glad of the protection of a wheelhouse.

As inspection was out of the question I was quite prepared to trust Mr. Beahan and agree to a three months' charter there and then, but unless we could be assured of fuel supplies, the boat would be useless. This was the insuperable obstacle. But by this time we had set our hearts on the idea and were not to be lightly discouraged. We examined every possible way out of the difficulty. We suggested to Mr. Beahan that he might convert the engine of his boat to burn paraffin, but he informed us that this was not only impracticable in this particular case, but that paraffin was as difficult to obtain as petrol. We could, I thought, bow-haul so light a boat through the canals or tow her with a donkey, but how could we cross the tidal river Liffey or the twenty miles of Lough Ree on the Shannon which separated one canal from the other? Some form of sail or power seemed essential. In desperation I tried unsuccessfully to find a small steam boat. I was accustomed to handling steam plant, and we could, I thought, fire her on turf.

Meanwhile the weeks slipped by and still Mr. Beahan received no reply to his application from the inscrutable Department of Supplies with whom the fate of the expedition now appeared to rest. By now we had arranged to move *Cressy* from her moorings on the Worcester and Birmingham Canal and to leave her at a yard at Banbury for repairs, so the situation was becoming desperate. I therefore agreed to charter *Le Coq* at a lower rate at her moorings, rising to the original rate if petrol was granted, or terminating the charter after one month if no supplies were forthcoming. At least, we reflected, we should see something of Ireland and would be able, meanwhile, to live very cheaply afloat. But it would be a poor alternative to the extensive journey which we had planned.

The fate of our voyage was still in the same state of uncertainty when, on the night of June 4th-5th, we stood on the deck of the Waterford steamer and watched the harbour lights of Fishguard slipping slowly astern.

INTRODUCTION TO IRELAND

ATHLONE AND LOUGH REE

Our first glimpse of Ireland was the bold promontory of Hook Point which we saw when we went on deck after an early breakfast. Thereafter we stood watching the steep hillsides and the little harbours of Duncannon, Arthurstown and Passage glide by as the steamer made her way slowly up the estuary of the Suir to her berth at Adelphi Wharf.

The name of Waterford to me means glass. Doubtless it will long continue to hold this association for many although the famous glasshouse of the Penrose family, that Irish seedling of far away Stourbridge which flowered in such crystalline beauty, has vanished long ago. Soon, even the site of it may be forgotten. But we had no time to search for recollections of the glass trade. Hiring a jaunting car for an extravagant sum we clattered along the grey waterfront towards the station to begin our long train journey to Athlone.

I have always been interested in railways, so that I looked forward to, and enjoyed, a journey which many people might have found tedious. I was prepared for antiquated rolling stock and hopeless unpunctuality, but I was wrong. Owing to the fuel shortage, the trains are slow and the service restricted but, in general, time-keeping was excellent. It may be thought that punctuality is easily achieved provided the timings are generous enough, but with only one train a day each way on most Irish lines, a far greater volume of parcels, luggage and mails has to be handled at stations than is usual on English railways. Consequently, as station stops are not unduly long, punctuality means smart work on the part of station staffs. Trains are clean and almost exclusively of corridor stock, while the broad gauge of five feet three inches (which was at once apparent to my eye) allows a wider corridor than is found on English coaches. The recently formed Coras Iompair Eireann have discarded the maroon livery of their Great Southern predecessors in favour of two shades of green, so that at present the trains have a mixed appearance which reminded me of the years which followed the English railway amalgamation.

Though we stopped at every station, we occasionally attained speeds which could not have been far short of the sixty mark because the average distance between stations is long. The stations themselves, clean, newly painted and bright with flowers in platform borders and hanging baskets, made me realize how grimy, drab and depressing the English railway station has become. I seem to remember when our country stations looked just as bright. At Carrick-on-Suir an enterprising tradesman boarded the train to sell chocolates and bananas, while at Clonmel a gentleman with a bright scarlet nose who moved in an aura of porter and turf smoke informed me in a hoarse whisper that I was missing the chance of a lifetime by declining to purchase his tip for the 2.30 at Limerick Junction.

The day was clear and sunny, and as we rumbled up the valley of the Suir and across the rich 'Golden Vein' lands of Tipperary a majestic succession of mountains moved slowly across the carriage windows. To the north, the Booleys and solitary Slievenamon; to the south, the Comeraghs, the Knockmealdowns and the Galtys, a magnificent range of peaks and ridges, purple as grapes against the sunlight in the clear air, which culminated in the 3000 feet summit of Galtymore.

At Limerick Junction we made our first prolonged stop to await connections from Cork and Dublin, and the entire train emptied itself into the refreshment room where bottles of Guinness and plates of ham sandwiches disappeared with astonishing speed. That Limerick Junction is over twenty miles from Limerick is a topographical detail which would occasion some surprise in England. It consists solely of the station, the racecourse and a cluster of cottages, and for the greater part of the day it slumbers like a strangely overgrown country station. But the meagre train service necessitates an elaborate system of connections, and for an hour or two at mid-day Limerick Junction becomes the scene of furious activity which few stations could equal as four trains converge upon it. This animated spectacle is further enlivened by the fact that the station is so designed that all these trains have to reverse into the platforms. When the Limerick and Waterford trains had manoeuvred into their respective bays, the Dublin and Cork trains thundered through and then reversed back to come to a stand facing each other at the single long platform. I wiled away the time of waiting by attempting without success to fathom the reason for this extraordinarily inconvenient track layout, and by watching the fires of the main line locomotives being virtually drawn and re-made while the passengers refreshed themselves. They were impressive six-coupled engines which reminded me of the original 'Royal Scot' class of the L.M. & S., and they had been built in the Great Southern shops at Inchicore in 1939. The war has left our own locomotives sadly blackened, so that the gleaming green paint and shining metalwork of these engines was a joy to the eye.

Eventually, the last passenger gulped his stout, the trains left Limerick Junction to wash up the crockery before resuming its interrupted slumber, and we continued our leisurely journey towards Athlone.

Two months later, an Irish friend at Portumna was to ask me what was the first impression I received when I landed in Ireland. It was a difficult question, and at this time I could not have answered it, for the multitudinous sights and sounds which clamour for attention on a long journey through a strange country do not allow the mind opportunity for the reflection necessary to register impressions. But when the question was put there had been

IRISH BROAD GAUGE. Cork-Dublin train at Limerick Junction. Gleaming green paint and shining metalwork were a joy to the eye.

ample opportunity, and I was able to answer without much hesitation that it was the slower pace of living which first impressed me. It had nothing to do with the slow speed of the journey. It was something much more profound; a fundamental characteristic of the Irish mind which has determined the rhythm of life. Very soon my own mind was to become attuned to it, and I was to find it illustrated in many ways; in the few public clocks which were almost always stopped; in the cheerful use of 'New' (Summer) or 'Old' (Greenwich) time whichever best suited the occasion; in the unhesitating suspension of any business for the sake of conversation or argument, and in the familiar rebuke to the hasty: or impatient: 'Time enough' - an expression which we soon used quite naturally ourselves. One of the symptoms of the effect of this altered rhythm upon, us was that we would murmur 'Time enough' with contented resignation in face of unpunctual trains or other unexpected delays, while examples of punctuality and efficiency positively delighted us, although by no means rare. On such occasions we would reflect that in England we took for granted an almost mechanical standard of efficiency and were frequently irritated beyond bearing when it was not forthcoming.

Now the bustling and efficient Anglo-Saxon may dismiss all this as mere evidence of the shiftlessness of the Irish race abetted by a mild, relaxing climate. He would say it was the reason why Ireland was 'backward,' 'unprogressive' and could never become a Great Power. Yet when I began to compare the serenity and ease of the average Irishman with the set-faced hurrying crowds of our own great cities, I wondered whether perhaps we have lost the measure of progress and of greatness. The average Anglo-Saxon is a materialist, and in his absorption with things temporal he has unwittingly become the slave of time. The Irishman, however, consciously or unconsciously, still holds the religious view of man *sub specie eternitas*. So long as he retains this vision he must remain the master of time. Who then shall say that he is not more truly civilized?

We spent our first night in Ireland at Limerick, as it was impossible to complete our journey in one day. Because our train for Athlone left early, we did not have much opportunity to see the city, but we knew that if our plans matured we should return again. Yet two things remain in my mind to recall this occasion. One is the excellent sherry we had before dinner in our hotel. It was the first good glass of sherry we had-tasted for five years. The other is the ticket we obtained for the trunk which we deposited in the cloakroom at the station. I have a habit of examining such unconsidered trifles, for sometimes, as in this case, they are unexpectedly rewarding. In small type on the reverse of this ticket was a scale of charges applicable to various items of passengers' luggage deposited. From this I learned that if I carried Hucksters' or Packmens' Luggage a mere threepence would suffice, whereas I should have had to expend the sum of eightpence if I had brought with me a Bass Viol, a Cash Register, a Harp, an Ice Cream Cart or ditto Freezer, an Organ (Street) or Piano (Street), a Scissor Grinder's Machine, a Sewing Machine (Treadle), a Side Car or a Violoncello. To deposit my Harmonium or Piano (other than Street) in the cloakroom would cost me twice as much, while I must be prepared to pay no less than four shillings if I was so rash as to allow my luggage to exceed twenty-five feet in length or girth. We often hear of strange articles being deposited (and often abandoned) at railway stations, and the Irish railways would appear to have instructed some sedulous clerk to prepare for every eventuality.

Next morning we journeyed on through the counties of Clare and Galway and the little towns of Ennis and Gort to Athenry. Poor country this after the rich lands of Tipperary which we had seen the previous day; a rolling, treeless, windswept land of lakes and bogs seamed by stone walls into a vast patchwork quilt of small fields. Some of these were under oats or hay, but the majority were permanent pasture and could never be anything else, to such an extent had the rock bitten through the meagre soil covering. In some places there was more rock than soil, and here there would be a wilderness of stunted scrub and thorn.

At Athenry, we had to change onto the old Dublin-Galway main line of the Midland Great Western, and as there was some time to wait we walked into the little town. It was fair day. Doorways and shop windows had been barricaded against the press of cattle and sheep which thronged the narrow streets, while upon the outskirts of this throng, rows of donkeys, harnessed to their little netted carts, waited patiently or slumbered with drooping heads. A hubbub of bargaining voices drifted from the overcrowded bars. The air was full of the mingled aroma of dung and turf fires. It was a scene with which we were to become very familiar in the weeks to come. Like so many places in Ireland, Athenry has seen greater days. Once it boasted a university, a castle and monasteries of the Franciscan and Dominican orders. Now, with the exception of the Dominican church with its fine decorated west window, only ruins remain and Athenry is only known to most Irishmen as a railway junction.

We returned to the station and embarked upon the last stage of our journey through Ballinasloe to Athlone. When I had looked up the timetables and found only one service each way per day on most lines, I had imagined that the trains would be packed to suffocation. But once again I was wrong, for on this, as on subsequent journeys, we never had difficulty in securing comfortable seats. The civilization of Ireland is predominantly rural and therefore stable. With livestock to be tended, the small farmer can seldom travel further than the nearest market town even if he has the means or the desire to do so. In England, however, rural de-population and the growth of urban industrialism have produced a rootless and nomadic civilization which places an increasingly heavy burden on transport. But when the Irish countryman does travel he travels with a vengeance. Finding that their native land cannot support them, the young men emigrate to England or America leaving rural Ireland to the old and the very young. This is the tragedy of Ireland, and in the course of our rail journeys we saw many tearful leave-takings at country stations.

When we reached Athlone we had envisaged leaving our luggage at the station while we went in search of Mr. Beahan and his boat. But this was unnecessary. No sooner had we stepped onto the platform than one of the station staff hurried forward and asked my name. When I told him he smiled and extended his hand. 'I'm Jack Beahan', he said, and forthwith helped us to carry our belongings out of the station. We had not far to go, for *Le Coq* was lying just above the great bridge with its swinging centre span which carries the railway over the broad Shannon.

Our first impressions were not very auspicious. When Jack had got his boat out of the water to repaint the hull, he had discovered that several of her strakes were rotten and must be replaced. Consequently she had only come off the slipway the previous day and had been run onto the mud until her seams took up. Her paintwork was still tacky, while owing to lack of fuel her engine had not been run for six years. Fitted up primarily for week-end cruising, there was very little stowage space in which to house the gear necessary for a protracted voyage, even though we had cut down our belongings to the minimum. However there were comfortable bunks and a generous supply of bedding and crockery, while we soon solved the stowage problem by constructing, by means of screw-eyes and string, two long racks, like the luggage racks in a railway compartment, under the cabin roof beams. Far more serious was the fact that there was not only no petrol to run the boat, but no paraffin to cook with. Without this we could not even live on the boat, let alone make our long hoped for voyage. It was a depressing prospect.

After an evening meal at an hotel in the town, we rowed up the river a little way in the dinghy, both feeling very disconsolate and in no mood to enjoy our new surroundings. We were returning through the dusk when we saw another boat pulling alongside *Le Coq*.

STARTING POINT. The Waterfront, Athlone.

It turned out to be Jack Beahan and his sister Dolly, bringing with them a can of paraffin, a wondrous pat of butter and other stores. They came aboard, and as we sat talking and smoking in the twilight of the little cabin we felt we were with friends that we had known for years. Our mood of depression vanished and we became optimistic. It was our first experience of that Irish kindness and hospitality which never once failed us throughout the whole trip.

Our experience was the same when we went down to the town the next morning for supplies. Our first call was at the barracks of the Civic Guards to obtain food ration books. The form of application for these books took nearly an hour to complete, but this delay was not due to bureaucratic formality or to the complexity of the form. The solitary guard whom we found seated at the table in the big bare room, jumped up and found us chairs, remarking that it was a grand day. Having seen that we were comfortably settled round the table, he then volunteered to fill up the form for us. In the intervals of this process of question and answer we discussed at considerable length our proposed voyage, food rationing and conditions generally in England, and the recent war. Normally, such protracted form-filling would have left us frustrated and irritable; here it was an excuse for a pleasant and mutually profitable conversation, while as to the delay, what occasion was there for hurry? Was there not time enough?

It was the same in the shops, and as practically every grocer in Ireland also runs a licensed bar, it was pleasant to discuss the grocery order (and the other topics which invariably arose) over a glass of sherry. It was possible to do this until comparatively recent times, in certain old-established grocers' shops in England. One of the last to perpetuate the admirable custom was, I believe, a grocer in Northampton who made a practice of offering his lady customers a glass of Madeira. But to-day we have neither time nor manners to spare for such civilized courtesies.

One of the shops we visited was O'Ferrall's whose frontage dates from the days when shop-fitting was not merely a business but an art, as the picture we took of it, with 'himself' in the doorway, clearly reveals. Old Mr. O'Ferrall was a tall gaunt figure. His hawk-like features had an aristocratic cast which was somehow enhanced by a long coat of archaic cut and a high stand-up collar. He had, we discovered, a great sense of the past, and as we sat together in the confined space of the small wooden cubicle to which, as in most

IRISH SHOP, ATHLONE. 'O'Ferrall's … dates from days when shopfitting was not merely a business but an art'.

Irish bars, women must retire in order to drink with propriety, he talked of the history of Athlone. Like that of most Irish towns, it has been stormy.

A curious parallel, both geographical and ethnological, may be drawn between the English Severn and the Irish Shannon. Both rivers in their courses from north to south form a natural border between the lowlands of the midland plains .and the highlands of the west. Just as the Roman and the Saxon drove the Celtic peoples of Britain westward over the Severn into the fastness of the Welsh mountains, so the Gael retreated before the Norman, the English of the Pale, Essex, Cromwell and Dutch William, to defy them in the wilds of Clare, Galway and Mayo. While, in England, the threat from the west and the power of the Welsh princes was extinguished by the fall of Owen Glendower, peace in western Ireland was never more than an uneasy truce. It was a wild country that provoked Cromwell's famous threat: 'To hell or Connaught'. The ancient crossing places of Severn and Shannon were natural strategic focal points of these struggles between east and west, and the parallel may be further extended by comparing Gloucester with Limerick, both the most southerly crossings, and Worcester with Athlone in the midlands. But Shannon with her great lakes, the largest river in the British Isles, is a far more formidable barrier than Severn, and this in no small measure accounts for the more stubborn defence of Connaught.

At Athlone, the town of Luan's ford, the Shannon narrowing as it flows out of Lough Ree, cuts through a low gravel ridge or 'esker' of glacial drift which forms a natural causeway across the great boglands of the central plain and the floodlands of the Shannon. This ridge was the course of the ancient road to the west, and for this reason Athlone has been rightly named 'the key to Connaught'. The fortress which still commands the bridge on the Connaught side of the town is a formidable reminder of the importance that was once attached to the possession of this key.

The last major struggle at Athlone was the famous 'Battle of the Bridge' when the Irish on the Connaught, or Roscommon side faced the forces of William the Third under General Ginkell on the Westmeath bank. After a ten-day bombardment, Ginkell forced a crossing, but the hero of the engagement was the Irishman Custume who succeeded in destroying the temporary bridgework which the enemy had thrown over the breached bridge. The garrison barracks, where the youthful Wellington once drilled his troops, are now named after Custume, while 'The Bridge of Athlone', like 'The Walls of Limerick' which commemorates another epic encounter, is a popular *ceilidhe* dance which you may see performed with great enthusiasm and gusto almost every Saturday night at St. Peter's or St. Mary's halls. To-day, shops, the new post office and the great new church of St. Peter stand west of the bridge, but in the days of the battle this was 'Irishtown', a huddle of thatched cabins where the native Irish were segregated. Athlone had for me a personal association, for it was at these barracks, early in the nineteenth century, that my great-grandfather, Sir John Rolt, was stationed as Colonel of the 2nd Queen's Regiment. I should never have known this but for my chance discovery, on the shelves of a second-hand bookshop, of a little book which he wrote entitled *Moral Command*. My family did not know of the existence of this book, and it proved moreover to be a presentation copy inscribed in his own hand on July 17th, 1843. It was in July, 1943 that I found it. The book advocates leadership by personality and example rather than by rigid discipline, but its theme is illustrated by so many anecdotes that it is virtually an autobiography. These reveal a humanity and a sense of humour which I should imagine were somewhat rare in the army of those days. The following is a typical example:

'When stationed at Athlone, in the autumn of 1823, I gave out an order "that the men's hair should be cut closer"; and on the following morning I went up to one of the companies on parade, and directed that the soldiers should take off their caps; when I pointed out to the captain four men whose hair had not been cut close enough, and said "that I should see those men again at the parade next morning".

'The day following, when I went up to the company, and directed the officer in command of it to call the four men to the front whose hair I had remarked upon the day before, I observed a sort of titter throughout the company, which broke out into a decided laugh, when on their being directed to take off their caps, the four fellows presented *four bare skulls*. In fact, thinking to have the laugh against me, they had cut their hair as dose almost as if their heads had been shaved.

'The attempt to turn an order into ridicule, is almost enough to try a commanding officer's *amiability*, but with a little effort I kept myself cool, for it occurred to me, that if I got angry I should have had "*the laugh against me*"; so, instead of showing that I was annoyed, I joined in the laugh, which then became both loud and general.

'After a little I said, "Well, you are, I am sure, four good-natured fellows, to have afforded us all so much amusement; but although I am very glad to have a laugh in this way amongst ourselves, yet I should not like to have strangers laugh at us". I then asked their captain how long he supposed it would take before those men's hair would grow sufficiently for appearing in public. He replied, "Six weeks". I then said to the four men "I should be quite distressed if your sweethearts were to see you in so unbecoming a plight, and therefore I am forced to order that you be confined to barracks for six weeks". The four fellows looked very silly; the tables were *turned* on them, and I do not think that they ever again tried to *turn* any order of mine into ridicule.'

Sir John served under Wellington in the Peninsula War. In later life he re-visited Ireland, for I possess a beautiful silver snuff box engraved with the arms of Cork, which was presented to him when he received the freedom of that city.

So far there seems nothing out of the ordinary about the life of this old soldier, yet his childhood and antecedents acre wrapped in a mystery which neither his book nor any family document can illuminate. During the seventeenth and eighteenth centuries the Rolts were lords of the manors of Sacombe and Cheslin Templars in Hertfordshire, but on the death of Thomas Rolt in 1735, the estate passed by the marriage of the heiress to the Hertfordshire family of Caswall. Two generations later, however, the Caswall male line also failed whereupon there appeared from Ireland an unknown and penniless young lieutenant. He was at once received at Sacombe, and shortly afterwards married the heiress, Anne Caswall. This was John Rolt whose early life in Ireland remained a jealously guarded secret. No doubt somewhere in Ireland there lurks a clue to this family mystery, but there was too much for us to see and to do in the brief time at our disposal for me to devote any time to genealogical research.

The church of St. Peter and St. Paul, which has only recently been completed, is, the pride of Athlone, but I cannot honestly say that I found its exterior satisfying. The great neo-Classical pile with its white walls, columns and campanile, and its dome of black Galway marble seems to have no roots in the Irish landscape, but to have been translated bodily from some sunnier southern climate. Unlike the tasteless and tawdry vulgarity of most of the Catholic church interiors which we saw in Ireland, however, I thought that the interior of St. Peter's (as it is usually abbreviated) was dignified and impressive. The reason for this is simple. The whole exhibits a sense of design and of craftsmanship. It is not just a nondescript building filled with the stock-in-trade of the Dublin church furnishers. Ireland could do with more craftsmen, particularly in her churches. The Catholic Church, which so rightly argues the value of vocational training, might well set a practical example by fostering local industries of stone masonry and wood carving and by patronizing them. *Laborare est Orare*; the crude Christ of the mediæval village mason is a prayer in stone, but a plaster cast is a worthless thing.

It is impossible to stay long in an Irish, town like Athlone without being made aware of the importance of religion in Irish life, and we soon saw incidents that were strange to us. The tumult and turmoil of a fair day in the main street suddenly hushed to a stillness almost uncanny by the ringing of the Angelus; vociferous groups of bargainers crossing themselves and standing with bowed and uncovered heads, then continuing the excited argument as though time for an instant had stood still. The congregation at Sunday Mass overflowing onto the steps of St. Peter's, a church which, in England, could cater for a town twice the size of Athlone. Windows and window sills massed with flowers on the Feast of Corpus Christi and the air full of incense as a long procession wound through the town while the people knelt-upon the pavements; a Franciscan monk zooming up the Shannon in an outboard motor-boat, his tonsured head gleaming in the sunshine.

This last scene is, I think, peculiarly typical of Athlone for it was, we discovered, the most river-minded town on the Shannon, if not in all Southern Ireland. It has a great reputation for boat-building, from ordinary rowing boats to four-oared racing 'pleasure boats,' outrigger fours and eights, and the little Shannon Class sailing boats. The town has its own sailing club with headquarters on the shores of Lough Ree, and a keen rowing club which sends crews to compete in most of the leading Irish regattas. Soon after we arrived, an Athlone crew were successful at Dublin regatta, and every evening, rain or shine, we heard the urgent cries of the coxes as practising fours or eights shot past our moorings. There were also more motor cruisers moored at Athlone than we saw elsewhere, and aboard these there was much activity as their owners, hoping, like us, that petrol would be forthcoming, re-furbished them after their long spell of enforced idleness.

We were soon able to leave our ignominious mud berth for permanent moorings out on the river, but the movement of *Le Coq*, the slap and gurgle of the water about her hull and the occasional rattle of her anchor chain as she swung into the wind, made our immobility the more tantalizing. Yet this period of waiting was not wasted; our new found Irish friends saw to that. The owner of a cruiser moored just ahead of us offered to lend us his outboard motor boat. He had, he said, a little petrol saved from his car allowance. Knowing how reluctant I should be to lend any boat of mine to a-perfect stranger, I marvelled at this generous offer but was very loathe to accept it. But he was insistent. 'Go on now', said he, 'Take her up to the lake for the day', and we could no longer resist the opportunity. So one bright morning we brought the outboard alongside *Le Coq*, stowed sufficient food on board for the day, and set off.

The Shannon at our moorings was about seventy yards wide, but upstream from this point it gradually widens for a distance of a mile and a quarter until it opens out into Lough Ree. Under normal conditions of flow with the weir sluices closed, the current is almost imperceptible. As we travelled upstream we soon passed the mouth of the old disused cut which rejoins the river below the weir and at the tail of the present lock to make an island of the Roscommon side of the town. Later, we were to see similar abandoned cuts at Roosky and Meelick. They formed part of the original line of the Shannon navigation until they were superseded by the present large locks which were built as relief work in the famine year of 1846 by the Shannon Commissioners whose powers were later invested in the Board of Works. Prior to this, navigation on the Shannon was controlled by three separate authorities, the Lower (tidal) Shannon from Kilrush to Limerick by the Limerick Navigation Company, the Middle Shannon from Limerick to Athlone by the Grand Canal Company, and the Upper Shannon from Athlone to Lough Allen by a Government appointed body, the Directors of Inland Navigation.

Above the entrance of this old cut the Shannon resembled a reed-fringed mere rather than a river. It was a landscape of wide levels and sun-dappled water whose only conspicuous feature was a low green knoll crowned with a clump of trees which some Athlone people maintain marks the very centre of Ireland. There was no lack of wild life on these waters. Duck rose from the reeds with a sudden whirr of wings or flapped across the water dragging an extended wing to feign injury and distract our attention from their nesting places. Several convoys of swans sailed past, the old birds jealously guarding their young. Occasionally some tall reed would suddenly swing and sway over the water under the weight of a clinging bunting, while the air hummed with the drumming of the snipe which soared and swooped overhead. But the most characteristic sound was the crying of the curlew. This plaintive piping was destined to be the familiar accompaniment of our voyage, translating into sound the loneliness of the Shannon levels and the wild desolation of the bogs.

Presently we sighted a cairn of stone surmounted by a black marker which indicated the river entrance to craft crossing the lake. Throughout the length of the Shannon, the navigable channel is marked in this way by red and black markers and buoys, red being to port and black to starboard when travelling upstream.[1] Lough Ree is eighteen miles long, and, at its widest point, seven miles across, so that as the flat country on its borders gives little shelter from the prevailing winds, it is seldom still. This morning there was only a light breeze from the west, but as we headed out from the lee of the land towards the wooded headland called Yew Point where we had planned to land for lunch, our little boat became alive as she danced over the waves, and spray came scudding over her bows. In theory, judging from a map or chart, it looks as though it would not be difficult to find one's way about on Lough Ree, but in practice it is very easy to lose one's bearings, as we soon discovered. There is a complete lack of conspicuous landmarks on the low coastline with which the numerous islands merge most confusingly. It is impossible to distinguish one from the other until, on close approach, the channels between them open out. However, we found our way to Yew Point without incident, and after a late lunch there, decided to cut across the lake to Hare Island. Accustomed to the narrow inland waterways of England, it was a unique experience for us to explore this lake which was more like an inland sea. Northwards, distant wooded islets floated as unsubstantial as a mirage in a waste of silver waters that stretched away to the horizon. Far away rose the solitary hump of a hill, blue and remote, which I judged from the map to be Slieve Bawn. We had already discovered that the margins of Lough Ree are very shallow and rocky and should be approached with caution even in a small boat. So we gave Hare Island a fairly wide berth as we skirted its northern shore looking for somewhere to run in. The map marked a landing place at the north-eastern tip of the island, but as it did not look promising we held on down the sheltered channel between the island and the mainland until we sighted the island harbour – 'Lord's Harbour' according to the map. With a narrow entrance between massive stone walls, it was a replica in miniature of the harbours in Cornish fishing coves. We ran in and beached beside a black tub of a boat which was obviously used for transporting livestock. From the water, the island had appeared to be completely clothed in dense woodland, but when we landed we discovered that its southern half consisted of meadow land screened by a narrow shelter belt of trees. The sward was of a wonderful green richness, and the condition of the young beasts which were at graze confirmed its quality. The grazing on these lake islands is generally good, so that it well repays the trouble of ferrying stock from the mainland. On our right as we walked up the path from the harbour were the ruins of a church, and on our left, a little way off, a thatched farmhouse with its outbuildings, from which came the familiar reek of a turf fire. It was warm and very still in the shelter of this

[1] It should perhaps be mentioned here that Captain Raven-Hart in his little book *Canoeing in Ireland* gives the relative position of these markers wrongly, an error which might lead to unfortunate results.

secluded ground, and save for the cropping of the animals the only sound was the murmur of the invisible waters of the lake as they lapped the shore. Something in the atmosphere of the place made us lower our voices and walk soft-footed. I felt I could understand why the youthful Yeats, exiled in London, was filled with nostalgia for the peace of his 'Lake Isle of Innisfree'.

In the centre of the wooded northern half of the island we found an empty fishing lodge. Rides radiated from it to afford glimpses of the lake between the trees. It had long been empty, we were told afterwards, and was used during the time of the 'Troubles' by the Fenians as a place of refuge and secret meeting. Certainly it seemed lost to the world.

By the time we had made a circuit of the island and returned to our starting point by a path which wound through the trees by the shore, it was time for supper. We built a good fire of driftwood in a sheltered spot near the harbour entrance and presently sat down to a repast of cold ham and freshly boiled new potatoes washed down with cups of tea and followed by strawberries and cream. While we were eating this meal the sky grew overcast and the wind freshened, for although we were out of it, the sound of the waves on the windward shore of the island rose from a sleepy murmur to a dull roar like that of heavy rain on a roof. Big fresh water lakes are very quickly responsive to changes of weather, and as rain threatened we decided to be off.

During all the time we had been on the island, the scent of the turf fire had been the only sign of life. The silence and stillness had been almost uncanny. But as we cleared the harbour entrance, an old man appeared on the wall above us. Long wisps of white hair floated out from beneath his battered hat. His face, lean, wrinkled and brown as a berry and his clear but deep sunken eyes made me think of an ascetic saint by El Greco. He might, indeed, have been a reincarnation of St. Ciaran of Clonmacnoise who built his first oratory here. We waved to him but he made no sign of acknowledgment, standing motionless on the lookout at the end of the harbour wall and gazing after us until we could see him no longer. I sometimes wonder whether he was real.

As we left the lee of Hare Island and headed into the wind we were glad that we had had the foresight to put on our mackintoshes and stow our gear securely in the locker in the bow, for the little boat pitched violently and covered us in spray as she punched her way through the short waves, while every now and again the engine raced as the propeller lifted out of the water. After half an hour of this hard going against wind and sea we rounded the marker at the entrance to the river and slid smoothly down its calm waters back to our moorings. It had been a memorable day.

We made one other noteworthy excursion in the neighbourhood of Lough Ree, this time on hired bicycles and in company with Dolly Beahan and her nephew Sean. We had read in the local paper that a Gaelic League Festival or 'Aerideact' was to be held in a field at the hamlet of Walderstown about ten miles distant from Athlone. As I was very anxious to see this, a fine Sunday morning saw the four of us setting off along the straight bog road. We arrived early, but we found, already holding a good strategic position by the gate, an old blind beggar of great decrepitude who generally occupied a pitch on the bridge at Athlone. How he had contrived to be transported thither I do not know, but we later came across other instances of the remarkable opportunism of Irish beggars. The Athlone tinkers, Greens, Smiths and Doyles, were also present in force, one of them running a miniature rifle range with great profit. Sean was quick to patronize this. He had recently left the Irish army, and it was, I think, a question of prestige.

Proceedings commenced with the arrival of a local pipe band who marched onto the field piping lustily. They wore green kilts, while streamers of orange, green and white floated from the chanters of the pipes which were of the Scottish type. The high-lights of the afternoon were a concert of Irish music by a number of celebrated Radio Eireann broadcasters including an Irish piper, an Irish dancing competition judged by Rory O'Connor the Irish champion, and a Gaelic football match between two local teams.

The dancing competition seemed endless as a succession of local girls, of ages ranging from six to sixteen, clambered on to the platform to perform under the critical eye of the great Rory. Many of them wore incredibly unbecoming garments and headdresses which evidently purported to be traditional. Two indefatigable fiddlers provided the music. In Irish dancing, footwork is all; the body remains as motionless as possible, the head poised and the arms straight and resting easily at the sides. Many of the dancers displayed footwork of remarkable agility and versatility, an excellent carriage and a fine sense of rhythm. But I could not help thinking that the convention of restricting all movement to the lower half of the body gave them a mechanical appearance, as if they were marionettes dangling upon invisible wires. I must admit that Rory's exhibition dance was a magnificent display, not only of sheer technical brilliance but of presence of mind. Half way through his performance the press of enthusiastic spectators caused the platform to collapse beneath him, bearing with it some of the dignitaries who had been accorded a ringside view. Rory, however, never faltered for a moment but danced across on swiftly flickering feet to that portion of the stage which remained standing.

When this was over and the pitch had, with the greatest difficulty, been cleared of spectators, the football match began. Gaelic football is a mixture of Rugby and Association. Thus the players can handle the ball but cannot, as in Rugger, run with it for more than three paces. Scoring can be affected either by shooting into the net in the mouth of the goal or by kicking over the bar and between the posts which, for this reason, are extended above the crossbar like rugger posts. But the most curious feature of the game to English eyes is that there is no offside rule. This enables players to lurk in menacing fashion round their opponents' goal irrespective of the whereabouts of the ball. As we presently discovered, the game, in its village version at any rate, is played with terrifying dash and ferocity. Casualties on this occasion were numerous, and the excited spectators were only with difficulty restrained from joining in the combat.

When we left I must confess to a slight feeling of disappointment, much as we had enjoyed ourselves. With the exception of the football match, the whole proceedings had about them a certain self-consciousness and lack of spontaneity which, in my experience, is inseparable from any attempt to apply artificial respiration to archaic traditional arts. The Gaelic revival is such an attempt, and by trying to put the cart before the horse, I believe that it will fail.

The arts of a people, their language, poetry, music and dance, are the spontaneous expression of their way of life. If that way of life changes or perishes, then these arts will change or perish with it despite all that the most ardent folklorists may do. But before this day was out I was to see for myself that these arts still live in Ireland without the stimulus of the revivalists.

Cycling back by a different route, we presently came to the village of Glasson which lies close to the shore of an inlet of Lough Ree called Killinure Lough or, more commonly, 'the inner lake'. The country hereabouts was well wooded and not so flat as in the immediate neighbourhood of Athlone. This district of the Lough Ree shore is notable for its association with the immortal Goldsmith. He spent two years in Athlone where his clergyman brother lived, while three miles along the Ballymahon road from Glasson, at Lissoy near the Three Pigeons, stands a dilapidated cattle shelter which was once the cottage where, as a child, Goldsmith lived for six years. In any other country but Ireland, the Lissoy cottage would doubtless have been preserved as a place of literary pilgrimage. It is a curious paradox of the Irishman's character that whereas he possesses a sense of the past so highly developed that he can speak of centuries old events as though they happened yesterday, he is commonly neglectful of the monuments of that past. Like so many great Irishmen before and after him, Goldsmith earned his fame abroad while he did not cease to dream of the Ireland to which he never returned. 'If', he wrote to an Irish friend, 'I go to the opera where Signora Columba pours out all the maze of melody, I sit and sigh for Lissoy fireside and "Johnny Armstrong's Last Good-night" from Peggy Golden. If I climb Hampstead Hill there, where nature never exhibited a more magnificent prospect, I confess it fine, but then I had rather be placed on that little mound before Lissoy gate, and there take in, to me, the most pleasing horizon in nature.'

Some Irish writers identify Lissoy as 'The Deserted Village', but with this I cannot agree. In my opinion the scene of this magnificent epitaph upon the death of rural civilization can only be in England. It portrays too faithfully the fate of the English village at the time of the Enclosures.

Though Irish towns and villages lack the regional diversity and beauty of English rural architecture, their characters differ very markedly. One will present a drab, dispirited, poverty-stricken appearance, a shabby display of ruined walls, tousled leaky thatch and broken windows eyeing an ill-made road. Another will be the precise opposite with its neat thatching and its trim houses bright with fresh paint, colour wash or plastering. Glasson belonged to the latter class without a doubt. The village street was still and deserted in the evening sunlight, but there was a significant stack of bicycles against the wall of the 'Select Bar', and from within came the sound of pipe music. Officially, only bona fide travellers can obtain a drink in Ireland on a Sunday. Consequently a generous proportion of the male population become travellers with the simple result that the village bars exchange their patrons and parties of 'regulars' pass each other upon the roads, each pedalling steadfastly towards the other's 'local'. This proceeding is known as 'doing a bona fide'.

As we were unquestionably bona fide we went into the house, attracted by the music of the pipes. The spotless, low-ceilinged bar with its floor of scrubbed stone flags was crowded, and on the wide window sill behind the bar sat the piper. With a check cap rakishly atilt over one ear and a cigarette in his mouth which drooped a long pencil of ash, he played and played, his head nodding slightly to the rhythm of his music. And what a wild lilting rhythm it was, a rhythm that could not fail to set heads nodding and feet tapping. It soon infected our young friend Sean who prevailed upon three of the company to join him in a 'half set'. They were heavily built men and had obviously consumed a generous quantity of porter, but they proceeded to foot it with a nimbleness which would have done credit to the platform at Walderstown had it been capable of supporting their weight. Every now and again they whirled about with such velocity in the confined space that they appeared to be in imminent danger either of dashing their brains out against the central pillar which supported the ceiling, or of sweeping all bottles and glasses off the bar counter. But there was no mishap; they finished the set amid great laughter and applause, and soon Michael the piper was off again with another lilting tune.

The pipes he was playing were the so-called Irish or Uilleann pipes, known in England (if they are known at all) as the Galway pipes. The bag which Michael held under the left arm was not mouth filled but was supplied by a bellows under the right arm to which it was strapped. In this the instrument resembled the Northumbrian pipe, but the arrangement of the drones was quite different to either Northumbrian or Scottish pipes. There were three of these drones sounding C in three octaves, the lowest being obtained by constructing the drone on the bassoon principle. By means of a series of metal keys worked by the pressure of his wrist, Michael was able to play a bass accompaniment of three-note chords on the drones while his fingers were left free to stop the sweet-voiced chanter with its range of two octaves. Presumably the instrument has been called the Irish pipe to distinguish it from the Scottish mouth-blown pipes, although historically the latter was used in Ireland and in England long before it was introduced to Scotland. But whereas in Ireland the mouth-blown pipe was extinct for many years until its recent revival, the Uilleann pipe continued to be widely played until the famine years of the 1840's when, though its use did not die out, it became much rarer. Michael's father had been a fiddler, he told us, but he himself had preferred the pipes. Angela took a photograph of him as he played in the bar, but unfortunately the light was poor and it proved unsuitable for reproduction. Just before we left, however, we took another picture while he sat on the mounting block behind the house, and this shows the instrument quite clearly.

We had heard the Irish pipes played that afternoon at Walderstown, possibly with greater competence for all I know. But for me, this mannered and polished performance upon a platform could not compare with our informal entertainment in the bar at Glasson. It was an evening to remember always.

IRISH PIPER. 'Michael sat on the mounting block behind the house.'

CHAPTER THREE

GALWAY AND CONNEMARA

As the days slipped by and no petrol arrived, we decided to take the opportunity of paying a visit to Galway. It seemed to be generally assumed among our Irish friends that we should stay at one of the several hotels in Galway's seaside suburb of Salthill. Yet, somehow, instinct told us that we should not like Salthill, and we installed ourselves in a comfortable old hotel facing spacious Eyre Square in the heart of Galway. When we did pay Salthill a fleeting visit we found it just as we had feared, a somewhat grim and grey version of an English seaside resort; a row of hotels, boarding houses and 'fancy-goods' shops straggling along a sea front promenade. No doubt the visitors enjoy the uninterrupted sea view and derive great benefit from the Atlantic air to which they are so freely exposed, but to my personal taste, any seaside resort of this type is anathema. Galway itself, on the other hand, is a fine city, in fact we preferred it to any of the larger Irish towns which we visited.

Galway has an immemorial history. Ptolemy described it as the principal city on Europe's western seaboard. During the Middle Ages the Normans settled in the city, driving out the native population, and during their occupation carried on a great trade with Spain, the influence of which is apparent to this day. These Norman families, Blakes, Bodkins, Brownes, D' Arcys, Ffrenchs, Kirwans, Joyces, Lynchs, Morrisses, Martins and Skerrets, became known as 'The Tribes of Galway' and Galway itself as 'The City of the Tribes'. A bye-law of 1518 which enacted 'that neither O' nor Mac shall strutte ne swagger thro' the streets of Gallway', shows that they believed in keeping the native Irish population firmly in their place. In this case that place was the Irish town of the Claddagh or, for the more turbulent, the wilds of Connemara to the west. The latter, however, were not to be so lightly dismissed, and from the inscription which once appeared over the city's west gate: 'From the fury of the O'Flaherties Good Lord deliver us', it would seem that the O's not only continued to strut in defiance of the bye-laws, but gave the Norman tribes a very uncomfortable time of it into the bargain. Throughout the time of the Civil War and for many years thereafter the city remained staunch to the House of Stuart and was twice beseiged, first by the Parliamentarians under Sir Charles Coote, and finally by that same General Ginkell who forced the bridge at Athlone.

Modern Galway does not speak of its long and colourful past so eloquently as the old towns and cities of England. Excepting the Spanish Arch by the quays, Lynch's Castle in Shop Street, which is an old stone mansion dating from 1320, and the Protestant church of St. Nicholas where Columbus is said to have heard Mass before setting out on his great

OLD GALWAY. The Spanish Arch.

voyage, few notable old buildings remain. Nevertheless, I found that the city possessed an atmosphere and a unique quality which I find it impossible to define. No Irish town can readily be likened to any English town; the differences are marked. Yet Galway goes further than this and in some strange way seems to declare itself a foreign city, foreign not only to England but to the rest of Ireland. Many things, not individually remarkable perhaps, combined to create this impression of strangeness. The almost unbelievable blue of the great arc of Galway Bay as we walked down to the harbour on a cloudless evening. The unfamiliar build and rig of the fishing boats, Pookawns, Hookers and Glothogues, which clustered in the harbour together with a great concourse, not of gulls, but swans. The swarthy, blue-jerseyed fishermen casting their ring nets for salmon by the mouth of the swift-flowing Corrib in the inner harbour near the Spanish Arch. The many bridges which carry the streets over the Corrib and its mill leats and over the disused Lough Corrib Navigation, which together make Galway a city of waterways. Last, but by no means least, the dark good looks of the people. I believe, rightly or wrongly, that this must be due to the admixture of Spanish with Celtic blood. Nothing else, I feel sure, could have produced the raven dark hair, the grey eyes and the dear, fair complexions of the most beautiful women I have ever seen. We have many pretty women in England but few that could truly be called beautiful. Too often, when the mask of make-up is dropped, even the prettiness disappears. The pace and strain of modern civilization is an enemy of beauty which requires not only physical perfection but serenity. Here, in the soft airs of the furthest west where life moves more slowly, beauty lives. It was an ironical example of modern economic chaos that in Galway, where their subtle aids were least needed, the windows of the

'Medical Halls' displayed such a wealth of costly cosmetics as the English woman has not seen for six years.

Galway, the nearest European deep water anchorage to America, has always aspired to become a centre of transatlantic trade. But the dream has never materialized and, now, with the establishment of the Atlantic airbase at Rineanna, it seems farther away than ever. Apart from a few vessels laid up in the inner basin, the only occupant of the harbour when we walked down the quay was the Admiralty salvage ship *Help*. She had been attempting to re-float a coasting steamer of the Limerick Steamship Company which had run aground in a fog off Black Head. Far out across the bay under the paw of the headland we could see the stranded ship, a black dot silhouetted against the sunset. The disgruntled crew of the *Help* told us how, after much labour, they had righted and re-floated her preparatory to towing her into Galway, when a sudden westerly gale had swept her away and driven her irretrievably upon the rocks. Such is the hazard and the heartbreak of this savage coast of storm and sea-bitten cliff.

While we were examining the *Help*, a small ship steamed across the bay and swung into the sea lock at the harbour mouth. She proved to be the *Dun Aengus* inward bound from Aran, and we walked round to watch her berth. Her aft deck was piled with sacks of potatoes and bales of wool, while the cattle crowded between decks gave her a heavy list as she was warped up to the quayside. The harvest of the islands. I judged that the potato sacks must weigh two hundredweight a-piece, but the islanders shouldered them and bore them up the gangway as though they had been filled with feathers. The menfolk wore the light-coloured suits of 'bawneen', home-spun from undyed wool, and one had about his waist the 'crios', a broad belt woven in bright coloured wools which reminded me strongly of the similar belts which English canal boatmen used once to wear. Their women wore skirts of 'bawneen' and wondrous brown shawls with ornamental borders of intricate design.

The modern reaction to an overdose of rural sentimentality is to deny that a prosperous peasantry ever existed except in fiction, and that in fact the life of the peasant has always consisted of heart-breaking toil for no better return than the poverty of want, hardship and squalor. The average Irish small farmer of the present day, for all his virtues and his ready wit, lends colour to this view. Generally he looks undersized and undernourished, often he is ragged and down at heel. But it should not be forgotten that for generations the Irish peasant of the mainland has been the sport of hostile economic and social forces which have virtually eliminated his brother across the Irish Sea. But the islands of the farthest west, too remote and too poor in natural resources to be exploited by these forces, are backwaters left by the floodtide of progress. While the rich lands are depopulated, while the small farmer on marginal lands struggles on in poverty against almost hopeless odds, on Aran, where fields must be built on naked rock with creel-borne kelp, men are rich in the fruits of their own skill, glory in their physical strength and move like princes. I do not exaggerate. There is food for thought in this.

We walked back along the quay and past the entrance lock of the Lough Corrib Navigation. Like most Irish canal works, it is large and massively built, and though never used, appeared still to be in good order. Construction of the navigation was begun by the Board of Works in 1848, as part of a scheme to connect Loughs Corrib and Mask with the sea. There is a subterranean connection between these two lakes through caverns worn in the porous limestone, and owing to this faulty rock formation construction of this section of the canal in the neighbourhood of Cong had to be abandoned.

Continuing along the towing path, we eventually worked our way round to the bridge which crosses the Corrib just below the weir by which the river starts its plunge from the lough level to the sea. The salmon, coming up the river to spawn, lie just upstream of the bridge preparatory to climbing the salmon ladder beside the weir. Looking down over the parapet we could see that the river was literally packed with great fish lying so closely that it appeared scarcely possible to drop a pebble without hitting one. A yard or so upstream we noticed a wire stretched across the river a foot above water-level, the purpose of which we could not fathom. We were enlightened later.

It appears that the Galway Salmon Fishery Board were much troubled by poachers until they adopted the time-honoured principle of 'set a thief to catch a thief' by appointing a celebrated poacher as bailiff. His first action was to erect this wire and the losses ceased. The technique of the poacher was as follows. He would saunter idly over the bridge and, having assured himself that he was unobserved, take from under his coat a coiled and weighted line carrying a vicious triple hook and sling it into the river. So thick lie the fish at this point that the sling and strike of a practised hand was very frequently successful. No doubt the new bailiff was a past master of this art, for he judged to a nicety the point at which a transverse wire would foul and prevent the line from being drawn up.

We felt we could not leave Galway without a glimpse, however brief, of Connemara. Obviously the only real way to see such a country is to walk through it, taking plenty of time over the journey, but our short stay would not permit this. It seems that the usual practice of the short-term visitor is to travel in the bus from Galway to Clifden and back. But we neither of us care for the motor bus as a form of transport, and never patronize it except with some ulterior motive or by force of circumstance. We studied the map and resolved upon a compromise. We would take the bus to a point called 'Canal Bridge' which lay directly beneath the Twelve Bens, scale one of the mountains and descend in time to catch the bus on its return. On the map it looked easy.

Next morning found us bowling along close to the shores of Lough Corrib, through the little town of Oughterard where a cattle fair was in progress, and out onto a desolate waste of rock and bogland pitted with innumerable lakes. The mountains began to loom closer on the right hand; Leckavrea above Maam Cross; the long ridge of the Maumturks marching away to the north-west, and beyond, blue and majestic in the morning sunshine, the clustered peaks of the Bens. The road followed fairly closely the line of the old Galway-Clifden railway. It is now a grass-grown causeway for the track has been taken up, and only the piers of the bridge across the Corrib at Galway remain. It would, I thought, make a good route for a walk through Connemara. Cross country walking is practically impossible, while it would be more interesting than the high road.

Recess, the last stop before we reached out destination, is aptly named, a little oasis of trees in this treeless land sheltering in a hollow by Lough Glendollagh. Canal Bridge, we found, consisted of nothing more than a stone bridge spanning the rapid stream which flows out of Lough Derryclare into Ballynahinch Lake. Why it should be called 'Canal' Bridge I do not know, as the most enthusiastic promoter of inland navigation would hesitate to contemplate the construction of a canal in this country. We leant over the parapet looking down at the purling peat-brown water while the bus, our last tenuous link with civilization, thrashed away up the narrow winding road until it disappeared over a brow and the sound of it was swallowed up in the silence. Mountains are always associated in my mind with the sound of the bleating of sheep, but here there was no such sound, only the voice of the stream and occasionally the cawing of a mountain crow or the pipe of a curlew. I can appreciate that Connemara could never support the same head of sheep as the mountain districts of Wales or Scotland, but nevertheless, the small sheep population of the district surprised me. I do not know the reason. Is it because they are apt to founder in the wet bogs which abound on the mountain slopes?

North of us lay the little valley of the Glencoaghan River closely encircled by no less than six of the Bens; Benlettery, Bengower, Benbreen, Bencollaghduff, Bencorr and Derrydare. Erosion had tattered and rent the meagre soil covering on their precipitous flanks to reveal gaunt ribs and massive shoulders of crystalline rock which glittered with flecks of white quartzite as with snow. They belong to the oldest geological formation, the product of some titanic upheaval so remote that the mind cannot compass the gulf of time. From afar off in the magic blue of distance they had looked like the peaks of fairyland, but from this close vantage they seemed as desolate, forbidding and primeval as moon mountains. One reason for the grandeur of the Bens is that no foothills detract from their height. Where we stood, little over a mile from their two-thousand foot summits, we were less than a hundred feet above sea level.

One or two lonely cabins crouched under the mountain walls, but the peaks themselves were obviously trackless. We had planned our day in the light of previous experience in the Welsh mountains, but we could see already that Connemara was a very different proposition, and that it would be a tough climb. It was, but we persevered. Squelching through bogs and clambering up slippery shelves of rock we eventually reached the summit of Bengower and sat with our backs against the leeward side of the cairn of stones recovering our breath. It was an extraordinary landscape which lay below us.

While we were climbing a blanket of cloud had come sweeping in from the Atlantic to banish the sun for good; but fortunately, though it seemed to lower close above our heads, it had not yet descended to the level of the peaks and the view was still clear. But the sombre light had drained all colour from the landscape to leave only the grey of rock and the silver of water and sky. Consequently no colour print could portray the atmosphere of the scene more clearly than does the photograph which Angela took from a shoulder of the mountain during our climb. From the dim humped shape of Aran, lying like a stranded whale beyond Galway Bay, to the Blaskets our eyes could follow the wild coastline torn by the fury of the sea into a maze of furrowed inlets. It was easy now to·realize that we stood upon the edge of Europe; that a hundred miles further westward the sea was of a depth of 1000 fathoms, and south-west, off the Kerry coast, 2700 fathoms or 16,000 feet, an abysmal depth compared with which the Irish Channel and the North Sea are mere lily ponds. Water and rock, water and rock succeeded each other into a distance where it was impossible to distinguish fresh water lake from landlocked arm of the sea. It was for all the world as though we looked down from some tremendous cliff upon a rocky shore studded with pools left by a receding tide. Never have I seen a prospect

CONNEMARA from BEN GOWER. 'Water and rock, water and rock succeeded each other into the distance.'

wilder or more desolate. It is not surprising that Connemara is a 'Congested District', that it cannot, in other words, provide sustenance even for the sparse population. Bitter indeed the struggle to win a livelihood in these wastes of rock and bogland, and it is difficult to see how any reclamation work could substantially increase its fertility. Yet so strong are the ties which bind a man to his own place that if one of these western men were to be suddenly transported to Eden, I believe that he would weep for Connemara and would ask to see again the peaks of the Bens.

By the time we had scrambled down the mountain and caught our bus back to Galway, the twelve Bens had vanished into the mists and a thin driving rain was sweeping across the bogs.

CHAPTER FOUR

THE VOYAGE BEGINS

ATHLONE TO SHANNON HARBOUR

When our train drew into the platform at Athlone, Jack hurried up with a smile which was even broader than that with which he had greeted us on our first arrival. The long awaited petrol allocation had arrived; an allowance of fifteen gallons a month. He seemed as pleased about it as we were.

Anxious though we were to start as soon as possible, to set off immediately was out of the question. Stores must be laid in, and, most important of all, *Le Coq's* long silent engine must be coaxed into life. The engine itself - an old Morris Oxford marine conversion - started with remarkable ease, in fact it was only after we had started it that our troubles began. First of all we could get no circulating water, but this was soon remedied for it proved to be simply due to a sheared pin on the drive to the circulating pump. The next trouble we discovered was much more serious. The original clutch and gearbox had been retained, the clutch being operated by the old handbrake lever. This exerted far more leverage than the original pedal but in spite of this the clutch would not withdraw. It stubbornly defied our combined efforts and every expedient of force or guile which we could devise. At length we realized that there was nothing for it but to withdraw the clutch housing and examine it. Anyone with experience of working on marine engines in situ will appreciate that this was quite an undertaking. But while the labour of dismantling and re-assembling was considerable, the actual work of freeing the clutch when we could get at it took no time at all. In course of time, the cork facings of the driven plate had literally 'grown' onto the metal driving surface, and to prise them apart and to clean and oil them was the lightest part of the job.

When we had got everything ship-shape once more we made a short trial trip up the river accompanied by Jack and the cheerful mechanic from a local garage who had been giving us a hand in the evenings. Everything now appeared to be satisfactory, and after we had successfully returned to our moorings we celebrated the event with some bottles of Guinness which we had previously procured, optimistically, for the purpose.

While this work was going on we were making plans for the voyage. I proposed going upstream to the limit of navigation, then travelling through the Royal Canal to Dublin, and returning to the Shannon through the Grand Canal. Had we set off we should have been unable to complete the round trip, and only a fortunate combination of circumstances prevented our doing so. A stranger, overhearing us discussing our plans in one of the

Athlone bars one evening, joined in the conversation and volunteered the depressing information that it was no longer possible to get from the Royal Canal on to the Liffey at Dublin because the lock at North Wall was disused. I at once despatched a letter of enquiry about this, not, for some unknown reason, to Coras Iompair Eireann, the owners of the Royal Canal, but to the Grand Canal Company at James's Street Harbour. It was lucky that I did so for, while they did not answer my question but referred me to the owners of the Royal Canal, they informed me that I should be unable to return by their canal because the entrance locks to the river at Shannon Harbour were to be closed for repairs on July 1st for two months. It was already the last week of June. If we were to carry out our plans, everything depended on our reversing our original itinerary and getting through these locks before they closed. But if we did so we must first make certain that we could get back by the Royal Canal, otherwise we should be stranded in Dublin. The consensus of opinion in Athlone on this point was not encouraging. Even if we could get onto the canal at Dublin, the western end of the Royal was quite disused and it was most unlikely that we should be able to reach the Shannon. Time was now desperately short, and to settle the matter I telephoned the Engineer's office of Coras Iompair Eirrean at Westland Row Station. The response was as encouraging as it was courteous. Of course the canal could be entered from the Liffey, while I could certainly make the passage through to the Shannon though the canal might be weedy in places. If I would let them know when I reached Dublin they would give me every assistance. After the unhelpful, if not positively discouraging, attitude of English railway companies towards anyone proposing to use their canals, this unsolicited offer of assistance left me almost speechless. Now it only remained for us to advise Richard and Marten, two friends from England who were joining us for a month in the first week of July, to meet us at Tullamore on the Grand Canal instead of at Carrick-on-Shannon as originally proposed.

With a strange and untried boat on a strange river, we were not disposed to cut things too fine but to allow for possible breakdowns or other mishaps and get under way as soon as possible. Accordingly on June 25th, though the morning was wet and unpromising, we let go our permanent moorings and moved down to Athlone Quay just above the lock. Here we took on stores, petrol and, thanks to our good friends, sufficient paraffin to keep our two primus stoves going for the whole trip.

There is not much traffic on this portion of the river. It consists. of an occasional Grand Canal boat trading up to the company's depots at Athlone, Lanesborough and Carrick with porter or general merchandise, and the regular passage of a larger craft, the *Eclipse Flower* of Limerick, carrying flour between Limerick and Carrick. Equipped with a wheel-house and engine-room telegraph, the *Eclipse Flower* might almost be described as a miniature sea-going coaster, better able to weather the storms on the lakes than the smaller Grand Canal boats. The latter are flush-decked craft, sixty feet long with a beam of thirteen feet and a cargo capacity of forty-five tons. A few of the older boats are timber built, but the great·majority are all steel. Hatches fore and aft give access to the crew's quarters and the engine room respectively, and they have tiller steering. Many of the boats we saw carried a drinking water barrel on deck painted-bright scarlet or green with the hoops picked out in white, but apart from this splash of colour they presented a very sober appearance compared with the gaily painted craft of the English canals to which we were accustomed. They are not even named, but bear numbers with the suffix 'M' for boats owned by the company and 'B' for those operated by independent carriers or 'bye traders'. Like so many English canal boats, they are powered by single-cylinder Bolinder semi-diesel engines, and it was this familiar exhaust beat that we heard coming down the river just as we were preparing to move into Athlone lock after an early lunch. As the lock is of great size, we locked down in company: with the canal boat, still leaving plenty of room to spare.

While the lock was emptying it was discreetly suggested to me that for a small consideration the captain of the canal boat would take us in tow. I felt a little loath to leave Athlone in this somewhat ignominious fashion, but as I had as yet no idea of *Le Coq's* appetite for petrol, I decided that it would be foolish to neglect any opportunity to economize fuel. So the matter was quickly settled; we threw the canal boat our bow line, and presently moved slowly out of the lock. We had agreed to cast off the tow when we reached the Seven Churches at Clonmacnoise which we had decided to make our first port of call.

The scenery along the Shannon, with the exception of Lough Derg, cannot be called spectacular, and this is especially true of the nine and a half mile reach from Athlone to Clonmacnoise. The country is so flat that in clear weather it is possible to stand on Athlone bridge and see quite distinctly the shape of the Slieve Bloom mountains thirty miles and more away to the south. The great river winds tortuously through reed fringed levels of water meadows interspersed with patches of bogland which, in time of winter flood, become a great inland sea. For this reason, frequent navigation markers indicate the course of the main channel but even so, we were told, at such times, boatmen who have navigated the river for years often fail to allow for the river's windings and find themselves aground in a field.

Yet despite its monotony there is, for the river lover, a curious fascination about this great stream of Shannon, the tall reeds rustling and bowing to the wind, the spaciousness of the illimitable levels and over all the wide Irish sky which, even on a sunless day, has a strange luminous quality. Owing to the risk of flooding, the few little white-washed, thatch-roofed farmsteads which we saw were well removed from the river bank and I experienced a feeling of loneliness and complete isolation such as I had never known on any English waterway, remote though they frequently are. Occasionally we passed little groups, a small farmer and his wife and children perhaps, tossing the newly cut hay in the waterside meadows. They would pause, leaning on their pitchforks, to watch our passing. Apart from this we had for company only the stalwart figure at the tiller of the steadily chugging barge ahead of us, but even he was cut off from us by the length of our towline.

At length we sighted a line of low green hills, another of the 'eskers' of glacial drift which interrupt the levels of the plain. Some time ago the rain had stopped, and now the sun suddenly burst out upon the hills so that their greenness seemed to shine with a brilliance that was almost unreal. A grey round tower over-topped the shoulder of the hill, and we knew that we were approaching Clonmacnoise. But there was still some way to go for the 'esker' deflects the river's course, causing it to wind round its flanks until, rounding a sharp turn, we saw the ruins of the Seven Churches directly ahead of us. I started up our engine and went ahead, creeping up to the stern of the canal boat while Angela stood at the bow coiling in the slack line until we cast off and waved good-bye to our 'tug'. While they disappeared from sight round the next bend, we came about in the wide reach and when we had headed into the current, dropped anchor near the fringe of the reeds. Where Shannon's margin is reedy the worst that can befall an approaching craft is either to run aground on soft mud or to become entangled in the reeds. But where the shore is bare it should be treated with caution and given a wide berth as this is almost invariably a sign that it is rocky.

After we had had some tea we rowed off in the dinghy, landing directly at the foot of the slope that led up to the ruins. As notices informed us, Clonmacnoise is now under the charge of the Irish equivalent of our Board of Works whose care of our historical monuments is usually exemplary. My first impression was that the Irish Board could profit by a study of our example in this respect. To reach the interior of the churches we had to beat our way through nettles. As a result of the desire for burial within the precincts, the ruins, including the famous High Cross, were almost submerged beneath a sea of unsightly tombstones of marble or polished granite. Furthermore, the demand for burial space had quite outrun the limited area available and in consequence the more recent dead displayed no reverence or respect for their predecessors in their anxiety to find room for themselves. Many of the older tombstones had been uprooted and broken by newcomers, while newly turned earth was-strewn with fragments of human bones. The fact that one's bones will, in all probability, be uprooted and flung aside by the next generation seems to me to make nonsense of the desire for burial at Clonmacnoise; only the belief that they will lie undisturbed in this quiet place until they rise with St. Ciaran when the last trump sounds makes it understandable. It seems to me that the only way of reconciling the dignity of Clonmacnoise with its continued use as a place of burial would be to do three things; firstly, to consecrate additional ground; secondly, for those that desire such memorials, to forbid the erection of unsightly tombstones and to insist instead upon some simple form of recumbent slab; thirdly, to keep the precincts properly mown and tended. I would add one further point. At one corner of the churchyard we came upon a shack-like wooden structure which we at first took to be a refreshment hut. But instead of a counter for the sale of fizzy lemonade it contained a jerry-built altar. It was, we understood, used on the occasion of organized pilgrimages to Clonmacnoise. What, I wondered, would St. Ciaran make of this latter-day product of the faith which once reared the great High Cross and these tall towers? To remove it would be a more fitting act of piety than a dozen pilgrimages.

From the point of view of the sight-seer the most noteworthy features of Clonmacnoise are the aforementioned High Cross, or the Cross of the Scriptures as it is called, to distinguish it from the other crosses within the precincts, and the beautiful doorway and chancel arch of the Nuns Church a quarter of a mile distant along an old causeway. The Celtic Cross is said to have been erected in the year 914 by Abbot Colman over the grave of King Flann Sinna, the Ard Ri. Between them, these two had founded the cathedral church of Clonmacnoise where, beneath the chancel, Rory O'Connor the last king of Ireland lies buried. The Cross, of elaborate Hiberno-Romanesque workmanship and displaying upon its shaft a number of symbolical groups of figures, is in a wonderful state of preservation. The doorway and arch at the Nuns Church belong to the twelfth century and are said to have been erected by Dervorgilla, wife of Tiernan O'Rourke who, because her faithlessness led to the Norman invasion, has been called the Helen of Ireland. With these exceptions there is nothing at Clonmacnoise to compare in glory of architecture with our medieval monuments. Yet, with the possible exception of Glastonbury we have nothing to compare with these ruins in their historical importance. It is for this reason that I have felt moved to speak so strongly about their present state. Clonmacnoise is a monument not of national but of European significance. Long before our great abbeys were thought of, this silent place beside the Shannon was a great seat of learning, culture and Christian faith, a lighthouse of the arts of living in the long night of chaos and barbarism which fell upon Europe after the collapse of the Roman Empire, an influence which transcended national boundaries. To-day, when Europe bids fair to fall into a similar state, there are those who believe that it will once again be Ireland's destiny to become a citadel of Christianity and the humanities. This may well prove to be true, but not until she is more mindful of these monuments of her past greatness, and erects beside them some more worthy symbol of her faith than a wooden shack, for by works are these things judged.

Despite recurrent plunderings and burnings by Dane, Munsterman and Norman, the great institution founded by Ciaran in A.D. 549 lived for a thousand years. As late as the twelfth century it flourished under the patronage of the kings of Connaught, a town surrounded the monastery and a bridge spanned the Shannon. But in 1178, the place was plundered by the Norman Hugo Constable, and throughout the next century Clonmacnoise continued to decline as a result of successive raids by the English. In 1214, a castle was built to the order of John de Gray, Bishop of Norwich, which dominated the monastery. But it was not until the sixteenth century that the end came. A Papal Commissary in 1515 found the monastery in great poverty, while in 1547 a terrific storm ruined the cathedral. Five years later the English garrison at Athlone completed the work of destruction leaving 'not a bell, large or small, an image or an altar, or a book or a gem, or even glass in a window'.

The ruined keep of John de Gray's castle now leans at a drunken angle having been, it is said, blown up by Cromwell. Surely no man in history has, rightly or wrongly, more ruins to his credit; they outnumber by far the beds where Queen Elizabeth reputedly slept or the hiding places of fugitive Stuarts. We clambered up the ruined stair of the castle that evening and sat upon the battlements looking out over the ruins and the river. The wind had fallen completely with the sun, the sky was overcast and it was very still. There was no sound at all but the distant pipe of the curlew crying over the darkening bogs. No landscape can have changed so little in a thousand years. In these days

ANCIENT IRISH UNIVERSITY.
Clonmacnoise, once 'a lighthouse of the arts of living.'

of chaos, arrogance, and confused thinking it is a pity, I thought, that more men cannot contemplate in quietness such immutable solitudes. Their influence is salutory and chastening. They make man aware of his creaturehood, of the brevity of a life 'bounded by a sleep', and of the vanity of ambition. But while it thus humbles him, the natural world enlarges man's humanity by enabling him to perceive the potential greatness of the human spirit with its unique creative capacity. It is a paradox that this perception should be born of humility and perish with pride, but it is so. I believe that it was for this reason that the Celtic saints sought solitude and built their churches in the loneliness of the bogs or upon the crags and islands of a wild coast. St. Ciaran was no exception, and he seems to have loved especially the Shannon, After studying under St. Finian of Clonard he became for a time a pilgrim, visiting St. Ninned of Lough Erne, St. Enda of Aran and St. Senan of Inis Scattery, a small island at the mouth of the river. He then stayed for a time with two brethren at Isel near Lough Ree before he founded his first settlement of Inis Aingin (Hare Island) on the lake itself. It was from here that he moved to Clonmacnoise, then called Ard Tiprait, or the Height of the Spring Well. Did he come as we had done, sailing down the river in a hide covered curragh?

This set me thinking of another more practical problem. The Danes are reputed to have sailed up the Shannon in their fighting ships to plunder Clonmacnoise just as they came up Severn to sack Worcester. But if this is true how did they ascend these rivers? The fall of the Severn between Worcester and the sea is not very great, but the Shannon falls swiftly 120 feet below Killaloe. Their long boats were surely too heavy to portage. Did they throw temporary dams across the river behind their boats, breaking them down one by one as they returned?

It was nearly dark by the time we rowed back to our boat. Not a breath of wind or eddy of current flawed the surface of the great river; silent it was, and so dark and still that but for the splash of our oars it might have been a sheet of black glass.

.   .   .   .

Shannon is not a river to be trifled with. When anchoring away from shelter it is advisable to remember the strong winds that blow over the exposed levels, and the fact that the river bottom often provides very poor holding ground for an anchor. We learned this lesson before we left Clonmacnoise. A stiff breeze got up in the night, and we awoke to hear the reeds rustling and scraping against our hull. *Le Coq* had dragged her anchor and settled herself comfortably in a reed bed with the wind dead on her beam. Thinking it would be sufficient, we had used our light anchor, but when we had breakfasted we got out the heavy anchor, rowed it out in the dinghy as far as the chain would allow; which was about mid-stream, and then let go. Returning to the boat we optimistically hauled on the chain, but instead of the boat moving out toward the anchor as we hoped, we merely hauled the anchor aboard without the slightest effort. It was a bright sunny morning so we decided to go for a walk instead of spending a lot of time and energy in getting off when the wind would in all probability drop towards evening as it had done the previous day. So we went along the bog road between honeysuckle scented hedgerows as far as the little village of Ballaghurt, making a detour to the shore of lonely Fin Lough whose waters were white with colonies of swans and black-headed gulls. We had grown very familiar with the latter birds while we were at our Athlone moorings. During the day there would scarcely be a gull to be seen, but every evening at dusk they would suddenly appear in their hundreds, swerving, swooping and dipping over the water after flies like so many swifts and melting away again imperceptibly as darkness fell.

When we returned to *Le Coq* and had disposed of a substantial high tea it was half-past seven, but although the wind had moderated somewhat there was still quite a strong breeze. However, if we did not make a move now it was obvious that we should not reach Shannon Harbour as we had planned before darkness fell. As we lay, if I attempted to move either ahead or astern our propeller would instantly become hopelessly fouled with reeds and, so far from getting clear, we should probably finish up in an even worse position. Somehow we had to get her stern clear. We tried shafting, but could get no purchase because the shaft simply sank in feet of soft mud. We decided to try to pull her clear with the aid of the dinghy in such a way that if we were successful we could keep going and not give the wind another chance to take us. We made the dinghy fast in her travelling position at the stern, and while Angela got ready at the oars I started up the engine. By pulling the dinghy hard astern, she managed to swing our stern clear, and as soon as she had done so I was able to go astern so that we travelled broadside across the river. When I judged that we had room to swing I went ahead and put the helm hard over. For a moment I was afraid that the wind was going to beat us, but we came about with a few yards to spare and sailed off down the river while Angela managed to scramble out of the dinghy on to the stern.

We kept going at a good pace until we sighted the many-arched bridge at Shannon Bridge and passed beneath the swinging span against the east bank. Just below, was the Grand Canal depot with a canal-boat lying alongside the quay. Opposite, and commanding the bridge was a gloomy fortress backed by a defensive wall of formidable proportions which extended westward like a grey comb along the crest of yet another of the green esker ridges. It was a symbol of the more peaceful times that have now come to the Shannon that, according to the signs displayed, part of the fortress had now become a village shop and bar.

A quarter of a mile below Shannon Bridge it is conceivable that an unobservant navigator might find himself proceeding up the river Suck instead of down the Shannon. The Suck is itself a broad river which was once used for navigation to Ballinasloe before the construction of the Grand Canal. Its mouth directly faces the traveller proceeding downstream, while the parent river at this point makes an acute right-angle turn, and soon widens out considerably. By now the light was beginning to fail so that it was becoming difficult to pick up the navigation buoys and markers. But we were able to slacken speed for not only was the river more sheltered by trees and higher banks, but the wind appeared to have died completely. A stormy sunset had been succeeded by a brooding grey dusk, and in the hushed stillness of this mysterious half-light we seemed to be moving, not upon a river, but through a succession of reed-fringed meres. Often we thought we had somehow missed our course and were heading into some broad backwater only to find another silver sheet of water opening out before us. To liken the Shannon to a long lake instead of to a river, is by no means fanciful. From its source at the Shannon Pot in the Cuileagh Mountains on the borders of Cavan and Fermanagh the river falls swiftly to Lough Allen, but in the

126 miles of its course through the great plain of Ireland from Lough Allen to Killaloe the total fall is little over forty feet. Most rivers of far less sedate and grandiose character become suitably adult and sluggish when they approach the sea, but in this respect the Shannon is a very remarkable river. For below Killaloe this great stream experiences a second childhood. As though suddenly recalling its mountain youth, it awakens and in a most undignified manner tumbles 110 feet between Killaloe and Limerick. It is this display of exuberance which has made possible the Ardnacrusha power station.

We were just beginning to fear that darkness would prevent us from reaching our objective when we saw, silhouetted against the sky above the bank on our right, the balance beams of a lock. We conjectured that this must be the entrance lock of the Grand Canal line to Ballinasloe. If we were correct, then the entrance to Shannon Harbour must be directly opposite, but all we could see in the gloom appeared to be a backwater spanned by a low wooden bridge and therefore obviously not navigable; also a small white cottage on the island which it formed. We slackened speed and held over to the west bank so that we should have plenty of water in which to manoeuvre. Very soon, the canal entrance opened out. It crossed the backwater, which we had first seen, at right angles, and cut off the tip of the island. The cottage stood on the larger portion and was connected with the mainland by the wooden bridge which carried the canal towing path. We swung across the river and ran in, mooring against the bank of the little island opposite the cottage. It was a snug and sheltered berth, and as we had made fast to a large tree it was impossible for any wind to worry us. Ahead of us, I could just discern the first of the two locks leading up to Shannon Harbour which had been the occasion of so much anxiety. So far so good; we had reached them with three days in hand.

Because there is night traffic on the Grand Canal and we were not lying at an accustomed mooring place, I lit a hurricane lamp and lashed it to the rail on the roof of the wheel-house. Then, to round off a successful day, we treated ourselves to tea and biscuits and a book in our berths. Reading in bed until the eyelids begin to droop with sleep (which is seldom very long) is one of my favourite indulgences: But the luxury of it can only be fully appreciated after a long day such as this had been and under such circumstances. I was just beginning to nod when I heard the steady exhaust beat of an approaching canal boat. Through the porthole I watched the dark shape slide past. Then I blew out the light and we fell asleep.

IRISH CANAL BOAT. A bye-trader on the Grand Canal.

CHAPTER FIVE

CLONFERT AND BANAGHER

As we had succeeded in reaching Shannon Harbour with time in hand, we resolved the next morning that we would walk to Clonfert Cathedral. We should not, I thought, lose the opportunity of making a pilgrimage to the burial place of one who was probably the greatest seaman and navigator that the world has ever known.

Brendan of Clonfert, or Brendan the navigator as he is more commonly called, made three voyages or series of voyages the story of which has been pieced together from tradition and by archæological research. Born by the shores of the Bay of Tralee and educated by Bishop Ere on the slopes of Kerry Head, it is safe to say that throughout the early years of his life Brendan was never out of sound of the sea. These early Celtic saints and *peregrini* were nearly all men of the sea for a reason which I have conjectured in the last chapter. Not only were they intrepid sailors, but they built their first oratories, forerunners of the great colleges of Clonard, Clonfert and Clonmacnoise, on remote islands or rocky headlands. Brendan established his first community on the slopes of Mount Brandon in Kerry, while it was his pupil Finian who was destined to build his cells on the crags of Skellig Michael.

It was from Brandon that Brendan set forth on his first voyage in a skin-covered sailing curragh in search of that mythical paradise of the farthest west which, under the names of Hy Brasil, Tir-nan-Og, Atlantis or the Isle of the Blest has haunted the imagination of men since time immemorial. According to tradition, Brendan made no attempt to influence the course of this voyage but allowed wind and current to steer him in the belief that God would guide him to these fortunate isles. It seems that it was Fionn-Barr of Ardfert who had told him:

> ...Tales, marvellous tales
> Of ships and stars and isles where good men rest,
> Where nevermore the rose of sunset pales,
> And winds and shadows fall toward the west.

But instead he found only the pitiless cliffs, the sea mists and the crying sea birds of the furthest Hebrides, Noss of the Shetlands, Iceland and the Faroe Islands. If we liken Brendan and his implicit faith in his drifting craft to our own civilization and its equally tacit belief in automatic scientific progress, this voyage in search of Utopia becomes a highly pertinent parable.

It is said that on his return, Brendan consulted his foster mother Ita and that it was through her that he realized his error in thus resigning himself blindly to the determinism of the elements instead of using his divinely bestowed gifts of ability and free-will. However this may be, Brendan's next voyage was evidently a much more purposive expedition. In his recent book, *Brendan the Navigator*, Doctor George Little illustrates a conjectural model of the type of craft which Brendan built for this second voyage. The hull of this vessel of A.D. 551 bears a remarkable resemblance to that of an ice-breaker Boat which I saw re-timbered at the yard of an English canal company in A.D. 1943. She was massively built of oak, iron fastened to the ribs, with a high prow and a whaleboat stern equipped with a steering paddle (the rudder had not then been invented). She was decked fore and aft, while the mast stepped in the well amidships bore a single lug sail. Her timbers were possibly skin-covered as the wooden curraghs of Inishbofin are to-day covered with canvas. She had considerable freeboard, and unlike the sailing curragh of the first voyage, she shipped no oars but depended upon sail alone. In this small but stoutly built craft, of which the Galway Pookawn of to-day is probably the direct lineal descendant, Brendan set forth once more to sail into the sunset, not this time at the mercy of the elements, but utilizing to the full all the navigational knowledge and skill of that time. Celtic knowledge of navigation was, in fact, much more extensive than is generally supposed, a knowledge inherited, cherished and developed no doubt from the remote past of their Mediterranean ancestry. There is much evidence to support the belief that on this voyage Brendan reached America nearly a thousand years before Columbus, that Newfoundland was his first landfall, and that he sailed from thence down the coast to the Bahamas and the everglades of Florida.

It was upon Brendan's return from this second voyage that he founded his monastery and college at Clonfert-Cluain Fearta Breannain or the Meadow of Brendan's Virtus. This was destined to become a great European University of three thousand students rivalled only by the similar institutions of Clonard and Bangor. Clear thinking was the liberal aim of education at this period, so that Clonfert was not merely an ecclesiastical college in the bigoted and dogmatic sense of the term. It is said that fifteen years elapsed before Brendan once more set sail to spend three years in Scotland where his wanderings are commemorated by many place-names such as Kilbrennan on the island of Mull and by a high cross which once stood upon Iona, From Scotland he passed to Wales, visiting the great Welsh scholars, Gildas the Wise and Cadoc of Llancarvan, and from thence to Brittany and the Cornwall of King Arthur. According to Bili, a ninth century Breton historian, Brendan, Machutus (St. Malo of Brittany), and Gildas joined forces with Arthur in his wars against the pagan.

Where Brendan voyaged after this is uncertain, but rumour and legend associate the name of this indefatigable traveller with the Canary Islands, Teneriffe, Egypt, Palestine and the Isles of Greece. Yet the patron saint of seafarers returned to Ireland to die in the convent of his sister Brigh at Annaghduin, ' "I fear", he said, "going alone, for the journey is dark. I fear the unknown - the presence of the King - the sentence of the Judge." When he had finished saying these things he blessed the brethren and his sister Brigh and, having gone out from that place, when he reached the threshold of the church, he said: "*In manus tuas Domine*" … Then he sent forth his spirit, having completed ninety-three years.' [From The Book of Lismore] And so Brendan set out fearfully and alone upon his last voyage while his body was brought home to Clonfert for burial.

The best way for us to reach Clonfert, I decided, would be to cross the river and walk along the canal towing path as far as Clonfert bridge. We therefore rowed over in the dinghy, mooring it at the tail of the western entrance lock from the river which had first given us our bearings the previous night. On our way over we had a look at the old manual chain ferry boat which was used for carrying boat horses across the river. By 1939, the present type of steel motor boat had virtually superseded the horse-drawn craft on the Grand Canal, but the war-time fuel shortage led to the construction of a number of wooden horse boats, usually described as 'emergency boats'. These were generally used for turf traffic over the eastern end of the canal between Dublin and turf loading points in the bog of Allen, but we were told that they had occasionally penetrated as far as Ballinasloe and so brought the old horse ferry into use once more.

It is, in fact, just under four miles from Fanning's Lock to Clonfert Bridge, but though I have walked many a mile along canal towing paths I have never known miles so long. Just above the head of the lock, the canal made a gentle turn northwards and then cut straight as an arrow across a vast expanse of bog. By the margins, the water was starred with the great white and yellow blossoms of water lilies while on the banks themselves grew innumerable spires of orchids - white, yellow and every shade of pink from crimson to palest rose. We walked and walked but the stone bridge in the distance ahead seemed to be moving with us. The weather looked threatening, but fortunately it held, for there was no shelter of any sort nearer than the bridge. We thought how pleasant it would be to get a lift on a boat, and listened in vain for the familiar beat of a Bolinder engine behind us. However, we at last reached the bridge and had struck off down the narrow lane sheltered by undergrowth just as the first drops of rain began to fall.

I do not regret that we visited Clonfert, if only for its associations, but the cathedral, which embodies all that is left of Brendan's Clonfert has, like so many of the old churches of Ireland, been very largely ruined by unsympathetic restoration. To my mind, no work of the ardent nineteenth century restorers in England that I have seen could rival the chill and arid bleakness of Clonfert's stony interior. The tawdry extravagance of Irish Catholicism would appear to have driven the protestant Church to the opposite extreme of drab puritanism. Even the great Romanesque west doorway which is the glory of modern Clonfert has been marred by the crass insertion of a small door whose vertical jambs conflict with the inclination of the septuple columns (symbolical, perhaps, of the seven sacraments) which support the arch. The oldest part of the building is now used as a vestry and occupies the position of a north transept in relation to the main body of the church. This has a low barrel roof of daub impressed with a mesh of interlacing grooves. Several theories have, I believe, been formulated to account for the origin of this curious surface effect. My own theory is that the thick wet daub was applied over a symmetrical framing or reinforcement of wattle work which held it in place while it set. When it had reached a certain degree of firmness, the uneven surface was levelled off down to the wattle frame thus ensuring an even and symmetrical roof. Finally, when the daub had hardened right off, the wattle framing was removed to leave only its impress upon the surface.

Close behind the cathedral and sheltering with it among the fine trees which make Clonfert an oasis in the bogland, stands the Bishops Palace, now a lay residence. Having been courteously granted permission to explore the grounds, we found Clonfert's celebrated yew walk which is reputed to date back to early mediæval times. The yews have attained unusual stature, and their interlacing branches curve outward and then upward towards the light to form a series of those ogee curved arches beloved of the Gothic revivalists of the Strawberry Hill period. As the main walk runs from east to west with two short transepts radiating from a central crossing, the effect is truly remarkable and resembles nothing so much as a great cathedral of natural growth. Moreover, the light within was appropriately dim and religious, the dark foliage excluding most of the light from an overcast sky. We found the silent twilight of this great nave of ancient trees strangely

CLONFERT – THE YEW WALK. 'A great cathedral of natural growth.'

impressive, more so, in fact than the man-made cathedral close by. In spite of the difficulty involved we decided to make this the subject of our pictorial record of Clonfert rather than the often-photographed west doorway.

As the weather appeared to be deteriorating rapidly we decided not to return by the exposed towpath across the bog, but to take the longer but more sheltered road through Banagher. It was well that we did so, for before we had gone far we were struck by a terrific squall of wind and rain out of the south-west from which we were able to shelter under a hedge. While we did so we consoled ourselves by thanking our stars that *Le Coq* was lying at a sheltered mooring.

The usual fortifications stand on the west bank of the river commanding Banagher Bridge. Opposite was the Grand Canal depot and the Maltings which are the town's staple industry, supplying malt to Guinness's Brewery at Dublin via the Grand Canal. Behind them, the little town wanders up a gentle slope in a single wide main street. The roadway was ill made, the houses looked seedy and drab, and an occasional derelict property gave the dingy facade of the street a gap-toothed appearance. The town seemed to have resigned itself to slow decay. In short, we thought it the most depressing small town we saw in Ireland. In fairness to the champions of Banagher, however, I should add that by this time we were both tired and hungry, that it was raining steadily, and that it was early closing day.

One August day in 1841 a carriage (or more probably a cart or a side-car) drew up before the hotel in the main street and there descended a shy, rather untidy young man of twenty-six. He had arrived to take up the post of clerk to the district surveyor, and his name was Anthony Trollope. I hope his first impression of Banagher was more favourable than mine.

CHAPTER SIX

THE GRAND CANAL

SHANNON HARBOUR TO TULLAMORE

On the morning following our visit to Clonfert we commenced our voyage through the Grand Canal. The history of the English canals and the story of their construction by our great civil engineers, Brindley, Telford and Rennie, though it may not be widely known to-day, is nevertheless much more fully documented than is the history of inland navigation in Ireland. In my view, some knowledge of the past is essential to the proper appreciation of the present. For this reason I think it well to preface the account of our journey from the Shannon to Dublin with a few notes on the history of Irish inland navigation in general and of the Grand Canal in particular.

'Much Ado About Nothing' would make an apt heading for the first chapter of this history, for although a number of high-sounding Acts to promote inland navigation were passed, practically nothing was accomplished beyond a few tentative surveys. The story begins with the appointment, on September 29, 1703 in the first Parliament of Queen Anne, of a committee to prepare a Bill for making the Shannon navigable from Limerick to Jamestown. In 1709 this Bill was presented and passed, but was not implemented. In 1715, the second year of the reign of George I, an Act was passed which established a general law authorizing inland waterway undertakings, and certain Members of Parliament were empowered to appoint undertakers to carry out waterway projects. It was intended that the waterways should serve the dual purposes of navigation and drainage, and the preamble is in this respect worthy of quotation. It is described as 'An Act to encourage the draining and improving of the Bogs and unprofitable low grounds, and for easing and despatching the inland carriage and conveyance of goods from one part to another within the kingdom'. In justification for this proposal it continues: 'Whereas the great tracts of bog and fenny waste grounds which encumber the midland parts of this kingdom are not only useless to the owners, but an occasion of corrupt air and a retreat and harbour for malefactors, and that it has been ascertained that navigable and communicable passages for vessels of burthen to pass through might be made from and through the said midland counties into 'the principal rivers, and that by the benefit of such master drains, the bogs and other lost grounds might be improved, and also a cheap and expeditious communication betwixt His Majesty's subjects inhabiting the several parts of his said kingdom might be opened, proceeds to authorize certain persons' … etc.

As a result, these 'certain persons' optimistically set to work to cover the map of Ireland with a mesh of inland waterways, in all no less than twenty projects. These included canals from Sligo and Galway to the Shannon at Carrick and Portumna respectively, and from the Shannon estuary to Cork. The germ of the Grand Canal project was also included in the proposal for 'a line from Dublin by the Rivers Liffey, Rye, Boyne, Mungagh and Brusna to Banagher on the Shannon'. But all this paper activity produced only one practical result, and even that proved abortive. Eight miles of the river Maigue from Adare to the Shannon estuary were made navigable. This was intended to form part of the Shannon-Cork Scheme which never materialized further.

Another Act was passed in 1729, but the only works actually constructed under it were in the north of the country, the navigation connecting Newry with the Upper Bann and Lough Neagh, and the Tyrone Navigation between Coalisland and Lough Neagh.

In the twenty-fifth year of the reign of George II, the Commissioners were constituted a body corporate with a perpetual succession and a common seal entitled 'The Corporation for promoting and carrying on an Inland Navigation in Ireland'. Their finances were to be derived from tillage duties. This body began work on the Grand Canal from Dublin to Ballinasloe, the Lagan Navigation from Lough Neagh to Belfast, the River Barrow Navigation from Athy to Scars, the River Boyne Navigation from Carrickdexter to Drogheda, and the Shannon Navigation from Limerick to Lough Allen. The enterprises of the Corporation, however, seemed to have been remarkable for their inefficiency, and the body was dissolved by Act of George III in 1787 whereupon, with the exception of the Grand Canal and the Lagan, responsibility for their works was vested in local corporations created by the same Act.

In 1800, a Board of Directors General of Inland Navigation was appointed 'to promote, complete and control Inland Navigation'. At this time there were eleven navigations either completed or under construction in Ireland. These were: The Maigue, Newry, Tyrone, and Lower Boyne under the control of the Board, and the Upper Boyne, Barrow, Foyle, and Lagan Navigations, together with the Grand and Royal Canals under private companies. Lastly, the Shannon Navigation was controlled jointly by the Board and the Grand Canal Company.

In 1831, yet another body, the Board of Public Works, was set up and assumed control of the properties hitherto vested in the Directors of Inland Navigation. Several new and abortive schemes were embarked upon including the Lough Corrib Navigation which has already been mentioned, and others to which I shall have occasion to refer later. In 1846, the Shannon came under the Board's exclusive control, and their appointment of the Shannon Commission who constructed the new locks at Meelick, Athlone, Tarmonbarry, Roosky and Jamestown was probably their most valuable achievement.

Now it seems to me that the great point of interest about this history is that long before the first still water canal was opened in England in 1761, ambitious canal projects had been promoted in Ireland under State patronage. Yet this initial advantage was wholly lost. While private venturers such as the Earl of Bridgewater, Earl Gower and Josiah Wedgwood secured the greatest civil engineering talent of the day and covered England with a network of canals, inland navigation in Ireland remained both literally and metaphorically bogged under successive Corporations, Directors and Boards who spent large sums of public money for practically no result. For example, the Commissioners incorporated by George II commenced work on the Grand Canal at the Dublin end in 1753. The work was inaccurately surveyed and badly engineered. As a consequence £50,000 of the original sum of £77,000 which was granted were squandered in costly errors. For example, the Corporation of Dublin granted an additional sum of £7000 to the enterprise upon condition that the canal should supply the city with water, but when water was first admitted to the works from the River Morrell, serious breaches and flooding occurred, and the canal had to be sealed off. After further work, another attempt was made with exactly the same result. Meanwhile the original contractor, by name Satterthwaite, had been succeeded in 1769 by a certain John Traill. Differences in the detail design of the locks which we afterwards noticed at the Dublin end of the canal no doubt recall these early efforts, while the larger size of the lock chambers of the first two locks west of James' Street Harbour are doubtless a reminder of the optimistic *éclat* with which the project started. Traill, apparently, fared no better than his predecessor, and in 1771 the Government abandoned the project as hopeless. In the following year, the present company was formed by private Bill. This 'The Company of Undertakers of the Grand Canal', which is still governed by its 'Court of Directors', has the distinction of being the oldest extant commercial corporation in Ireland. The first act of the new company was a wise one. They commissioned John Smeaton to resurvey the line of navigation and to advise upon the works which thereafter proceeded slowly but surely under the company's engineer, General Tarrant.

With the aid of grants totalling £83,776, the company completed the mainlines of canal from Dublin to the Shannon at Shannon Harbour in 1805 and to the Barrow at Athy in 1791. Ringsend Docks, beside the Liffey at Dublin, and the branch canal to connect them with the main line were completed in 1796 at an additional cost of £18,231. Finally, the extension of the main line to Ballinasloe in 1827, and the branches to Mountmellick (1830) and Kilbeggan (1834) were undertaken as poor relief work supported by grants. In all, the capital expended is said to have been £1,137,680. In 1894, the company purchased the Barrow Navigation from Athy to Waterford Harbour for £30,000. To-day, the Grand Canal Company claim that, including the River Shannon where, although they do not control the waterway, they have their own depots, they operate a greater mileage of inland waterway than any other company in the British Isles. Besides heavy bulk traffic such as turf, wheat, malt and Guinness, a very considerable volume of general merchandise of every description passes through the Grand Canal. In this respect, the interiors of the waterside warehouses which we saw during our passage through the canal exactly resembled a railway goods depot in the variety of individual consignments - cases of groceries, pieces of machinery and the like which we saw awaiting shipment or delivery. The fuel shortage which is a result of the 'emergency' has placed the canal in a strong position because for sheer fuel economy road or rail cannot compete with the canal boat. But in the years between the wars when road and rail competition was keen, the Grand Canal Company held their own by means of energetic goods agents at their local depots combined with an efficient local road delivery service from and to these depots.

The boatman of the Grand Canal approximates much more closely to the seaman or the river barge master than does his counterpart on the English canals. This is understandable, for his voyages are not confined to the canal but include the river Barrow down to the salt waters of Waterford Harbour, and the inland seas of the Shannon lakes. The family boat with which we are familiar on our English waterways is unknown in Ireland. The boats are manned by an all-male crew of three or four, the man in charge being known as the captain and not, as in England, the steerer. The junior member of the crew, as like as not, will be the small son of the captain. His job is to brew interminable pots of tea, peel the potatoes which form the staple diet afloat, mend the cabin fire with turf or run ahead to set the locks. But one day he will become a captain like his father, and so the skill of the boatman passes to successive generations. Most of these men will be found to have a cottage near the canal somewhere between Lowtown and Dublin which they contrive to visit quite frequently in the course of their passages to and fro.

The Canal was originally opened for traffic from James' Street Harbour, Dublin, to Tullamore Harbour, and the line from Tullamore to the Shannon is a subsequent extension. Its completion is commemorated by an inscribed stone set in the wall of the first of the two locks leading from the river to Shannon Harbour. Unfortunately, it had so weathered that I could not decipher the lettering. These locks were built with larger chambers than the other locks on the canal to enable the steamers which once plied on the Shannon to come up into the harbour. It is manifestly only possible for self-propelled craft to navigate the Shannon, so that in the days when traffic through the canal was horse-drawn, goods destined for places on the river were transhipped into steamers at Shannon Harbour. It was this necessity which created the ranges of stone warehouses and the single short street which is Shannon Harbour in the midst of the bleak windswept waste of the Shannon callows. Since nearby Banagher has its own quay on the river, Shannon Harbour serves no purpose except as a place of transhipment. Consequently, when the diesel-engined boats ousted the horse-drawn craft and began to ply direct between Dublin and the Shannon quays, Shannon Harbour suffered eclipse and became little more than a toll office and refuelling point. Yet at the time of our visit, as we soon discovered, this original activity was just about to be resumed. For the canal boats are not capable of weathering the violent storms which whip up the Shannon lakes into raging seas. The consequent delays, particularly in winter, are sometimes so great that, in the opinion of the company, they justify the labour of transhipping cargoes destined for the Shannon into larger craft capable of making the passage through Loughs Derg or Ree under any conditions of weather. To admit those bigger boats to Shannon Harbour, the two entrance locks from the river were to be still further enlarged, and it was this decision which had enforced our rapid change of plan. When we passed through that morning, baulks of timber, heaps of gravel, sheer-legs, portable air-compressors and pumps had already been assembled on the lock sides ready for the work that was due to begin in two days' time. I asked how traffic would be handled while the work was in progress. A certain number of boats would remain on the river, and through traffic would be transhipped by road from Shannon Harbour to be re-loaded at Banagher Quay.

SHANNON HARBOUR. The Grand Canal Hotel.

When we had got through the locks we tied up to the quay at the harbour for I had to pay my toll through to Ringsend Docks. We also wanted to make one or two purchases from the little shops and procure some stamps from the sleepy post office. I also decided to make some adjustments to the carburettor of our engine before we travelled any further. On her run from Clonmacnoise I had discovered that *Le Coq* had displayed an appetite for petrol which soon threatened to dispose of her slender ration. I had hoped we should reach Dublin on our first month's allocation, but we certainly should not do so if we continued to consume it at the present rate.

After the customary gossip, I paid my toll, £3 17s. or, in other words, 1s. 9d. per lock for the forty-four locks. We then walked across to the post office and in doing so passed the doorway of the most notable building at Shannon Harbour. This is an enormous stone house of three storeys with a front portico approached by an imposing flight of steps. A semi-derelict tenement, with the steps to the door cracked and broken, this was once an hotel built by the company in the days of the passenger 'packet' boat traffic; one of five, the others being at James' Street Harbour, Portobello, Robertstown and Tullamore.

Passenger traffic once formed a very considerable part of the Grand Canal Company's revenue. The service was inaugurated on June 9, 1788, when the Lord Lieutenant made a state progress through part of the canal in the new packet boat *Buckingham*. He took luncheon on board, and was further regaled by the strains of a band of musicians who had installed themselves in a second boat the *Mercury*. The imagination revels in the contemplation of this wondrous spectacle. Thereafter, the boats plied regularly and traffic increased steadily until, in the year 1837, a total of 100,695 passengers travelled over the canal. For a few years more the figure remained practically constant and then traffic began to fall off. The great famine seriously affected trade; in 1853, passenger traffic ceased entirely, and the coming of railways precluded any revival. Athy, Tullamore, Shannon Harbour and Ballinasloe were the most important stages, and boats left Dublin for these destinations in the morning and afternoon from James' Street Harbour and from Portobello. There was first and second-class accommodation, first-class passengers being allowed eighty-four pounds of luggage and second-class forty-two pounds. First-class fare from Dublin to Tullamore was 9s. 2d., and second-class 4s. 9d. 'Second-class' was the equivalent of 'outside' travel on a stage coach, although it is said that they had the advantage of a roof over their heads. Engravings of the period, however, would appear to suggest that they merely sat on the open cabin roof in imminent peril of having their heads knocked off when passing under bridges. The traffic was certainly organized on precisely similar lines to the stage coaches, and the company's hotels were simply the posting houses of this water-road. Like the stage coaches, the 'expresses' of the water were the narrow 'fly' passage boats by which the first- and second-class passengers travelled. By means of four horses travelling at the gallop, and by frequent changes, they managed to average eight miles per hour including the passage of locks. They travelled only by day. No doubt in winter the morning boat from Dublin rested at Tullamore, and the afternoon boat at Robertstown. Meanwhile the impecunious travelled in the equivalent of the road waggon, a slower and heavier craft which carried parcels as well as passengers and which travelled night and day.

In those days there was considerable interchange of passenger as well as goods traffic at Shannon Harbour. Travellers changed here from the Dublin passage boats into Bianconi's 'long cars' which operated between Birr, Shannon Harbour and Athlone in connection with the boats. Alternatively they might board the paddle steamers *The Lady Lansdowne* or *The Lady Burgoyne* which plied between Killaloe pier head and Athlone, calling at a jetty on the river near the mouth of the canal. Smaller craft sailed from Killaloe pier head to the transatlantic port of Limerick, and so the Grand Canal became a link in the route between Dublin and America. Shannon Harbour became celebrated for its oaten bread which passengers purchased in large quantities to take with them on their long voyage across the Atlantic. The departure of a passage boat from Shannon Harbour was heralded by the ringing of a large bell in the now empty cote over the stables. This was tolled three times, once for the horses to be harnessed, twice for the passengers to board, and thirdly as a signal for departure.

To-day, all that remains to tell of this once extensive traffic, apart from the gaunt hotels, are the early records and a few relics, such as an old menu card or a blunderbuss once carried by a postilion, which are preserved at the offices of the company. Yet the passage boats have left their mark in contemporary literature. Charles Lever in his novel *Jack Hinton* sends his hero on a passage boat from Portobello to Shannon Harbour where he attempts to find accommodation at the hotel, then already in decay. I am fortunate in possessing a copy of this forgotten novel, and am tempted to quote at considerable length from the fascinating though derogatory chapter which describes this journey. I will confine myself to a brief passage depicting the arrival at Shannon Harbour. He describes:

> '... the sedgy banks whose tall flaggers bow their heads beneath the ripple that eddies from the bow ... the loud bray of the horn ... the far-off tinkle of a bell. We near Shannon Harbour, and all its bustle and excitement. The large bell at the stern of the boat is thundering away ... the banks are crowded ... the track rope is cast off, the weary posters trot away to their stables, and the stately barge floats on to its destined haven without the aid of any visible influence. A prospect more bleak, more desolate, more barren it would be impossible to conceive -a wide river with low and reedy banks, moving sluggishly on its yellow current between broad tracts of bog or callow meadow-land; no trace of cultivation, not even a tree to be seen. Such is Shannon Harbour.'

Trollope, too, in *The Kellys and the O'Kellys* sends Martin Kelly from Portobello to Ballinasloe. His description of the journey, which is as derogatory as Lever's, may well be auto-biographical for it is possible that he travelled through the canal as a young man to take up that first post at Banagher. Mr. Kelly, he tells us, travelled continuously for twenty hours, arriving at Ballinasloe at 10 a.m. whence he caught a Bianconi car to Tuam. He complains of the tedium of canal travel:

> 'I hardly know why a journey in one of these boats should be much more intolerable than travelling either outside or inside a coach; for, either in or on the coach, one has less room for motion, and less opportunity for employment. I believe the misery of the canal-boat chiefly consists in a pre-conceived and erroneous idea of its capabilities. One prepares oneself for occupation - an attempt is made to achieve actual comfort - and both end in disappointment; the limbs become weary with endeavouring to fix themselves in a position of repose; and the mind is fatigued more by the search after, than the want of, occupation.'

Trollope's opinion of Grand Canal catering abilities also appears to have been low:

'He [Martin Kelly] made great play at the eternal half-boiled leg of mutton, floating in a bloody sea of grease and gravy, which always comes on the table three hours after the departure from Porto Bello. He, and others equally gifted with the *dura ilia messorum*, swallowed huge collops of the raw animal, and vast heaps of yellow turnips, till the pity with which a stranger would at first be inclined to contemplate the consumer of such unsavoury food, is transferred to the victim who has to provide the meal at two shillings a head. Neither love nor drink - and Martin had, on the previous day, been much troubled with both - had affected his appetite; and he ate out his money with the true preserving prudence of a Connaught man, who firmly determines not to be done.'

James Johnson, M.D., in his *A Tour in Ireland* (1844), describes a departure from Portobello in less disparaging and more informative terms:

'At Portobello ... the head of the Grand Canal ... there was bustle enough. Passengers of all descriptions with their diversified luggage were tumbling into the fly-boat on the quay. This same boat is curiously constructed, and a very slight inspection of it would prove its Hibernian origin. In all other boats - even canal boats - in England, the best cabin is in the stern; but here it is on, not under, the forecastle. The Captain's cabin is amidships and the cabin of the crew, with caboose and all kinds of stinkables and filth, is in the stern. The cabin of the passengers, although rather small, is far from uncomfortable, and in fine weather you may sit outside on the small forecastle or platform. When passing the locks, however, which are numerous, or, rather, innumerable, all hands are crammed into the cabin, and the: door is closed to prevent the spray coming in, while a regular cascade tumbles headlong down close to the head of the boat and splashing over the forecastle.
'The horses were put to, and away they went at full gallop exactly at 7 o'clock. But the locks in the first ten or fifteen miles are very numerous, though it must be confessed they passed through them with wonderful rapidity. They will get through a double lock even on the ascent in five minutes, and on the descent to the Shannon in three minutes or less. The dress of the postilions, the measured canter or gallop of the horses, the vibration of the rope, the swell that precedes the boat, and the dexterity with which the men and horses dive under the arches of the bridges without for a moment slackening their pace, all produce a very curious and picturesque scene such as I have never seen equalled in Holland or any of its canals.'

After an early lunch, we cast off and began our eighty-mile journey to Ringsend. The canal climbs up the valley of the River Brosna which joins the Shannon at the same point. The first lock at Colony Bridge came soon and was equally soon negotiated. Not so the next lock at Bellmount, two miles further on. This was what is called in Ireland a double lock. To anyone not accustomed to the waterways, the description is misleading, for here a double lock does not imply a pair of locks side by side such as are found on the Trent and Mersey Canal on the Cheshire side of Harecastle Tunnel or in the Oxford Canal at Hillmorton. The Irish double lock is the equivalent of our 'staircase' or 'riser', that is to say it consists of two successive lock chambers having an intermediate pair of gates. It is thus, in effect, two locks although for toll purposes it counts as one. Towards the upper end of the lower chamber, the lock walls rise to the level of the upper chamber so that it will be appreciated that at this point the lock is very deep. But even in the lower portion it is difficult to scramble on to the lockside from the deck of a small boat when the lock is empty.

Added to this, for some unknown reason, no Irish lock is provided with a landing platform and steps at the lock tail such as is found on almost every English lock and which enables a member of the crew to step ashore and set the lock as the boat comes in. Instead, he must jump as best he may from the boat to the bank when nearing a lock. Boats travelling by night on the Grand Canal are only permitted to carry a red light for'ard on the grounds that a white headlight would dazzle oncoming craft. Imagine, then, the hazard of these deep locks and this hit-and-miss leap from the boat. It is said that at least one man is lost in this way on the Grand Canal every year, and that there is scarcely a lock on the main line which has not within living memory claimed a victim either by drowning or by being crushed to death between steel boat side and lock wall. This tragic toll could easily be reduced. At many, if not all, of the locks, landing places could readily be built, while a lesson could be learnt from our own Grand Union Canal where night 'fly boats' operated perfectly satisfactorily with electric headlights before the war, and where bridge-holes, steps and locksides were outlined with whitewash so that they could be distinguished at night. But to return to Bellmount lock. This was made particularly awkward by an overbridge, the arch of which spanned the lower chamber, springing sheer from the lock walls on either side. This made the lock extremely difficult for a crew of two to work, and almost impossible, with a boat the size of ours, to get bow and stern lines ashore and make fast while the lock was filling. A boat that filled the lock chamber, on the other hand, could easily put out lines above and below the bridge respectively. Just to add to our difficulties the lock keeper was out, while a following wind, blowing in through the open bottom gates, swung the dinghy round till it jammed broadside between the walls. The dinghy was just the most awkward length in this respect and proved to be little more than a nuisance on the canal section of our voyage. But since it was absolutely essential on the Shannon, and as we should be rejoining the river at a different point, we could not leave it behind. Angela, who had got ashore, closed the bottom gates while I managed to right the dinghy with a boathook. By this time a volunteer from a neighbouring cottage had appeared and drew the paddles while we kept the boat as steady as possible. As soon as the lower chamber was full, the intermediate gate could be opened, and we could move into the upper lock, our difficulties were over. Bellmount, as we had been told at Shannon Harbour, is the only double lock on the canal's western descent to the Shannon. There were a number of double locks on the Dublin side of the summit, but by this time we should have a crew of four. Moreover, we never encountered another lock, either on the Grand Canal or on the Royal which had another such awkward bridge.

When I said that our assistant at Bellmount 'drew the paddles' I used the English term for the rack-operated sluices which let the water in or out of the lock. If these are mounted on the bank beside the lock, admitting water through a brick culvert they are called 'ground paddles' in England. If they are mounted on the lock gates they are called 'fly-paddles' or 'flashers'. But in Ireland, we learned, the equivalent terms are 'land racks' and 'breast racks' respectively. By comparison with some of our English locks, those on the Irish canals were well provided with large sluices and were therefore capable of being filled or emptied remarkably quickly. There were two 'breast racks' on each of the four gates and two 'land racks' beside the top gates. But if, when we were locking up, as now, we had lifted all six top racks together, for a few moments the lock chamber would have become a mill race in which our small craft would have been dashed about uncontrollably. A canal boat which is built to fit the locks cannot swing more than a few inches and can therefore draw faster. We found by experience that the best technique when ascending these locks was as follows. We would lie against the lock wall with fore and aft lines ashore as near the lower gates as possible; only so far in, in fact, that the stern of the dinghy would clear the bottom gates. We would then lift the land rack on the side opposite that on which we were lying, opening it half way at first and then fully. Next we would lift the other land rack and only begin to raise the four breast racks when the water in the lock had made up considerably.

In just under a mile from Bellmount we came to the single lock at Glyn's Bridge after which we knew that we had a level pound of ten miles ahead of us. For a time we travelled through sheltered waters, but presently emerged onto a desolate expanse of bogland. The morning had been bright and sunny with a stiff breeze, but now the wind had dropped and the sky was overcast, threatening rain. The canal constructors deliberately chose to carry their waterway across the bog wherever practicable with the idea of saving the cost of earthworks. But this proved to be false economy. Subsequent draining, and the turf cutting which was stimulated by the canal itself have between them lowered the level of the bogs. This has meant costly maintenance work which has resulted in the canal being carried on an embankment high above the surrounding country. It was on such an embankment that we travelled for some distance, crossing over the Silver River by a stone built aqueduct which, as we saw from the inscribed stone on the parapet, was called Macartny's. Without exception, all the Irish canal works are of stone and of truly massive proportions. Unlike our brick-built bridges and locks which tend to crumble with age, these works, built on a monumental scale with great blocks of the hard, fine grained, marble-like grey limestone of the central plains, are as sound as the day they were made. They are enduring tributes to the craft of stone masonry. Nearly all the over bridges bear a name and the date of their construction carved in a square block over the keystone. Sometimes they carry the local place name, sometimes that of some defunct, landed proprietor in the neighbourhood, and sometimes an obscure surname. Do these latter, one wonders, also refer to some local inhabitant or to the foreman mason responsible for the bridge?

We travelled on; silver water ahead, grey sky above, on either hand a brown sea of bog. A desert could scarcely have appeared more lonely or more desolate. We met two or three canal boats, and once we passed an isolated wharf where boats were loading turf. But apart from these and an occasional solitary cabin the only sign of civilization in these ten miles was the little hamlet of Pollagh, a school house and a handful of cottages beside the canal.

By the time we reached Cornalaur Lock at the end of the level it was nearly seven o'clock and we were in two minds whether to continue or not. *Le Coq* decided the matter for us. When I made to start up the engine, to come out of the lock, the chain on the overhead starting gear broke, so we bow-hauled her out and moored up to the bank clear of the lock head. It was a satisfactory mooring place for we were clear of the bog at this point and sheltered by trees. There was a lock cottage on one side of the water and a peat thatched farmhouse on the other with a pump in the yard where we could get drinking water. When I went to it later with our bucket I discovered that it was a wooden pump which had obviously been bored out of the solid tree trunk with a huge auger in the manner which Walter Rose describes in his book *The Village Carpenter*.

But before I went in search of water I concerned myself with the broken chain. I should explain that whereas *Le Coq* possessed an electric starter, this was out of action because the battery had become defunct while the boat was laid up, and Jack had been unable to replace it. The hand starting gear was constructed of cycle parts; a pedal crank for handle, a free-wheel sprocket and a long length of cycle chain which disappeared downwards into the bowels of the vessel. While it was an ingenious adaptation it was hardly man enough for the job of swinging a 14 h.p. engine, being obviously intended for emergency rather than for continuous use. The alignment of the sprockets was not too good with the result that the slender chain emitted ominous creaks and cracks of protest whenever used. But it was going to get a great deal of use in the next few weeks because I could not afford, on our meagre petrol ration, to keep the engine running in the locks. I resolved to try and obtain a heavier chain when we reached Tullamore, but meanwhile, without rivet punches or an extractor, the existing one must be repaired before we could move again. In this difficulty I was helped by the fact that everybody rides a bicycle in Ireland. 'Himself' from the cottage next door to the farm enquired what was wrong, bore off the chain and returned it a few minutes later neatly repaired. I fitted it on again but dared not test it, deciding it would be better to conserve all its energies for the following morning when it would really be required.

We were awakened next morning by the sound of the paddle racks at the lock being drawn, although we could hear no approaching boat. Looking out through the port-hole I saw the first horse boat we had encountered in Ireland. It was presumably one of the wooden 'emergency boats' and was travelling light, probably to load turf at the wharf on the bog which we had passed the previous day.

When we had breakfasted, the tense moment arrived. Would the chain break again or would the engine start? She started, but I decided to take no more chances and keep her running, locks or no locks, until we reached Tullamore.

We came to the next lock at Ballincloghan in less than a mile. Then followed a four-mile level. The canal had now left the bog and was pleasantly sheltered by trees and undergrowth. We passed occasional thatched cabins, the cottagers' donkeys, cows or geese grazing the narrow strip of sward beside the water. Often a rough road ran along both sides of the canal to connect these cottages together and was obviously their only means of access. The provision of accommodation bridges is by no means so liberal on the Irish canals as in England, and moored beside most of the waterside cottages and farms which we passed on the journey we saw small ferry punts; oblong wooden boxes which were pushed across the water with the aid of a pole.

Just before we reached the end of the level at Ballycowan Lock with its trim whitewashed lock cottage we crossed the Huband Aqueduct over the Clodiagh River which we had been following for some distance and saw on our left the extensive ruin of Ballycowan Castle. In the ordinary course of events we should have stopped to inspect this, but not only was I anxious to keep our engine running, but by this time it was raining steadily and we were glad of the shelter of the wheel-house. Also we were now quite close to Tullamore where we should have three days to wait for the arrival of our friends, during which time we might walk back to Ballycowan and see it under more favourable weather conditions.

IRISH CASTLE, Ballycowan. A seventeenth century fortress by the Grand Canal.

Beyond the next bridge there was a fine stand of beeches, on the left bank, a tree which flourishes on the limestone of the central plain, and it was here that we caught our first glimpse of Tullamore, the lofty spire of the church and the distant bulk of the whisky distillery which is the town's principal industry. There are two locks at Tullamore, and we asked the lock keeper where we should lie so as to be not only out of the way of traffic but as free as possible from the inquisitive attention of the Irish small boy. He advised us to leave the main line of the canal and enter Tullamore Harbour. At first sight, the word 'harbour' seemed to be an exaggeration, for the short arm into which we turned appeared to come to a dead stop in front of a small warehouse, and to be in no way protected from unwelcome attention. However, when we reached the apparent terminus we found that a narrow cut at right angles communicated with a basin of great size surrounded on three sides by ranges of warehouses which, with their heavily barred windows, looked as strong as a prison. On the fourth side there was a dry dock in which a freshly painted boat was lying. Here we were able to find a reasonably secluded berth which was out of the way of boats coming to the quays. In this connection I ought to mention that, because of the heavy traffic on the Grand Canal, 'pleasure boats' (or 'yachts' as they are generally called in Ireland), are not customarily permitted to lie up on the canal but are expected to make the passage between the Shannon and Dublin in three days. In our case owing to the closing of the Shannon Harbour Locks and the fact that we had to meet our friends at Tullamore, this rule was courteously waived.

Though we saw plenty of activity during our stay, the traffic in the harbour was certainly not commensurate with its size, and the greater part of the floor space in the warehouses was unused. In the early days of the canal great quantities of wheat are said to have been handled here. But in Ireland, as in England, arable acreage declined steeply after 1870 and this must to a great extent account for the eclipse of this traffic. It has been estimated that in 1870, 5,659,796 acres of Irish soil were under rotation crops. By 1902 the figure had fallen to 4,641,937 acres, or in other words over a million acres had gone back to grass. I do not know, but would be interested to learn, what the figure is to-day. During the 'emergency', Ireland pursued a 'plough-up' policy similar to our own and one which is open to the same criticism. Farmers were ordered to plough up a certain percentage of their total acreage, and the result demonstrates the fallacy of attempting to impose any measure of arbitrary uniformity upon a craft so variable. While the larger farms on the rich lands of the east and south might well have exceeded the prescribed arable acreage, the small peasant farmer on the poor lands of the west has frequently been compelled to expend fruitless labour in cultivating land so poor as to be incapable of repaying the cost of the seed.

One evening I was talking with the captain of a boat which was lying at the quay loading sacks of malt for Dublin. Though the boat bore the letter 'M' after her number, it transpired that he was, in fact, a bye-trader who had chartered the boat from the company and was working her on his own account. This, I understood, was a not unusual arrangement.

TULLAMORE. The Grand Canal Harbour.

Wages on the company's boats are low, and the captain striking out on his own has the chance of earning a larger return. But it is a chance that depends on the luck of securing remunerative cargoes and quick turn-rounds because the outgoings are considerable; hire of the boat and fuel, wages of the crew and the tolls paid to the canal company. This man had worked on the canal all his life and now his small son was working with him. He took me through the fore hatch and down the vertical steel ladder into his cabin. Though bare it was spotlessly clean and much more roomy than the external appearance of the boat would suggest. A cheerful turf fire glowed in the stove making the cabin very warm and snug. There were four bunks, two on each side, the upper ones folding up out of the way during the daytime. The only ornament was the inevitable highly-coloured 'Holy Picture', in this case a vivid and almost anatomical rendering of the Sacred Heart.

I liked Tullamore. It is a trim, spacious town. I liked the broad square in the centre of the town, and the gentle slope of the wide main street. There were good shops where we were greeted with the same kindliness and courtesy as we had enjoyed at Athlone and which enabled 'those people on the yacht' to take aboard sufficient stores to see them through to Dublin. Here I was also able to acquire a chain of the variety known as 'Carrier cycle' which effectually disposed of our engine-starting difficulty-for the rest of the trip.

As the day following our arrival was a Sunday, and the morning brilliantly fine, we decided to walk through Charleville Park and from thence to Ballycowan. The park is extensive and lies about a mile to the south west of the town. It is not open to the public, but I obtained written permission to walk through it from the estate office. It is heavily and finely timbered; indeed, as we walked up the drive towards the castle I thought I had never seen oaks so magnificent in girth and stature. This was the more surprising because as a general rule the oak does not flourish in Ireland as it does in England. Doubtless the shallow limy soil does not favour this deep-rooted tree as it does the surface-rooted beech. There are red deer in the park, but they are very shy, and we only caught sight of one hind moving between the trees.

When we rounded a bend in the drive and found ourselves confronted by Charleville Castle, my immediate reaction was to stop in my tracks and stare fixedly at it. There was such an air of fantasy about this extraordinary manifestation of latter-day Anglo-Irish feudalism that I felt it might dissolve and vanish if I looked away. Despite its massive limestone walls it somehow looked as unsubstantial as a film set. It is a building to make a Hollywood film magnate's eyes light up, for were he to purpose a film based on one of the Waverley novels he would undoubtedly conjure just such a facade out of lath and plaster. The 'Gothick' portico was flanked upon one side by a lofty octagonal keep, and

IRISH CASTLE, Charleville 'Georgian Baronial'

on the other by an even loftier round tower which resembled nothing so much as a crenellated lighthouse. In addition to octagonal towers at the other two angles of the rectangular block, there was also a massive square central tower, a corner of which appears in our photograph.

The castle has long been unoccupied, but is jealously guarded by an ancient retainer who lives in what were once the coachman's quarters over the stables. From the little we could see of the interior, it appeared to be of a style which I can best describe as Georgian Baronial. Judging from the maturity of the oaks in the park, this astonishing structure must occupy the site of an earlier building.

We progressed from the replica at Charleville to the genuine at Ballycowan Castle. When we had passed this building in the boat the previous day I had judged it to belong to the fifteenth or, at the very latest, the early sixteenth century. But I was to learn that it is dangerous to apply English architectural standards in Ireland. When in England the lords of many manors had long ago left their gloomy castles to the owls and jackdaws and built great houses that lacked even the defensive of a moat, their fellows over the water were still embattling themselves against the 'wild Irish'. Except for the size of its stone mullioned windows, Ballycowan is nothing more than a mediæval keep, yet it was built by Sir Jasper Herbert in 1625. His escutcheon surmounts the doorway together with the truculent motto: 'By God of Might I hold, my Right'. This doorway now opened directly into a farmyard, while what had once evidently been an extensive underground magazine had become a cow byre. The building above displayed ample evidence of Sir Jasper's intention to live up to his motto. The immensely thick walls bristled with gun ports, while on the battlements, machicolations over the doorway and near the angles promised the unwelcome visitor a warm reception of boiling pitch, molten lead or some similar form of largesse. Part of the magazine, I noticed, had a daub ceiling similar to that which we had seen at Clonfert Cathedral. This would seem to indicate the continuance of this form of construction in the seventeenth century, unless the magazine formed part of an earlier building.

We walked back to Tullamore beside the canal. Since we had passed that way the previous day, a family of tinkers had pitched their low tent beside the bank. The man and his wife were sitting in the evening sunlight before a turf fire on which was planted a smoke-blackened pot. The woman wore a black shawl over her head and was lilting softly to the child cradled in her lap. On the day following, we visited both Catholic and Protestant churches although, as we anticipated, they proved to be characteristically unrewarding. The former exhibited the customary copious display of Catholic repository bric-a-brac. The Protestant church stands some little distance from the town upon the summit of a huge mound which has every appearance of being artificial but concerning which we could discover nothing. As usual, it was locked, and the interior, damp, fusty and decaying, scarcely repaid the trouble of obtaining the key. A colony of wild bees had made their hive over the south door and filled the empty church with their humming. The only other object of interest was an enormous white marble group by Van Nost which practically filled the small south transept. Muses mourned over the idealized, gracefully reclining figure of Moore, first Lord Charleville, Baron Tullamore; the group, we were informed, being a token of the gratitude of his nephew and heir Burton, second Lord Charleville. Sic transit … only the bees sing dirges for him now and his castle is desolate.

Few things have a greater attraction for my eyes than a distant range of hills or mountains. Whether they merge into the blue of the horizon, whether they veil themselves in mist or stand stark in the storm light they entice me to scale them and to discover what country lies beyond their far skyline.

> But who are ye in rags and rotten shoes,
> You dirty-bearded, blocking up the way?

asks the Master of the Caravan in Flecker's *Hassan*, and the Pilgrims answer:

> We are the Pilgrims, master; we shall go
> Always a little further: it may be
> Beyond that last blue mountain barred with snow ....

I, too, know well this urge to go 'always a little further', and the particular objective in this case was the ridge of the Slieve Bloom Mountains which seemed to have marched along beside us in tantalizing fashion all the way from Shannon Harbour. They were about eleven miles distant from Tullamore, so we proposed to hire bicycles and visit them if the weather held fair.

The only cycle Tullamore could offer us was an ancient tandem, a type of vehicle which neither of us had experienced before. We were prone to wobble perilously when starting off, while we struck each other some agonizing blows on the shins by inadvertently rotating the pedals while the other was unprepared. Apart from an occasional fellow cyclist or a creaking donkey cart we had the road to ourselves so that our erratic course was not fraught with any great danger and by lunch time we had reached the village of Clonaslee at the foot of the mountains without mishap.

It was a glorious day, and having fortified ourselves with a glass of porter in the village bar, we rested in the sunshine on the parapet of the bridge which spans the same Clodiagh River that we had crossed in the boat at Ballycowan. Then we began the long ascent of the mountain road that leads to Mountrath on the other side of the ridge. It was a long up-hill walk of four and a half miles to the 1400 feet summit where the road cut through the narrow spine of the ridge by a deep rocky defile. The smooth shoulders of Slieve Bloom with their even fleece of heather were a contrast to the naked rocks of Connemara, while the prospect from the summit, which well repaid the labour of the ascent, was also very different from that wilderness of lakes and sea upon which we had gazed from Ben Gower. In the direction from which we had come, the great central plain spread away like a blue sea in the haze of the summer afternoon. Southwards, beyond the pass, the landscape was more varied. We could distinguish the distant Galtees on the far horizon, while to the south-west and nearer at hand we could identify the cleft summit of the Devil's Bit Mountain. It is this cleft which gives the mountain its name, and the rock thus bitten out, says the legend, was subsequently let fall to form the rock of Cashel. Like our own Wrekin, this is only one of the many titanic tasks which tradition credits to the labours of the industrious fiend.

Less than a mile from our vantage point was Barna Mountain where the River Barrow rises, and there is legend here also. It is said that the river has its source in a well which is singularly temperamental. To touch its waters, or even to look into it, is enough to make it overflow and to induce a deluge of rain into the bargain. Once disturbed in this way, the well can only be set at rest and the countryside saved from inundation by the saying of Mass on the spot.

Another legend of the Slieve Bloom district relates to St. Molna's Monastery at Clonfert-Mulloe. Here there is a millpond which was said to make lepers of all who bathed in it except the monks. I confess that I suspect these holy men of fostering this reputation in order to ensure exclusive bathing rights.

If our ascent of the pass had been slow and laborious, our descent was swift and perilous. Our machine boasted only one ineffective brake on the front wheel, and to actuate this with any appreciable effect called for a grip such as one applied to those 'Try your Grip' machines which used to stand on sea-side piers. Before we had gone far, momentum increased, we began to bounce alarmingly on the rough road, and my clutching hand became almost paralysed with cramp. We managed to stop somehow, and then contrived to lash the brake lever to the handlebar with a leather strap which we luckily had with us. After a certain amount of adjustment this expedient answered the purpose. We returned intact to Clonaslee, and from thence proceeded in more sober fashion back to Tullamore which we reached just as dusk was falling.

SLIEVE BLOOM. 'If our ascent of the pass had been slow and laborious, our descent was swift and perilous.'

THE GRAND CANAL

TULLAMORE TO DUBLIN

Did our proximity disturb that cantankerous well on Barna Mountain? All the signs had seemed to promise a spell of fair weather, yet the morning of our friends' arrival dawned grey, still and ominous. Richard and Marten had hardly set foot on board before the first stealthy raindrops began to patter on the cabin roof. It rained heavily and unremittingly all that night, all the following day and most of the next night. To have moved off under such conditions would have been no pleasure. We hauled *Le Coq* under the projecting roof of a loading shed, which silenced the depressing tattoo of the rain on the roof and stopped the irritating leaks from hatch coamings and opened seams, and here we waited for better weather.

Nearly thirty hours of continuous rain was followed by an April-like morning of fresh clear air and hurrying white clouds which parted to reveal windows of blue sky and whose swift shadows chased the dazzling sunlight across wall and roof-top. We lost no time in getting under way, heading slowly round the acute turns out of the harbour and back on to the line of the main canal. In the first three miles we climbed six locks. Just above the last of these, at Ballycommon, the Kilbeggan branch, eight and a half miles long and now disused, leads off to the north. Here we moored. Though my adjustment of the carburettor at Shannon Harbour seemed to have reduced our petrol consumption considerably, I was still uncertain whether our petrol ration would prove sufficient. It seemed prudent to seek another tow while we had the chance, and this was the best place to do so because there lay ahead of us twenty-five miles of water with only one lock. I was anxious to conserve plenty of fuel for our return journey through the Royal Canal, for if we ran short there, there would be no alternative but to bow-haul.

We did not have to wait long. Richard had resigned himself to a long wait and was getting out his fishing tackle, but before he had baited his hook we heard the sound of a boat corning up the locks from the direction of Tullamore. A short colloquy with the captain while his crew were filling Ballycommon Lock was sufficient to clinch the bargain and so we soon resumed our journey. As we went we ate a simple lunch of fresh brown 'soda cake', country butter, cheese and coffee in the wheelhouse, taking turns at the wheel.

We soon discovered that our 'tug' was the canal equivalent of an 'ordinary goods' train on the railway, and in consequence our day's journey proved as slow as it was eventful. Our first stop was at Philipstown Wharf to pick up some empty porter barrels. ('Philip' was King Philip of Spain who is also the King of King's County.) After performing this arduous task the crew adjourned to the bar which was conveniently situated near the canal bridge and proceeded to do their best to empty another porter barrel. Richard and I gave them some small assistance, but for my part I found porter too heavy a drink to consume in any quantity on a summer noon.

Until now, the landscape had been unremarkable, but when we eventually left Philipstown it improved, Croghan Hill (769 feet) with its ancient church and castle away to our left is a notable eminence in this region of bogs and we passed through a finely wooded reach where the canal skirts Toberdaly Park. At the next bridge, which was just beyond the limit of the park, we stopped again, this time to deposit two sacks of sugar. There was no wharf or warehouse, in fact no sign of habitation. Apparently the sugar was destined for the shop in the little village of Road just over a mile distant. Here there was no convenient bar to detain us, and we were just congratulating ourselves on having got under way smartly when our 'tug' suddenly slewed across the canal and ran her bows into the bank while one of the crew jumped ashore. He had apparently arranged to call at the neighbouring cottage upon some errand or other. Having by now become inured to this erratic behaviour, we were prepared to fend off at any moment, otherwise we would certainly have rammed their stern with more damage to ourselves than to them.

When we were once more ready to move off it was found that the canal boat was fast aground at the bow and she resisted all the efforts of the crew to get her off. In English canal parlance, she was 'stemmed up'. At length we shafted *Le Coq* to the bank so that Richard and I could go to their assistance, and our united efforts succeeded in floating her off. We wondered what would have happened had we not been there. Presumably they would have waited for a passing boat to pull them off.

We passed a delightful little group of thatched cabins on the canal bank at Cartland Bridge, Ballykine, and presently reached the junction of the mile long branch to the town of Edenderry. Here the crew signified their intention of turning up the branch, suggesting that we should cast off the tow and await their return. As I never neglect an opportunity to explore any length of canal however short, we signalled back our intention of coming up to Edenderry with them. As things turned out, this was an unfortunate decision.

The canal terminated at a depot on the edge of the town, and here we proceeded to load the usual empty barrels. This accomplished, one member of the crew departed on a bicycle for his home which was not far away, while the other invited Richard and me to join him in a drink. The captain, who did not drink, remained on board looking impatient. Not caring to refuse the proffered hospitality, we accompanied our friend to the nearby bar. We fondly supposed that after one quick round we should be away again, for we had been promised a tow as far as Lowtown which was still nine miles away, and the evening was already far advanced. But once he was securely propped against the bar a charge of dynamite would scarcely have shifted our host. We could hear all the while the sound of the Bolinder engine idling in the basin, and imagined that by this time the captain was calling us unprintable names for luring away his crew however clear our consciences might be. Nor was this all. The news of our arrival appeared to have spread round the town like wildfire with the result that it seemed as if every child in Edenderry had crowded onto the towing path to look at the 'yacht'. Angela and Marten were having a struggle to keep them at bay. The dinghy seemed to be the chief attraction, strangely enough, and it was only with the greatest difficulty that they could be restrained from leaping into the 'wee boat'. The situation was most difficult, but our tactful suggestions that it was time to make a move were of no avail. 'Och'! he would reply, 'Time enough; let's be having another one now'.

At length it became obvious that there was only one thing to be done. We left the crew entrenched behind yet another pint of porter, started up our engine and beat a hurried retreat from the clamourous youth of Edenderry. So ended our second and last tow. Obviously our friend made a night of it, for our tug did not pass us by until the early hours of the following morning.

Having rejoined the main canal we journeyed across a great embankment high above the darkening bog until we reached the solitary lock at Ticknevan just above which we moored for the night. We had now reached the heart of those tracts of bogland which are called collectively the Great Bog of Allen. The ordnance map of the district showed, upon either side of the canal, vast blank spaces devoid of any track or habitation and patterned only with the thin blue lines of drains or sluggish streams.

It will already have become apparent from my frequent mention of them, that bogs are the dominant feature of the midlands of Ireland. Some people may wonder why this should be so when bogs scarcely exist at all in England. The reason is that in the great geological changes and upheavals of pre-history, Ireland fared badly in respect of the richness, depth and variety of her soils and in mineral resources. As in England, rich coal measures were laid down in Ireland at the end of the Devonian epoch, but a subsequent period of land lift produced what geologists call the Hercynian folds, in consequence of which practically all the coal measures were weathered away from the central area to survive only as cappings on the Arigna mountains which flank Lough Allen. Furthermore the particular inclinations produced by the folds largely prevented the deposition of subsequent strata. Thus, during the Permian and Triassic periods when the Oolitic strata were being laid in England to provide her with some of the best and most beautiful building stone in the world, Ireland was further denuded instead of enriched. For the same reason there is no chalk in Ireland. The only equivalent is the 'white limestone' of Slieve Gallion in Londonderry and of the cliffs near Portrush and in County Down. This is really chalk baked and crystallized by molten lava which welled up through fissures in the limestone floor during the upheavals which formed the English chalk Downs. The lava itself formed the great columnar basalt crags of Slemish and the Antrim Cliffs. In the Eocene period when the London clays were being laid in England, Ireland was rocked by a further series of earthquakes, eruptions and upheavals which threw up the high plateau of Antrim, the Mountains of Mourne, and separated first Ireland from England and finally England from Europe. When all these convulsions were over, Ireland emerged as a great natural amphitheatre, a ring of mountains, seldom far from her coastline, enclosing a central plain of carboniferous limestone, level, and lacking any well-defined watershed. Over half the area of Ireland, in fact, lies below the 309 feet contour. Hence the bogs. Though the arterial drainage scheme of the early nineteenth century reduced their area considerably, they are still very extensive. The soils of the plain, though shallow, are rich in lime and lime phosphates and therefore make excellent pasturage, very largely accounting for the reputation of Irish horse-flesh. Where land is reclaimed, there is thus no lack of lime to counteract the acidity of the bog. Yet, short of a nation-wide hydro-electric scheme; Ireland could not afford to dispense with her bogs, even if this were possible, because she depends on them for fuel. Despite the great consumption it seems unlikely that supplies will be exhausted, in fact it is said that certain worked-out bogs are very rapidly manufacturing fresh turf.

The vast bulk of Irish turf supplies are cut by hand in the traditional manner, but because the turf blocks require plenty of wind and sun to dry them before they can be carted from the bogs, the quality and quantity of the turf harvest is dependent on the season, and a prolonged spell of wet weather can produce a serious shortage. The countrymen, and the people of the smaller towns, generally cut their own supplies from neighbouring bogs, but the inhabitants of Dublin and the other larger centres of population are dependent upon turf drawn from the 'Government Bogs', bogs, that is, which have been taken over by the Turf Board. This Board is experimenting with new methods of winning and utilizing turf, and we passed the scene of one of these experiments at Lullymore soon after we left Ticknevan the following morning. The turf is cut from the bog by mechanical means and drawn to the factory where it is dried, pulverized, mixed with a binding agent and compressed into oblong briquettes which are about three inches thick, have a glazed surface and are comparatively clean to handle. From the point of view of the urban consumer perhaps the greatest advantage of these briquettes over natural turf is that they are of uniform quality. Natural turf absorbs water like a sponge. This property is a great source of profit to some unscrupulous dealers selling turf by weight.

We moored for lunch that day at Lowtown Wharf, between the junction of the canal to the Barrow and Lowtown Lock which would presently raise us to the summit level of the canal. I am told that the valley of the River Barrow is singularly beautiful, being narrow, deep and well wooded. It was thus a great source of disappointment to us that our limited fuel supplies would not allow us to explore it. For the benefit of those who may be more fortunate, I have included the Barrow Line in the itinerary at the end of this book. I was told, however, that navigation of the Barrow is by no means fool-proof, but calls for considerable experience and local knowledge. Whether the boatman who told me this exaggerated the hazards of this river I cannot say, but it is certainly true that the great majority of the boatmen working between Dublin and the Shannon never navigate the Barrow. Barrow traffic is virtually the monopoly, or one might almost say the craft, of a distinct class of boatmen who are usually referred to by the Dublin-Shannon men as the 'Barrow Boys'.

The history of the Barrow navigation is very similar, in the infirmity of purpose which marred its construction, to that of the Grand Canal. The length of the canalized river from the junction of the Grand Canal at Athy to the tidal river at Scars Rock is forty-three miles with a fall of 169 feet which is overcome by twenty-three locks. Prior to 1759, the river was only navigable in summer by boats of from two to three tons burden, but in that year work was commenced under the direction of a certain Thomas Omer with the idea of making the river navigable by seventy-ton boats. By 1790, only seven locks had been built, a company was incorporated to complete the work, and William Chapman appointed their engineer. He proposed the more modest load limits of fifteen tons in summer and thirty tons in winter, but subsequently the promoters again changed their minds by raising the limit to eighty tons. To this end, locks eighty feet by sixteen feet with five feet of water over the sills were designed, though for what reason is not clear because the Grand Canal locks above Athy were smaller so that these larger locks would be useless for through traffic between the two systems. However, ten of these locks were built and four of the earlier locks rebuilt, though by 1812 the navigation was still unfinished. Even when it was eventually completed, boats could not load fully in summer owing to lack of water. It has been said (and James Brindley, the father of our canal system would doubtless have concurred in this) that it would have been cheaper and more satisfactory to have constructed a parallel canal down the Barrow valley. In recent years, following their recent acquisition of the navigation, the Grand Canal Company have deepened the river so that fully-laden craft can now navigate at all seasons. As the river bed consists of solid rock in many places, this work involved blasting and considerable labour.

There are some who believe that the water which is used in the making of Guinness's Stout comes from a well beneath the brewery in Dublin. Others subscribe to the more cynical theory that supplies are drawn from the neighbouring River Liffey. Neither of these superstitions is correct, though the peat dark waters of the Liffey certainly lend colour to the latter belief. Actually, Guinness is made from canal water and should therefore be the staple beverage of all inland waterway enthusiasts. As this may sound even less inviting than the waters of the Liffey I must hasten to explain the statement. Near Milltown on the Curragh of the County Kildare are a series of seven springs known as St. James's Wells.

These springs supply both the brewery in Dublin and the summit level of the Grand Canal via the Milltown Feeder which enters the canal just above Lowtown Lock. This water, apparently, is ideally suited to the brewing of stout which requires a softer water than beer.

All the way from Ticknevan to Lowtown the water in the canal had been growing clearer and clearer. When we entered Lowtown Lock after lunch, the clarity of the water was quite extraordinary. No English chalk stream that I have seen could compare with it. Our boat appeared to float in air, and even when the lock chamber was full, the sunlight still penetrated to the very bottom. This should reassure Guinness drinkers. We had travelled

GRAND CANAL 'We saw ahead, framed by the arch of a bridge, the canal hotel at Robertstown.'

less than a mile along the summit level before we saw ahead, framed by the arch of a bridge, the canal hotel at Robertstown. It is an almost exact replica of the Shannon Harbour hotel, but is in better repair being at the present time a Turf Board hostel for workers on the bogs. Robertstown itself, a whitewashed canal depot, a post office and a shop and 'select bar' or two strung along the canal waterfront beside the hotel, is a canal village. The Grand Canal has made Robertstown just as our Trent and Mersey Canal made Fradley. Like Fradley there was, for me at any rate, a fascination about Robertstown which I find difficult to define and which our photograph can scarcely convey. A particular atmosphere, melancholy, nostalgic yet captivating, always invests a waterfront no matter whether it is that of some old seaport town, some cliff-walled fishing cove or merely, as in this case, some inland village beside a still canal. It captivates because it is a doorway to the unknown and so appeals to our sense of adventure and that nomadic instinct which lies buried in all of us. It is nostalgic because it recalls memories of places visited and never perhaps to be re-visited. It is melancholy because it is redolent with the unnumbered farewells which it has witnessed; a reminder that life, in the words of some poet whose name I cannot recall, is a perpetual farewell. Only the waterside possesses this evocative power in full measure. Certain railway stations, perhaps, exhale a little of it, but the motor road and the airport for some reason have no such atmosphere. Perhaps this is because they convey, not the sense of travel, but the sense of ceaseless and restless movement which, having no beginning and no end, is not travel but merely a symptom of social sickness.

Only an occasional cargo boat now calls at Robertstown to deliver and take on goods at the warehouse, but it was easy here to imagine that thunder of galloping hooves, waxing louder in the still evening air, which heralded the arrival of the Dublin passage boat. Easy too, to see the bustle on the quay before the hotel as the passengers disembarked, some of them on the first stage of that long journey to America; then lights springing up in the hotel bedrooms, as the steaming horses were led away to the stables.

The situation of Robertstown contributes more than a little to its charm. Tree-clad slopes rise behind the village to shelter and frame it, while to the south east the land falls away in a great sweep to the levels of the Liffey valley and the rich plain of Kildare. Beyond these levels lay the whole range of the Wicklow Mountains, blue and magnificent against the skyline.

We had made fast to the quay, intending to continue on our way after we had made a few purchases from the village shop, but so fine was the day and so pleasant the place, that we moved no further than the grassy bank on the opposite side of the canal just beyond the hotel. Here we lay for the night.

Early that evening the quiet of Robertstown was startlingly shattered by the loud but unintelligible sound of raucous American voices coming from somewhere near at hand. Upon investigation this proved to issue from a travelling cinema, a phenomenon which we were destined to encounter again and which might be called the mechanized successor of the old 'gaffs' of the strolling players. In 1932 I was lucky enough to see what I now believe to have been one of the very last of these old 'gaffs'. They pitched on the Common at Hungerford in Berkshire. They had drawn their waggons up in the form of a square arid tented over the enclosed space to form the auditorium. The side of one waggon let down to make stage and proscenium, while the waggon opposite acted as pay box, having a central gangway through which the audience was admitted. Here I witnessed a harrowing melodrama entitled, to the best of my recollection, 'Only a Mill Girl' and which

IRISH CANAL VILLAGE, Robertstown, 'We made fast to the quay.'

depicted the seduction of the innocent mill girl by the dissolute son of the villainous mill owner. Unlike its modern successor, the tough gangster film where the cop is as unscrupulous as the crook and the sympathy of the audience frequently goes to the latter, 'Only a Mill Girl' still possessed some tenuous link with the old mediæval morality play; all ended for the best; villainy was confounded and virtue triumphant. Apart from the quality of its subject matter, celluloid is a poor substitute for flesh and blood.

The entertainment business was evidently promising in Robertstown, for this cinema appeared to have settled down semi-permanently, and its bills were headed 'Robertstown Cinema'. The auditorium and projection room was part hut, part tent and part waggon. Its sound-proofing qualities were therefore not very high, in fact anyone content to hear without seeing might sit on the canal bank and be entertained for nothing. He might, however, find the sound of the generating plant a little distracting. This consisted of an elderly Lister single-cylinder hopper-cooled petrol engine. 'Tuff-tuffing' indefatigably, it rocked so much on its unstable wooden mountings that water spilled over the rim of the steaming hopper.

The performance finished early, and peace was restored. We strolled about the village as dusk began to fall. It was one of those rare occasions when time, place and the weather combine to distil pure magic. With us, the sun had set, and only toward the west was the clear sky still flushed with a faint afterglow. Yet although the first stars were beginning to prick through the eastern sky and night's shadows to gather in the plain, the summits of the Wicklows were still fired with light. We stood leaning over a gate looking across to the mountains until the last light had left their topmost pinnacles. From the doorway of a cottage there appeared an old woman. Anything from seventy to a hundred years might have been required to form the furrows that seamed her face. Her head and shoulders were draped in a black shawl and she carried a stick as knarled as the hand that clutched it. Such was the enchantment of the half-light that I should not have been unduly surprised to see her whisk away over the roof tops astride that stick or to find that the cat which lurked by the door had transformed itself into an imp. Another cottage in the street we had thought empty when we had first seen it earlier in the day. The thatch was ragged, the windows boarded up and we could detect no sign of life. But now, as we passed it by there suddenly came from within the sound of fiddling. We stopped to listen. It was utterly toneless and tuneless, resembling the wailing of a banshee rather than any music, and the effect was eerie in the extreme. Perhaps it was a banshee. In this way ghost stories begin and soon grow into legends.

Being a Saturday night the village bars were well patronized, and as closing time came the two village guards went the round of the saloons encouraging the convivial patrons to 'go along quietly'. In one, a party of tinkers were celebrating, and their cart, drawn by a great raw-boned horse, waited outside. They were ejected with some difficulty. One member of the party; an old woman, was so much the worse for drink that she could not stand, but her male companions bundled her up into the body of the cart as though she was a sack of potatoes before clambering unsteadily on to the driving platform. But when they drove off at a perilous pace along the quayside she proved sufficiently sober to hurl derisive abuse in a shrill cracked voice at the guards who stood watching their departure. We watched them, too, as they went spanking down the long straight road beyond the hotel. It was a dizzy and death-defying progress, weaving uncertainly from one side of the road to the other while the body of the cart itself swung and clacked to and fro on the loose axle trees. For a moment we thought that all was over when a particularly violent swerve landed one wheel in a gulley beside the road. But although the company reeled and the incident provoked a fresh torrent of abuse from the old woman, the equipage righted itself and passed out of sight with unabated speed.

The last of the revellers had just made his unsteady way homeward when an empty horse boat appeared from the direction of Dublin, a black shape gliding silently over the mirror smooth surface so that only the plodding of hooves could be heard. Here the towing path changes sides, but Robertstown Bridge not being a 'roving bridge' the towline had to be detached. Having passed under the arch, one member of the crew led the horse back over the bridge and down the other side. Then his mate threw him the towline from the boat.

When, leaning over the parapet, we had watched them disappear into the darkness, we returned to our boat and to bed.

We awoke to a golden morning. Except for a group of boys who were playing handball against the wall of the warehouse, Robertstown slumbered in the bright sunlight which already promised a hot day. Doubtless most of the inhabitants were at Mass. The weather was much too fine for hurry, and it was not until 11 a.m. that we cast off after a leisurely breakfast which we ate in the open. At the end of the long embankment which carries the canal away from Robertstown we passed the junction of the Blackwood Feeder. This, the second main source of supply to the Grand Canal, draws water from springs and from a storage reservoir in the parish of Ballynafagh about four miles distant. Another mile and a half brought us to the eastern summit lock, and here we began the long descent to Dublin. We had now said farewell to the bogs. For the remainder of its course to Dublin the canal passes through richer country which is much more reminiscent of English landscape, except for the towering Wicklows which are seldom out of sight. From the point of view of scenery there can be no doubt that the section of the canal which we were now traversing from Lowtown Lock as far as Sallins is easily the most attractive. Above the next lock at Landenstown, a belt of magnificent beeches grow beside the canal, and as the sun was now really hot, we decided to moor for lunch beneath their shade.

It was an idyllic mooring. Shafts of sunlight striking through the brilliant foliage of the trees made entrancing patterns of light and shade in the clear water and on the emerald green moss of the woodland floor. We were beguiled into prolonging our stay until tea-time, and throughout that languorous afternoon we lay at ease either on cushions on the deck of the boat or on the equally soft moss on the bank with backs propped against the smooth silver boles of the beeches. Once a red squirrel came to peer at us from the cleft of a branch.

My map told me that beyond this screen of woodland lay Landenstown house, and when I found a path through the wood, my curiosity overcame my indolence. So far nearly all the 'big houses' which we had seen were either blackened reminders of the 'troubles' or had been partially demolished by the Land Board, their demesnes divided into small holdings. So it was not with any very high expectations that I went exploring. Had I known what I should find I should not have trespassed so boldly. Landenstown, indeed, is a beautiful house beautifully maintained. The house itself and its flanking outbuildings are linked together by archways to compose a perfectly symmetrical and harmonious group. With the exception of the porch and the 'oeil de boeuf' in the centre gable (a masterly touch, this) the facade is quite devoid of ornament and affords, in my opinion, an object lesson in what may be achieved simply by right proportion, particularly in the relationship between windows and wall space. The house reminded me, not of any English building, but of illustrations I have seen of certain country houses which were built in America towards the close of the eighteenth century. If the owners of Landenstown should ever chance to read this I hope they will forgive us our trespass and the liberty which we took in photographing the house from the cover of one of the trees in the park. I was anxious to include among our photographs an example of the Irish country house, and I doubted whether we should see a worthier one.

IRISH COUNTRY HOUSE, Landenstown. 'A beautiful house, beautifully maintained.'

We felt quite reluctant to leave Landenstown, but after tea we journeyed on through Landenstown and Digby Bridge Locks to the Leinster aqueduct over the River Liffey. It was an attractive pound, the canal skirting a ridge of high ground on our right with a view over the valley to the left until it turned to cross the river. As there was little traffic about, we stopped for a few moments on the aqueduct, an impressive structure of four arches, to look down at the swift flowing peat-stained waters which we next should see, and enter, in the heart of Dublin. On the river bank was a small pumping station which the canal company have recently installed to supplement their water supply for, even in this well-watered country, the Grand Canal has occasionally suffered from water, shortage in the past.

Beyond the aqueduct is Soldier's Island, junction of the short branch to Naas; next comes the village of Sallins and then, having traversed a deep cutting, the canal, which until now

GRAND CANAL. The Leinster Aqueduct over the River Liffey.

has pursued a tortuous course from its summit, cuts straight as an arrow across levels of rich grazing land. The cattle which we saw here, mostly Herefords or Shorthorns were remarkable both for quantity and quality. Many of the bullocks were as massive as bulls.

There is a fly in every ointment, we are told, and here we experienced the only trial of an otherwise perfect day. The particular fly in this instance was the horse fly (called 'clags' hereabouts, 'clegs' in Wales, or 'brees' in Warwickshire). Doubtless the hot weather combined with the proximity of the cattle was responsible, for they assailed us in force and with most bloodthirsty intent. Fellow sufferers will no doubt endorse my opinion that no other insect makes a more resolute but at the same time more subtle assault upon its luckless quarry. It attacks swiftly and silently and alights so softly that the victim is only made aware of its presence too late by the needle prick of its bite against which a thin summer shirt is no protection. We kept a wary eye on each other, and at times there developed such a quick succession of mutual swatting that a chance onlooker might have been pardoned for thinking that the four of us had come to blows and that violent mutiny was imminent on our small vessel.

We moored for the night in a tree-sheltered stretch of water where the canal skirts the large demesne of Lyons House, and a very pleasant mooring it proved to be. As the canal

GRAND CANAL, Lyons House Lock. *Le Coq* enters the lower chamber.

hereabouts is dead straight, and as the trees line both banks for nearly two miles, the effect is that of a great avenue with water for a carriage way. After dinner a satisfactory day ended with a walk through the dusk to the old round tower of Oughterard which, standing on a hilltop above Lyons House, commands a fine prospect of the Liffey valley on the one hand and the Wicklows on the other.

The double lock at Lyons House which we passed through on the following morning is of somewhat curious construction, the walls of the upper chamber having a 'step' in them. I can only conjecture that this represented some theory of resistance to lateral pressure which sometimes, owing to frost in the ground or for other reasons, causes lock walls to cave inwards. Detail differences in the construction of locks and bridges are noticeable in passing through the Grand Canal, and are said, doubtless correctly, to be due to the different contractors who were employed and often bankrupted, during its construction. I have seen an engraving which shows a passage boat entering this lock. Except that the trees have grown up and thickened, the scene looks much the same to-day. But the picture did not show the trim whitewashed lock cottage on the lower level to the left or the delightful houses with their bright gardens and climbing roses which face the canal a few yards above the lock, though doubtless they stood there then.

There followed six and a half miles to the village of Clondalkin with only one more lock, but thereafter, in the last five miles to Dublin, the locks both single and double, came thick and fast. The locks themselves were no difficulty to us for we had perfected a simple routine. Angela and Richard went ashore to work the locks while I stayed by the engine and kept the boat under control, and Marten sat on the stern to prevent the dinghy from getting out of hand. But we had not reckoned with the strike of school teachers in Dublin which had then been going on for many weeks. Instead of being in school, every child in Dublin seemed to be on the towing path of the Grand Canal that afternoon. Like most navigators of inland waterways I have suffered from the unwelcome attentions of small children when passing through towns, but never before, and I sincerely hope never again, did I experience the like of this descent into Dublin. Hordes of shrieking little ruffians (I can call them by no other name) pursued us along the towing path, and whenever we drew into a lock we had the greatest difficulty in keeping them off the boat while they swarmed on gates and lock-sides so that we could hardly lift the paddles or move the gates. Inevitably, one small boy fell into the canal. He sank like a stone but made no struggle and when he came up for the first time, all we could see was his hair floating like water weed. We fished him out by the scruff of the neck like a half-drowned puppy, but his misfortune did not in the least deter his companions. When the boat sank in the locks they were no

longer able to attempt to board us, but we were subjected to another ordeal for they would then begin to spit at us or, worse still, to throw stones. How the wheelhouse windows or the large glass lights over the fore cabin escaped breakage was nothing short of a miracle. We all heaved prodigious sighs of relief when we emerged intact from the last of the main line locks at Griffith's Bridge. From this point, the terminus of the canal at James' Street Harbour is under a mile distant, but we turned to the right onto the Ringsend Branch which leads down to the Liffey, and here we shook off most of our pursuers.

There is a basin and a dry dock at Portobello, just above the bridge and lock. We swung in here and came about to moor alongside the wall of the dock, protected by a locked iron gate from any intrusion. We had arrived. We celebrated the event and our deliverance from the ordeal at the locks in an excellent tea.

GRAND CANAL, Lyons House Lock. *Le Coq* ready to leave the lower chamber.

CHAPTER EIGHT

DUBLIN

Portobello Lock is the first of the flight which descends to Ringsend, and beside it stands the now familiar Grand Canal Hotel, in this case a hospital. Portobello Bridge crosses the canal immediately below the lock chamber, and owing to subsequent widening, the balance beams of the lower gates have had to be cut short and winches installed to open and close them. Here there once occurred a notable disaster when the horses of a coach which was crossing the bridge took fright with the result that the whole equipage plunged over the parapet and into the lock. According to the version I was told, the lock was empty at the time and the lock-keeper, instead of throwing ropes to the unfortunate passengers so that they might be hauled up, is reputed to have filled the lock with the misguided idea that by this means they would float to the top. Instead, all were drowned.

Apart from the fact that we were secure from intrusion, Portobello was a convenient mooring because it was only a short tram journey from the Nelson Pillar in the heart of the city. But the custodian of the basin could give me no authority to remain there, and advised me to visit the head offices of the company at James' Street. Here I was informed politely but firmly that no 'yachts' were permitted to moor on the Grand Canal. I explained that we had none of us visited Dublin before, and that we were anxious to see something of the city before leaving. It was then conceded that, while under no circumstances could we remain at Portobello, we might, *sub rosa*, lie at Ringsend but only upon the understanding that we would not remain there longer than three days.

I do not blame the Canal Company for their attitude in refusing to countenance pleasure boat facilities which might impede the movement of their own traffic. Moreover, I was told how mooring rights once granted in the past had been abused. In this way do we often suffer for the thoughtlessness and bad behaviour of others. Yet this is a good example of the difficulties which invariably beset the water traveller when he visits any large city in the British Isles. A crying need exists for the establishment of centrally situated commodious yacht basins adequately protected from inquisitive intruders and equipped with those facilities such as drinking water which the water traveller needs. In no case that I am aware of would great capital expenditure be required but merely the conversion of disused docks or basins already existing. A portion of such a basin might be made available for permanent mooring, but a part should always be reserved for the use of visitors.

I have no doubt that many English owner boatmen would be encouraged to visit Dublin if good mooring facilities were available, and later, no doubt, extending their voyage to the Shannon Lakes or the west coast via the Grand Canal. Also, we subsequently met several Dubliners who own boats and who are accustomed to take them through to the Shannon in the summer. But at present the stranger appears to be confronted with only two alternatives. Either he may take his craft to Dun Laoghaire in the hope of finding an anchorage in the harbour, or he may (presumably) anchor on the Liffey just below O'Connell Bridge. Dun Laoghaire is some distance from Dublin, while to judge from a melancholy photograph which appeared in the press during our visit showing a number of small craft sunk after dragging their moorings in an easterly gale, the yacht harbour there leaves much to be desired. The River Liffey is certainly central, but a tidal river in the heart of a city is not the ideal mooring, while there is nowhere against the quay where a boat's dinghy could be left with safety if the crew went ashore.

Not wishing to invite another audience such as had attended our arrival in Dublin, we contrived to slip quietly and unobtrusively down the seven locks between Portobello and Ringsend in the early morning before breakfast. We emerged from the narrow canal into the wide waters of the inner basin from beneath a bridge, passed close under the lofty bows of a sailing vessel *Oranmore* which was lying at the quay, and moored beside the bridge-keeper's cottage where a swing bridge carries the Ringsend road over the channel dividing the inner and outer basins. We were fortunate indeed in this choice of mooring, for Mr. Plunket, the bridge-keeper, proved to be so unfailingly cheerful and helpful that Richard, whose knowledge of hagiology was more extensive than mine, christened him 'Blessed Oliver Plunket' and as 'Blessed Oliver' he will always be remembered.

During our brief stay in Dublin we did most of the things that visitors are expected to do. We climbed the dark stone stairs of the Nelson Pillar to emerge blinking in the bright morning sunshine on the narrow parapet whence we could look out over the roof-tops to the blue waters of Dublin Bay to the east, or southward to the equally blue Wicklow Mountains. We trotted in a side-car round Phoenix Park whose green spaciousness we found somewhat marred by the vast mounds of turf stored there by the Turf Board. We walked the quays and watched a steamer loading barrels of Guinness in the shadow of Gandon's Customs House, Dublin's most magnificent building. We went round Guinness's enormous brewery at St. James' Gate where I was most interested in the cask-making shop and in the ingenious little narrow gauge overtype steam locomotives. These were originally designed by an engineer of the brewery for handling traffic on the extensive internal railway. One of their most interesting features is that the complete locomotive can be lowered bodily into a broad gauge frame which it drives by friction so that it can perform shunting duties on the sidings which connect with the Irish Railway system. We explored the great Georgian Squares, those exemplary illustrations of eighteenth-century design and town planning. In the case of some of the houses, notably those in Upper Mount Street, I thought that the first floor windows were strangely out of proportion. I admired most the delicate ironwork of the balconies and the beautiful doorways with their fanlights.

Many of these doorways were enhanced by the gay green or red and white striped canvas coverings which protected the paintwork of the doors from the heat of the sun, a custom which seems almost to have died out in England since my childhood. Particularly noteworthy was a row of houses in Herbert Place which faces the canal and which we had remarked as we locked down to Ringsend. And in the intervals of this orgy of sightseeing we refreshed ourselves in a shop in O'Connell Street with exotic ices piled with whipped cream, for the weather was hot.

It was astonishing to discover that three and sixpence would buy the best seats at the theatre. We attended a good performance of 'Heartbreak House' by Lord Longford's Company at the Gate, a small house which nevertheless has about it the authentic atmosphere of the theatre. We also patronized the Abbey in which I must confess that I was disappointed. The bucolic comedy of Irish rural life which we saw there, though it was amusing enough and competently performed, was hardly of the standard which one expects from a national theatre which the Abbey now claims to be. A national theatre can fail by putting too narrow an emphasis upon the word 'national'. By all means encourage the work of national actors and dramatists for that is the first duty of such a theatre. But this duty is not fulfilled by presenting exclusively national work which may often be of mediocre quality. It can only be accomplished by aiming at the best in drama and acting irrespective of national boundaries. Without such a living theatre, the drama cannot flourish; lacking the stimulus and inspiration of such a qualitative standard, the work of native actors and dramatists will tend to fall to the level of provincial amateurs. This does not imply any disparagement of the provincial amateur, particularly in Ireland where the Irishman, more mercurial, emotional and less self-conscious than the Saxon, has a natural gift for the theatre. It means that however great the national gift may be it will never be fully exercised unless it receives the finest inspiration from the top of the dramatic tree. I think the founders of the Abbey, for all their passionate nationalism, would agree with me in this.

As for the Abbey itself, I thought it a gloomy and depressing theatre. While I am by no means opposed to original schemes of decoration, I prefer the orthodox red-plush-and-rococo to this austere, quasi-religious atmosphere of Celtic twilight and Art Nouveau. After all, we go to the theatre to be entertained. To herald the rise of the curtain with the stroke of a deep-toned gong is, I should guess, a customary survival of the Yeats period. In the presentation of serious drama it would be an effective device calculated to silence the most ill-mannered audience, but when the curtain goes up on some trivial comedy the effect is one of bathos. And why is J. M. Synge omitted from the portrait gallery in the foyer? Is there no portrait available, or has Ireland still not forgiven him for that 'Playboy of the Western World' which created such ludicrous commotion? Like Ireland itself, the Abbey Theatre, its battles fought and its position assured, has grown complacent, has lost vigour and enterprise. What next? Where do we go from here? It may be that if dramatist and producer could be found to set Dublin by the ears as Synge did, the Abbey would live again.

It would be presumptuous of me if, upon the strength of so brief a visit, I attempted to discourse at length upon the past and present of Dublin. Instead I will attempt to sum up my personal impressions of the city. Like our own cities, Dublin is beginning to sprawl. We found the answer to the empty crofts of Connaught in the serried housing estates of Goldenbridge and Kilmainham which we saw from the canal as we entered Dublin. Affluent Dubliners escape to fashionable suburbs while the beautiful Georgian houses of the Squares become offices or degenerate into tenements.

When our industrial revolution was fairly launched, we fouled our cities. We forsook the country for the town and while we forget the art of country living, we also lost the art of living in cities. We made a compromise which made the worst of both worlds by evolving the suburb which sucked the life out of both town and country. To-day the bulk of our population exist in these sterile suburbs where the arts of living die, where a wedge is thrust between that once intimate relationship of town and country, and where the one is looked upon as a workshop and the other as a playground. Because of her lack of coal, Ireland's Industrial Revolution is only just beginning under the stimulus of hydro-electric power, and it remains to be seen whether she will succeed in avoiding our mistakes. The first symptoms of the disease of industrialism are already apparent in Dublin. The city stands in the same relation to the rest of Ireland as did the London of Cobbett's day to rural England, and indeed I believe that a twentieth-century Irish Cobbett would be justified in calling it a 'Wen'.

The many English people whom we saw in Dublin and whose presence, I fear, was not due to any love for or interest in Ireland but to the desire to eat her food and buy her goods, must carry away a false impression of Irish prosperity. The spectacle of plenty which the Dublin shop windows present is largely illusory. They are filled with goods which provincial Ireland cannot afford. If they could afford them there would be scarcity instead of the illusion of plenty. The real wealth of rural Ireland is draining into Dublin just as London sucked dry the riches of Cobbett's England. In return, the country receives only money, and precious little of that.

How this drift of people and wealth from the country to the city might be checked is a social and economic problem of general and not local importance, and it would thus be irrelevant to discuss it here. So far it has not seriously smudged the individuality of Dublin. Starting from the Nelson Pillar, a man could still reach open country in the course of a morning's walk. No city should grow larger than this; if it does so it becomes a mere agglomeration of bricks and mortar. From the broad streets and the green islands of the squares, for which we have to thank the Wide Streets Commissioners of 1757 and the genius of the eighteenth-century planners, the stroller catches unexpected glimpses of the river or of distant mountains. Thus, instead of that claustrophobic sense of being insulated from the surrounding country by an endless warren of streets, he is repeatedly made aware of the topography of Dublin and its surroundings. On a fine morning it is as though Dublin borrows something of the clarity of the mountain atmosphere so luminous and pellucid is the light that warms and glows upon the old lime-pointed brickwork. But as dusk falls the mountains retreat, and it is the river that distils the city's magic. For a hyacinthine haze veils the quays, the mountains are forgotten and it is Dublin of the sea and the waterfronts of which we are aware. The ripples of the flowing tide make glowing serpent trails of reflected lights, while darkness lends airy grace to the flights of the bridges that leap from quay to quay.

To-day, when the tree of our civilization is rotten at the root and tottering to its fall, instead of planting anew we are forever devising fresh props which we fondly suppose will avert the inevitable. The latest of these is planning. Every problem can be solved by an appropriate plan. Because it is an example of deliberate planning, a Georgian city such as Dublin encourages this belief. There are those who believe that to do likewise it is only necessary to make a plan on a drawing board and then assemble on the site x men and y tons of material and prefabricated parts. How pathetic is this fallacy! Georgian Dublin was created under the inspired patronage of men who were the heirs to generations of good taste and sensibility, and who knew the arts of living in cities; men such as the Duke of Leinster, Viscount Fitzwilliam of Merrion, Lord Ardilaun, Luke Gardiner, Doctor Mosse and Viscount Mountjoy. These men could command architects nursed in the great tradition of their art, Gandon, Cassels, Cooley, Sir William Chambers, Ralph Ward, the Ensor brothers and others. Last, but by no means least, the conception of the patron and the design of the architect received tangible shape at the hands of craftsmen and master builders such as Charles Thorp, Michael Stapleton or Pemberton, and were beautified by stuccodore and decorator, by a Francini or a Bartholomew Cramillion. It was, in fact, a common qualitative conception shared by patron, architect, craftsman and decorator that made possible these squares. To suppose that a semi-illiterate bureaucracy with the aid of a horde of machines and unskilled labour can go and do likewise by the mere flourish of a pencil is lunacy. Our new barbarism whose goal is always the lowest common denominator can no more create work of this order than palæolithic man could have reared the Acropolis. Even if the design was forthcoming, there would be no executants.

If we accept the narrow canons of the ardent Irish Nationalist, then the Georgian architecture of Ireland must be called Anglo-Irish and we must say that since the age of Hiberno-Romanesque Ireland has produced no vernacular architecture other than the thatched cabin. But I have no patience with these racial purity theories. We are all of mixed blood, and stronger than any bonds of blood are the ties which bind a man to his own place. It is thus the organic life of a country itself which turns fresh blood into old channels so that the invader of one generation becomes the patriot of the next. Thus England assimilated successively the Celt, the Saxon and the Norman, and it was only political folly, the greater blame for which must lie with us, that perpetuated racial hostility in Ireland. Even so, the list of Irish patriots in the ranks of the so-called Anglo-Irish is a long and impressive one. I think of Parnell or of W. B. Yeats. Thus, too, I think of Georgian Dublin, which has its own distinctive quality, as Irish and not as English or even Anglo-Irish. Modern Irish domestic architecture is slightly less offensive than our own, but that is the most that I can say of it. There is little evidence as yet of any attempt to gather up the threads of this great tradition, but I hope that Ireland will do so rather than follow us into the neo-concrete or sheet metal ages.

.   .   .   .

DUBLIN BRIDGES. (1) Rolling lift bridge, North Wall.

The day before we were due to leave our moorings at Ringsend I thought it as well to reconnoitre the entrance from the Liffey into Spencer Dock at North Wall. The channel into the tidal lock was barred by an enormous rolling lift bridge over which an endless procession of carts and lorries was rattling and thundering. To my eyes it appeared as though this formidable barrier was seldom or never moved. In any case it seemed optimistic to suppose that this ponderous mechanism would be operated, and the traffic along North Wall suspended, merely to allow the passage of our small craft. Looking up the dock I saw yet another obstacle; a drawbridge this time operated by two steel beams high overhead which looked at this distance, with their long rods linking beams to bridge, like a pair of slender, long-beaked birds. This carried Sheriff Street, another busy thoroughfare, across the dock. I could not see whether there were any further obstacles, but it looked as if our passage bade fair to dislocate the traffic of Dublin. I thereupon visited the engineers department of Coras Iompair Eireann at Westland Row Station where I tactfully suggested that if I came up to North Wall at low tide we might just be able to get under the bridge there. But I was received with that same helpful courtesy which had answered my first telephone enquiry, and matters were quickly arranged. Of course the bridge would be lifted, that was no trouble at all. And when did I wish to come up the river. To-morrow? High tide was at noon; if I would undertake to be at the bridge at that time, it would be opened at once. Arrangements were made on the spot by telephone.

DUBLIN BRIDGES. (2) Drawbridge, Sheriff Street.

Next morning 'Blessed Oliver' announced that he had business across the river and volunteered to accompany us. We gladly accepted the offer and set off, our extra crew looking very efficient and workmanlike in a clean boiler suit. We found that there was no need to open the Ringsend Bridge because we could just get under it with a few inches to spare. We crossed the broad waters of the outer basin and entered the tidal lock. Actually there are three locks of different sizes here, side by side, and we entered the smallest of them which was on our port side. The lower gates opened, we paid a final farewell to the Grand Canal, and were soon dancing over the little waves of the Liffey mouth. It was our one brief taste of salt water. Having made sure that no steamers were on the move to or from the quays, we headed straight across the channel and came up the river close in to the North Wall side, I had noticed the previous day that the position of the bridge allowed just sufficient room for *Le Coq* to lie in the slack water of the dock entrance while we waited for it to be opened, we swung straight in and got our lines onto the quay precisely at the time appointed. Everything went like clockwork. The bridgeman clambered up into his overhead cabin, men appeared from nowhere armed with red flags to stop the traffic, and in a few moments, with a rumble of machinery, the bridge opened remarkably swiftly. We passed through into the lock, and the bridge as quickly closed behind us. While the lock was filling, I paid my dues, two pounds for the ninety-two miles and forty-seven locks to Richmond Harbour. This done, the Sheriff Street Bridge drew up with similar despatch and we sailed through into the inner dock basin where we moored till the following morning when we should begin our journey through the eccentric shoe-maker's canal. Probably very few of the thousands who pass over the North Wall Bridge or board the steamers for Liverpool or Glasgow at the nearby quay suspect that this is the gateway of a forgotten water road which leads through the heart of Ireland.

CHAPTER NINE

THE ROYAL CANAL

SPENCER DOCK TO MULLINGAR

I have already quoted that account by Samuel Smiles of the inception and construction of the Royal Canal which first prompted us to make this journey. The shoe-maker's Company was incorporated in 1789, but the subsequent history of the project is the reverse of that of the Grand Canal; for whereas the latter was begun by a public authority and completed by a private company, the Royal Canal from its summit level to the Shannon was completed by the Board of Directors General of Inland Navigation. Doubtless the Board were responsible for calling in John Rennie to make good the errors of his predecessors. How grievous those errors were, and how great the difficulties of construction, may be judged from the fact that the Royal, which boasts only one short branch canal to Longford, is reputed to have cost £1,400,000; more, in fact, than was required for the construction of the whole Grand Canal system excluding only the Barrow Navigation which it had not then acquired. Though the canal can never have justified the capital expenditure, for some years it carried a very considerable traffic, and with average tolls of from 1d. to 1½d. per ton per mile, income doubled expenditure. In 1836, total receipts amounted to £25,148 as compared with the figure of £37,557 for the Grand Canal in 1837. Passenger passage boat services were operated between Dublin, Mullingar and Longford, but the traffic was never so great or so profitable as that on the Grand Canal, nor do the same grandiose facilities for travellers appear ever to have been provided. In 1837, when the Grand carried over 100,000 passengers, only 46,450 travelled by the Royal. I conjecture that there were no opulent galloping fly-boats on the Royal, but that traffic was handled exclusively by the slower passenger and parcels boats travelling night and day. This would account for the lack of hotel accommodation along the route.

In 1845, the canal was acquired by the Midland Great Western Railway whose main route from Dublin to Athlone and Galway follows the line of the waterway closely as far as Habsborough beyond Mullingar. Thereafter, canal traffic dwindled until the principal function of the Royal became the supply of water to the stand-pipes of the railway stations along the route. During the 'emergency' the canal enjoyed a temporary revival when a number of horse-drawn turf boats were put into service, plying between Dublin and the midland bogs. Power-driven commercial craft are not permitted to use the canal upon the grounds that the banks would not withstand the wash. By the time of our journey, the 'emergency' boats had ceased work and were laid up in the pound above the Cross Guns Locks. Only two boats were at work on the canal, a boatman named Cafferty carrying general cargo between Dublin and Mullingar and occasionally as far west as Keenagh Harbour and Leach of Killucan loading bog ore into Dublin.

No one can approach the Royal Canal without meeting, or at least hearing about Cafferty. We met him on that last evening in Dublin as we lay in Spencer Dock, for it appears that he was unloading there at the time and that he had been informed of our intended passage. Richard and I were strolling on the quay in the half-light before turning in when we saw the short stocky figure coming purposefully, if a little unsteadily, towards us. When he reached us he stopped short, regarding us fixedly, rocking slightly from heel to toe the while, and announced 'I'm Cafferty'. We nodded and looked suitably impressed. He told us how he had worked on the Royal all his life and how his father had done so before him. He then went on to speak of the wonders of the canal in so intimate and affectionate a manner that one might have supposed that he not only owned it but had built it with his own hands. He waxed eloquent and poetic. 'You'll be travelling' said he, with a sweep of the arm towards the western sky which was still faintly bright, 'the west and I'm telling you now, sir, that's a wild country you'll be seeing, and you can be travelling the whole day and only the birds and the wild things for company. Then you'll come to a place,' he went on, warming to his theme 'you'll look down, and you'll see a hundred feet of bog down that side, and you'll look up this side and see a hundred feet of rock, and that's the truth I'm telling you'. As he said this he pointed dramatically first to the ground at our feet and then to the sky over our heads while our eyes instinctively followed his gestures as though the earth should open beneath us or mountains rise out of the waters of Spencer Dock. He asked us when we proposed starting and we told him that we were leaving early on the following morning. At this he took my arm and I was irresistibly reminded of c's *Ancient Mariner* 'You've twelve locks ahead of you now', he vouchsafed, 'and then' - he lowered his voice impressively – 'you'll be travelling through the rock'. As he went on to dilate upon the hazards of 'travelling through the rock' in a manner that made the perils of Scylla and Charybdis seem small beer, it became that Cafferty's concern for our welfare was not wholly disinterested but that he was quite prepared to delay his departure from Dublin if there was any chance of a profitable job of pilotage. I do not suggest, however, that his reason for thus visiting us was wholly mercenary. His was a genuine enthusiasm and an honest impulse to give strangers the benefit of his knowledge, but if they could be turned to practical profit so much the better. When it became clear that his services would not be called upon he was not in the least put out. 'Ach well', said he, 'if you are in any trouble at all, don't be forgetting that I shall be behind you' He seemed confident that he would overtake us in some dire difficulty, and I must confess that after his emphasis upon the hazards of this deserted and semi-derelict canal it was rather a consoling thought that he was following us and might at least give us a tow if the weeds proved too much for our propeller. He stood for a few moments more puffing at the glowing cigarette I had given him, and then he turned and disappeared into the darkness with a 'Good luck to ye and good-bye now'. And as things turned out, that was the last we saw of Cafferty.

Just ahead of our mooring was yet another drawbridge; this time a curious steel skew bridge with one long balancing girder which carried a single line of railway across the canal. This was a heavily graded and curved goods loop line connecting the C.I.E. goods lines down to North Wall depot with the Great Northern Railway of Ireland at Amiens Street Station. Where we lay we were within a yard of the metals but nothing passed during the evening. That night, however, I was awakened with a start by a volume of sound which at first suggested to my sleep-fuddled mind that an earthquake or a tidal wave was about to overwhelm us. It was a goods train beating up the incline with a banking engine assisting in the rear. The train engine which had wakened me had passed before I sat up and looked through the port-hole, but I could dimly see the whirling spokes of the waggon wheels as they clanked rhythmically over the rail joints. Then came a renewed crescendo of labouring sound as the banking engine went by and a glimpse of thrashing coupling rods through a drift of steam. A few cinders from the ash pan remained to glow for a moment between the metals as the sound of the train faded. I have been an inveterate train-watcher since my earliest childhood, but I never thought that I should one day lie in bed and watch the driving wheels of a locomotive pass almost within my reach.

We had arranged to make an early start with the idea of clearing the Dublin locks before too many spectators got about. We felt that the passage of a 'yacht' up the Royal was likely to prove too much of a nine days' wonder for our comfort. Punctually at 8 a.m. two men arrived and proceeded to remove the rail clips from the bridge so that it could be lifted and allow us to move through into the first lock. We found the Royal Locks similar to those on the Grand except that they were longer and were provided with rings on the side walls which are a convenience for a small boat such as ours. There are forty-eight locks between the Liffey and the Shannon by the Royal route as against forty-four on the Grand, while the height of the summit levels above the sea are 322 feet and 279 feet respectively. Of the eighteen locks on the Royal between the Liffey and Ferrans Bridge, no less than ten are double, so that, in effect, the total is twenty-eight. The climb out of Dublin is particularly steep, the first single lock out of Spencer Dock being followed by a flight of five double locks in quick succession. From the summit of these we found we could look back over the city to the waters of Dublin Bay. Our ascent was not without incident. The regular lock-keeper was on holiday, and we were assisted by a youth who did not prove to be very competent. We were in the lower chamber of the first double lock which was being filled from the top gates, the intermediate gates being open and the water cascading over the sill. Eventually, the water covered the sill and our assistant, standing on the top gates, signalled me to move ahead into the upper chamber. I foolishly obeyed without using my own judgement, but the water had not made up sufficiently, with the result that our stem made violent contact with the sill, fortunately without doing any damage. The moral of this incident for those who may follow after is never to move forward until the lower chamber is full. This may be judged by keeping an eye on the water level against the bottom gates.

When we had risen to the top level of this lock we discovered that the short pound above was practically empty, and we had to wait for a considerable time while additional water was drawn from the top of the flight, thus losing much of the advantage of our early start. However, we had our breakfast while we waited, and as it happened we did not suffer unduly from unwelcome attention. Once we had got under way again we made splendid progress, far better, in fact, than we had anticipated. The water so far was weedless and, so soon as we left Dublin behind beautifully clear. We moored for lunch by the double lock at Blanchardstown where, although we had only travelled six miles we were in the seclusion of the country once more and Dublin had already become a memory. Moreover, we had broken the back of the locks, for there lay before us a level of seven-and-a-half miles.

Soon after we left Blanchardstown we discovered what our friend Cafferty had meant by 'going through the rock'. For the best part of two miles, as far as the little village of Clonsilla, the course of the canal had been hewn and blasted through almost solid rock. The channel was so narrow that two boats could not have passed each other, and looking down through the clear water we could see that the bed of the canal was rock, while jagged rocks projecting at the margins emphasized the importance of keeping a straight course, Though narrow, the channel was deep, and in places the rock walls rose practically sheer from the water, the towing path being carried along the bank twenty to thirty feet above. It was certainly not the place to choose to make an error of judgement as did the steerer of a passenger passage boat in the darkness of a November night in 1845. This I should imagine, was the worst accident in the annals of canal passenger transport in the British Isles and comparable, in its tragic results, with a major railway disaster. The steerer ran the bow of the boat into a rock with the result that it slewed across the narrow

ROYAL CANAL. Filling the lower chamber, Blanchardstown Lock.

channel and instantly capsized. The passengers in the fore cabin managed to scramble ashore, but sixteen luckless travellers were trapped and drowned in the aft cabin.

There have been other fatalities in the Clonsilla cutting caused through cargo boats striking rocks owing to inexpert or negligent steering. These did not prove fatal to the boats or their crews, but to the men and horses on the narrow towing path high overhead. The sudden dead check on the towline brought them toppling over the edge onto the rocks below. These disasters were recounted to me by an ex-Royal Canal boatman whom I subsequently met in a little bar at Jamestown on the Shannon. He was also able to answer for me a question which puzzled me as we went through the cutting. I could not understand how in the days when there was considerable traffic on the canal, the contingency of two boats meeting each other in the middle of the cutting and being unable to pass, was avoided. The boatmen of those days carried horns ('trumpets' he called them) and when a man reached either end of the defile he sounded a blast. If there was no reply he proceeded, but if he heard an answering call he waited until the other boat had passed him.

The construction of this cutting must have been a prodigious undertaking, and when I consulted the map later I came to the conclusion that an alternative line might have been surveyed which would have considerably reduced this labour. I recalled Samuel Smiles' account of the canal. No doubt these were the 'limestone rocks' where Rennie found the works at a standstill, and one of the 'difficulties, mostly unnecessary, which had marred its construction'.

Soon after we emerged from the shelter of this impressive defile we crossed an exposed embankment past a railway station appropriately named 'Coldblow and Lucan'. Here we recognized the tower of Lucan church which we had noticed as we entered Dublin by the Grand Canal. At this point the two waterways are only three miles apart, the village of Lucan lying midway between them.

Looking at the course of this canal on the map, and observing how closely the railway accompanies it for mile after mile, anyone might conclude that it would prove a dull waterway to travel upon. But this is not the case, at least it was not so far as we were concerned. In fact my verdict is, having travelled through both canals, that the Royal is a much more interesting waterway than the Grand. It is more beautiful, the country it traverses is more varied and of greater interest, while the railway does not detract from it and is often invisible, being carried on different levels. Again, the magnitude of the Royal Canal works, though they may have been uneconomic and unnecessary, certainly enhance it from the traveller's point of view. Thus we presently crossed the Rye Water by an aqueduct of most impressive height from which we looked down upon the village of Leixlip beside the Liffey and beyond to the now familiar shapes of the Wicklow Mountains destined soon to pass out of our sight. The canal at this point is a hundred feet above the level of the river beneath.

Decy Bridge and Lock marked the end of the level from Blanchardstown. If the tidal lock from the Liffey into Spencer Dock be discounted, this is the thirteenth lock above Dublin. I cannot say that I noticed anything unusual or sinister about it. It was simply a single lock, a bridge below, the usual lock cottage, and beyond on the right the fine woods of Carton Park. But my Jamestown boatman told me afterwards that it was reputed to be haunted, and that none of the old Royal Canal boatmen would ever moor beside it. He obviously took the lock's reputation quite seriously and was not merely 'telling me the tale '. Nothing would induce him, he said, to remain at Decy Lock for the night. But either he could not or would not tell me the source of the belief, while as to the nature of the haunting he would say no more than that if I had remained there I should have been 'disturbed'. When we passed through it was broad daylight, but perhaps if we had stayed there after nightfall …. Had I known of this tradition at the time we would have moored there; now I must leave to others the pleasure of making this experiment. One of my earliest literary efforts was a ghost story about a haunted lock which appeared in a magazine that specialized in such cheerful trifles. In this, the victims were warned by a local lock-keeper to follow the example of the boatmen and give the lock a wide berth. It was strange to find that my fiction had come to life, not, perhaps, as fact, but certainly as a living tradition.

A couple of hundred yards above the lock we found the answer to the freedom from weeds which we had so far enjoyed. A weed-cutting gang had been working along the canal from Dublin and we had now overtaken them. It being past five o'clock, they had knocked off for the day leaving their boat moored to the bank where great cocks of fresh cut weed were lying. At the sight of the canal beyond the boat our hearts sank. From bank to bank it was so thickly overgrown with reeds and rushes that at a distance it was difficult to see any water. We had only covered fourteen of the ninety-one miles to the Shannon; suppose it was to be like this all the rest of the way? However, there was no use despairing so we put on speed and plunged into the jungle. *Le Coq* battled her way along much better than I had expected, covering about two hundred yards before we finally lost way, with the propeller hopelessly fouled. I gave her a momentary kick astern, an expedient which will often clear a propeller, but although we saw a lot of weed float away as I did this, Angela, who was leaning over the stern, reported that the blades were still almost invisible. Richard thereupon armed himself with a sharp knife, descended into the dinghy and from this convenient vantage cut the weeds away. He remained where he was as we proceeded, and every hundred yards or so I slipped out of gear while, at a signal that it was safe to touch the propeller, Richard cut it free again. In this way we forged slowly on until we arrived at Maynooth Harbour. Here, it being a Saturday evening, we stopped and went into the village to purchase milk, bread and other stores. When we returned we found that the signalman at Maynooth Station, whose box was close beside the canal, had been successfully keeping at bay the inevitable small boys. We had resolved to explore Maynooth at leisure the following morning, but we now decided to push on a little further to a more secluded mooring whence we might easily walk back to the village. We therefore re-embarked and continued for just over a mile to lie at the head of the next lock at Jackson's Bridge. It had begun to rain but we were encouraged by the fact that the canal was much clearer. I managed to keep the propeller free by judicious reversing, so Richard was spared a wet journey in the dinghy. When we had made fast for the night we felt we had earned our dinner. Seventeen miles and fourteen locks on a strange and practically disused waterway, was, we decided, a satisfactory day's progress.

Maynooth College is the twentieth century equivalent of Clonmacnoise or Clonfert, and in the influence which it exercises over Irish life and thought, I would say that while it is one of the least publicized of Irish institutions, it is the most important. Here, to live under strict rule and discipline, come six hundred of the bright boys of Catholic Ireland; from Dublin to the most remote parish of the furthest west. Here for seven years they study Philosophy and Logic, the Classics, Moral and Dogmatic Theology, Sacred Eloquence, and the tenets of Plato or Aquinas; all that vast store of learning which the Old Religion has accumulated in the course of centuries. If he stays the course, the Maynooth student returns to the Irish village as a patriarch, a man of unquestioned authority, a man no longer as other men but regarded as the veritable deputy of Christ. It is to the credit of Maynooth that this authority is not more grievously abused than it is. At his best, the parish priest is a patriarch in the truest and finest sense; at his worst he is an extortionate petty dictator ruling by superstition and fear. Human nature being what it is, variation between these extremes is inevitable; what must be considered are the merits or demerits of this patriarchal system and the faith upon which it is based in this twentieth century.

I have never had access to those vast treasure-chests of learning which are stored at: Maynooth, and such slender share of mother wit as I possess is largely self-acquired. With so poor a brief it may therefore seem impertinent of me to comment upon the faith and philosophy for which Maynooth stands. But because no visitor to Ireland can escape the impact of Catholicism, this book would be incomplete if I did not attempt to define my own reactions to it.

Those who expound upon and espouse the cause of freedom without any very clear idea of what they mean by freedom, dismiss Ireland very simply as 'priest-ridden'. When asked to expand this statement they will point out that the priest rules by superstitious fear. (I picked up a Catholic tract in an Irish church whose lurid cover portrayed the flames of hell as vividly and realistically as a medieval mural.) They will also point to the wealth of the Church, its many monasteries and its great new churches like those at Athlone or Mullingar, and contrast them with the poverty of the people, the wretched cabins lacking any civilized amenity in which many live, or the struggling peasant farmer in his ragged clothes. They will say that this theocracy is supported by 'voluntary' church dues wrung from these poor by the dread of having their names included in the list of defaulters read from the altar. They will maintain that this rule can only be upheld by keeping its subjects backward and ignorant, and in support of this contention they will instance the book censorship and the low standard of education.

There is justice in all these criticisms, but it is always easier to see the faults of others than to be aware of our own, and it would be wiser for the freedom lovers to consider whether they were not themselves ridden by something worse than priests before coining catch phrases like 'clerico-fascism'. The great temples of bureaucracy place a similar and steadily growing burden on the people, and their rule must be enforced by a torrent of rules and orders against which there is no appeal. And as this octopus grows in Europe it moulds education by propaganda and imposes censorship in order that it may the better enforce its will. By exchanging the priest for the bureaucrat we have merely jumped from the frying pan into the fire.

The chaos in Europe appears likely to resolve itself into a struggle between the Catholic and the Communist, and in this Ireland sees herself as an island bulwark of the true faith in a naughty world. Yet the commissar and the Jesuit have this much in common; they believe that any means justifies their end which is the world imposition of their respective philosophies (or rather their version of them). This is a fallacy. The end is invariably lost in the fanaticism and bigotry of the means long before it can be reached. Moreover, both Communist and priest display a puritanical and masochistic attitude to life which results in the loss of the humanities and the eclipse of the arts of living.

Though I could never be a Catholic I am, I hope, a Christian, so that, in the unhappy event of my having to take sides in this encounter I should be compelled to support the priest. Communism, with its deification of mass material ambition incarnate in the State (which so far from 'withering away' becomes omnipotent) is the most potent manifestation of positive evil that the world has ever seen. On the other hand, within these tomes at Maynooth there lies the germ of truth, however sorely it may be misapplied. The Church may or may not enshrine the principles of eternal truth, but though these truths may be changeless they must be perpetually renewed, developed and interpreted in the light of new knowledge and new problems so that they may refute falsehood which is forever putting on a new guise. Christianity was once a stream of thought steadily growing in volume as fresh minds, like tributary streams, made each their contribution. But that once bright stream became sluggish and now it is dammed up. Maynooth is a still pool of dogma, deep it is true, but dead, and the minds that come to her are so many empty buckets to be dipped and filled. Seldom or never do they spill over. Occasionally, bright rivulets do appear. The Report on Vocational Organization was one, and the Association known as Muintir na Tire which supports the principle of self-sufficiency and the values of the family farm and the family workshop, is another. Little of practical value has yet been achieved, but Ireland's hope lies in this attempt to find a Christian alternative to the disease of industrialism. It will certainly not be found in the attempts to seal Ireland off from pagan Europe by means of rigorous book censorship, restriction of education and a puritanical mistrust of the arts of Europe. The Irish are an artistically gifted race, yet how many Irish artists of recent times have been Catholics? Neither Catholic nor Communist to-day can produce great art for the same reason. Those Irishmen to-day who believe that these measures and the width of the Irish Sea will protect Ireland from the contagion of our world disease are living-in a fool's paradise, unaware of what is going on in the world. The disease is not only contagious, it is infectious, and-its germs are borne by the cinema, the radio and the machine. A people jealously protected from exposure will contract the disease all the more rapidly and virulently when inevitably, sooner or later, they are infected. The only defence is attack. The choice of purpose before Ireland is typified by the controversy between the dogmatist Manning and the visionary Newman. If the dam can be broken and the reservoir at Maynooth become a river once more, then Maynooth might become a second Clonmacnoise and Ireland again set an example to a continent.

Such were my reflections, right or wrong, as we strolled in the sunlit gardens of St. Joseph's Square, over the echoing flags of Pugin's cloisters, and through the nave of the bewilderingly over-decorated nineteenth-century Gothic chapel. The cloister walls were hung with the portraits of past dignitaries of the Church robed in the splendour of full canonicals. They looked down at me sternly, disapproving, I am certain, of my heretical notions. Only one of these portraits - by a contemporary Irish painter - was really alive; the rest had been painted with the painstaking but lifeless accuracy and detail of coloured photographs.

It was lucky for us that the students were down (if that is the correct term at Maynooth), and that the porter at the lodge, with typical Irish courtesy, admitted us freely and left us to wander unaccompanied through the quiet courts.

A fortress of massive, towering walls guards the gateway to Maynooth. It was the castle of the Norman FitzGeralds, Earls of Kildare. There is a curious tradition that when the castle once caught fire, the infant heir was rescued from a blazing upper room by an ape, and that the event is commemorated by a figure in the FitzGerald coat of arms. It was the ninth Earl who founded the first college at Maynooth in 1518, but it had a short life, being suppressed at the Reformation twenty years later. The chapel of the FitzGeralds then became the Protestant church which stands to this day, unabashed, within the very precincts of this Catholic stronghold. Close beside it grows an ancient yew beneath whose shade, so the story goes, Lord Thomas FitzGerald - called for some reason 'Silken Thomas' - was accustomed to play the harp. He eventually sailed to England for an audience with Henry VIII, and like so many others who tried conclusions with that monarch, his journey ended at Tyburn.

The present College was established at the close of the eighteenth century as a consequence of a parliamentary measure entitled: 'An Act for the better education of Persons professing the Popish or Roman Catholic Religion'. In 1795, the College trustees purchased the house of a certain Mr. Stoyte, steward of the Leinster estate, at the same time acquiring the lands surrounding it from the Duke of Leinster, twenty-first Earl of Kildare. In memory of his ancestor's endowment, the Duke parted with the land at one-third of its value. This, the original nucleus of the College survives substantially unchanged and is known as Stoyte House. With an annual grant of £8000, the College can scarcely be said to have been richly endowed. Nevertheless, with the aid of private bequests it began slowly but steadily to expand. First, wings were built onto each side of Stoyte House, and later two wings at right angles were constructed so that the garden now called St. Joseph's Square was enclosed on three sides.

MODERN IRISH UNIVERSITY, Maynooth. The chapel and part of Pugin's range from Stoyte House.

Peel, who carried the Catholic Emancipation Act of 1829, was largely responsible for the improvement of the fortunes of the College in the mid-nineteenth century. By his efforts in 1845, the English Parliament approved a handsome annual grant with the addition of a special grant for new building. The result was Pugin's great block which closes the fourth side of the square and which, with its cloisters, created a new quadrangle beyond.

In 1869, the Act of Church Disestablishment withdrew the grant and left the College with a capital sum which, though large, could never produce an income equivalent to the grant. Nevertheless, it was after this date that the chapel was completed on the north-west angle of St. Joseph's Square.

I am afraid I must profoundly disagree with what appears to be the prevailing opinion of Irish Catholics and Maynooth men as to the architectural merits of the College. One of these, writing of Stoyte House and its flanking wings, describes it as: 'that tame and undistinguished-looking front which completely hides from view the subsequent growth and the hand of Pugin'. Speaking of Dunboyne House, part of the next portion to be built, the same writer says: 'Its appearance is non-committal, being a replica of New House which faces it across St. Joseph's Square'. It is all a question of personal taste, no doubt, but, for my part, I could not disagree more strongly with this judgement. I doff my hat to the memory of those unknown architects and builders who were responsible for the simple but assured dignity of Stoyte House and who had the manners to build the wings and both New and Dunboyne Houses in accordance with this original. The whole group is an essay in restraint and good proportion which is only marred by the unsightly skylights which have been crassly super-imposed upon the roof-tops of the Stoyte House wings. They resemble two green houses perched there by some freak storm. By contrast with this earlier work, Pugin's great neo-Gothic block which forms the fourth side of the square seems to me to be an excellent example of architectural egoism and bad manners, a display of self-confidence that ignores any precedent and which did not hesitate to confront the hipped roof and bland eighteenth-century facade of Stoyte with squinting Gothic windows and a serried rank of dormers set in a high-pitched roof. It was originally proposed that the old buildings should be demolished, and Pugin's first plans were made on this assumption. From his point of view it is a pity that funds did not enable the project to be carried out. At least the result would have been homogeneous; as it is, his work invites comparison with that of his predecessors. Of all the neo-Gothic work at Maynooth I liked best the spire of the chapel, a graceful work by a later hand.

Readers will have gathered from this that I am not an admirer of the work of Augustus Welby Pugin. I am aware that he is considered the master of the nineteenth-century Gothic, but while no one could have a greater admiration for medieval Gothic, I cannot appreciate its latter-day revival. For the soul of the Gothic, that felicity in invention which could invest the most ponderous masses with an inimitable quality of aerial grace and lightness, for this we, look in vain. Instead we find only the gloom of great heavy buildings to which a mechanical Gothic convention has been applied like a thin spread of jam on a thick slice of stale bread. I incline to believe the story that Pugin once made a drawing of the front of Lincoln College, Oxford (Gothicized in 1819) in the belief that it was an exemplary specimen of original Gothic.

Among the traditions of Maynooth is a ghost story, and a gruesome one at that. Unlike the mysterious 'disturbance' at Decy Lock, I was able to unearth the details of it, and this is the version that I was told. (I have no doubt there are others.) One morning, a student of the College was found with his throat cut in his small study-bedroom. His open razor lay beside him. Some time after, another tenant of this room met the same fate. Another interval of time and a third student occupying the room made a similar attempt upon his life. But this time the self-inflicted wound did not prove mortal. The victim was quickly found and promptly treated. When he had recovered, he told the following story. He was standing before his mirror shaving when he saw, reflected in the glass, a figure standing behind him and gazing over his shoulder. As he looked, this figure raised its arm and drew the extended index finger across its throat, whereupon, without being aware of what he was doing, he was impelled to make the same gesture with the hand in which he held his razor. After this, it is said, the party walls of this grim chamber were pulled down so that it is now an open lobby. Was the room haunted? Or did the first student take his life for some extraneous reason and leave behind him some powerful force of auto-suggestion? We shall never know.

I liked the little village of Maynooth. Its street, wide as all Irish village streets are, has been happily planted with trees so that it forms an avenue from the gates of the College to those of Carton Park. On our way through the village to the canal I noticed, lying abandoned in a small builder's yard, the chassis of an old Martini car whose date I judged, from details of the engine and from the final chain drive, to be about 1910. I have never seen an example of this rare Swiss car in England, and I pondered on the circumstances that could have brought it to this last resting place in an Irish village. Had it originally accompanied some visiting member of the Continental Catholic hierarchy?

We surprised a party of village boys round the boat when we returned from our tour of Maynooth. Though she was locked, we afterwards discovered that they had succeeded in opening one half of the wheelhouse windscreen and had stolen Angela's fishing line and spinner from the shelf beneath. The morals of Maynooth do not appear to extend very far beyond the College precincts.

It was evening by this time, but we decided to get under way and lie for the night at the village of Kilcock, two-and-a-half miles ahead. We moored at the top of the double lock there and enjoyed an excellent pint of porter - a legitimate 'bona fide' - in the 'select bar' on the waterfront. Exploring the village later, I observed that the sanctuary lamp in the Catholic church had been electrified. I am not versed in Catholic ritual, but it seemed to me that this example of mechanization which made the continuance of the light dependent upon the possible vagaries of distant power-house and transmission lines, effectually disposed of any symbolical significance which it might possess.

Next morning we got under way in good time and soon passed through McLoghlin's or Ferrans Double Lock, beyond which we knew there lay ahead of us a level of over twenty miles. The water here was once more clear of weeds. Having finished his labours at the locks for the time being, Richard got out his short pike rod and a spinner and settled himself in the dinghy as we travelled along. He was very successful, for although he caught nothing over three-quarters of a pound in weight, his catch made up in quantity what it lacked in quality, and by the end of the day it totalled nine perch and six pike.

We lunched near the village of Enfield, then crossed over the River Blackwater and entered a beautiful tree-shadowed reach which continued as far as the little village of Moyvalley with its trim freshly painted railway station beside the canal. Here we met Leach of Killucan bound for Dublin with a load of bog ore. Bog ore is technically described as 'a limonitic deposit of bogs and stagnant pools which occurs where the water in the locality is, or has been, charged with salts of iron'. It is used in the process of purifying town gas. As soon as I sighted Leach's boat I eased up, but his two horses were so disconcerted at our unprecedented appearance that they stopped in their tracks, turned about on the narrow towing path, and were only restrained from bolting by prompt and skilful handling.

Between the fine and lofty aqueduct over the River Boyne and the bridge named Blackshade (does this perpetuate another haunting?), we met a second weed-cutting gang. This gang was at work, cutting the reeds with scythe blades drawn along the bed of the canal from the banks. For the next two miles through Hill of Down we had more trouble with propeller fouling, though the weeds were never so thick as on the first bad length before Maynooth.

Hill of Down must derive its name from the little conical hill which stands close to the canal's right bank and which is of such symmetrical shape as to look artificial though I do not believe this to be the case. With a small thatched and ivy-covered farmstead sheltering below, it was an attractive place, and we stopped for a few moments beneath the arch of the bridge while Angela bought bread at the village shop. Beyond this point, and until they finally part company, railway and canal become less closely associated. While the former takes a line of rigid straightness, the course of the latter becomes more tortuous, roaming across the country in a series of wayward loops. We crossed a tract of bogland where there was a little lonely lough called Croboy, but the bogs along the course of the Royal are nowhere so extensive as those traversed by the Grand, the country being much more diversified. Thus we very soon left the bog and found ourselves approaching D'Arcy's Bridge under the shelter of the trees of Hyde Park. We had come twenty-two miles from Kilcock, and knew we must be nearing the Killucan Locks, so we decided to make this our resting place for the night.

As our photograph shows, it was a happy choice. On the grass between the canal and the lane which ran beside it, Angela set to work to prepare some of Richard's perch for supper. A man coming home from his work in the fields to his cabin on the bog got off his bicycle and with delightful informality knelt beside her and demonstrated the art of scaling and preparing them. 'Och! 'Tis a simple thing now, no trouble at all … ' and in a very short time the fish were ready for the pan. He was rewarded with some of them, for we had

THE ROYAL CANAL. Moorings at D'Arcy's Bridge.

more than enough for our needs.

This wholly unselfconscious and unreserved friendliness and generosity of the people of rural Ireland is one of my most cherished recollections of this voyage. The lock-keepers along the Royal, particularly on the western section, are mostly peasant farmers, for on this disused waterway their duties are light and their pay low. They gave us bunches of young onions or 'scallions' as they called them and kept us supplied throughout the journey with milk and potatoes. Though many looked pitifully poor we had the greatest difficulty in inducing any of them to accept money for their produce. It was offered freely and so liberally that had we accepted all, we could have sunk the boat under the weight of potatoes or floated it in milk. There was little else that they could have offered us.

That evening, to round off a successful and delightful day, we went rowing in the clear and windless dusk. It was one of those times when the atmosphere is so calm, so silent and still, that one instinctively lowers the voice to a whisper as though for fear of disturbing some secret and soundless activity. Once, indeed, a heron rose from the reeds close behind us and wheeled away into the gloom, and once the dark shape of an owl swept overhead in noiseless, mothlike flight. We rowed slowly and softly while Richard, encouraged by his day's catch, began spinning from the stern. For some time none of us spoke, and the only sounds that betrayed us were the faint creak of the oars in the thole pins and the occasional whirr of the ratchet of Richard's reel as he let out more line. Suddenly there came a swirl in the still water, the trailing line sprung taut and the rod flexed into a quivering arc. At once, indolence became tense excitement and activity. Angela who was rowing at the time, backed water while Richard played the fish, and in a few moments a pike of two and three-quarter pounds was floundering in the bottom of the boat. Certainly it was no fish to make an angler's legend, but nevertheless, however many monster fish I may see landed, I shall never forget the excitement of that catch in the semi-darkness.

We soon ascended the eight single locks at Killucan the next morning and so reached the summit level which we found to be clear, deep and weed-free. After a stop for lunch in a tree sheltered reach near the demesne of Woodfort, we continued over a stretch of bogland and presently entered a long cutting. This was not so sheer and rocky as the Clonsilla cutting but was nevertheless a work of considerable magnitude. At the end of it we saw ahead of us Mullingar, the county town of Westmeath. Mullingar is the only town along the line of the Royal between Dublin and the Shannon, and being approximately the half-way point, it is a useful port of call where we had arranged to collect mail and replenish our stores of food and fuel. The canal here makes a great loop which encircles the town on three sides, and we had travelled more than half-way round before we came to the harbour where the helpful Cafferty had advised us to moor and to seek the assistance of Mr. Stenson the harbour-master.

It was a contrast to the busy harbour at Tullamore which had been the half-way house on our eastward journey. We had to dig for the mooring rings on the grass-grown quay, while the warehouses were empty and forlorn, one corner serving as a sty for Mr. Stenson's pig. Our harbour-master proved to be a delightful old man of charming courtesy whose brilliant twinkling blue eyes belied his white hairs and his infirm legs. He held the keys of the iron gates which were the only landward means of access to the harbour so that the mooring was satisfactory in every way, *Le Coq* being able to lie at the quay secure from interference.

I prefer to remember Mullingar by the kindness of Mr. Stenson, who, in addition to entrusting us with his keys, pressed upon us fresh vegetables from his garden, gifts for which we endeavoured to make some small return by presenting our scraps to his pig. For the rest, I thought that, for a county town, Mullingar was a mean place. It had a shabby ill-kempt appearance reminiscent of Banagher, nor did we find here (our harbour-master excepted) that same friendliness among the people which we found everywhere else in Ireland.

The new Catholic cathedral at Mullingar is similar in style to the new church of St. Peter at Athlone. The interior is of even more impressive magnificence, while the lighting arrangements are cleverly disposed to display this to the best advantage. But the exterior is much less satisfactory. The roof of the nave is too long and low pitched in proportion to the height of the dome and of the twin campanile at the west end. As a result, instead of a compact and balanced association of masses leading the eye upward to soaring pinnacle, tower or spire to which they should be organically related, these various elements are disintegrated and the cathedral sprawls clumsily. In this respect, St. Peters, Athlone, is a much more satisfactory composition. One of the Mullingar campanile carries a clock with a singularly sweet chime, but the architect has not succeeded in solving the problem of what to do with the space occupied by the clock faces on its twin, and this gives the west facade an unbalanced one-eyed appearance.

The town is situated midway between two large lakes, Lough Owel on the north and Lough Ennell on the south. By means of a feeder a little over two miles long, the former provides the main source of water supply to the summit of the Royal Canal. This feeder enters the canal close beside the harbour, and on the day before our departure we decided that we would attempt to navigate it in the dinghy. The water in the feeder was deep and clear and there was quite a strong current, but it was much too narrow for the use of oars. One legacy of Richard's term at Oxford, however, is a proficiency in the art of punting which I envy but cannot emulate, so it was arranged that he should propel the dinghy up to the lake while we walked. To navigate a punt on the 'Char' is one thing, to stand on the stern of a light dinghy and coax it up a narrow channel against a strong current with the aid of a clumsy pole which had once been *Le Coq's* wireless mast, was quite another story. However, Richard performed wonders, achieving a slow walking pace. Occasionally, as a variation, he performed feats of 'legging' or 'handing', disappearing beneath bridges which were no more than culverts while we anxiously awaited his emergence at the other end. Finally we had to make a portage round the sluices and into the lough. This was successfully accomplished although we had some difficulty in launching because a breeze, blowing across the lake directly into the mouth of the feeder, was creating quite a swell. However, we all embarked safely and rowed across the lake to Church Island where we had a picnic tea beside the much overgrown ruins that give the island its name. Perhaps the most enjoyable part of this outing was the return journey when, having transferred the dinghy from the rough waters of the lake back to the calm feeder, we all clambered on board and floated serenely on the current down to the canal, occasionally crouching in the bottom of the boat as we went under a culvert. I doubt if many people can claim to have navigated the Lough Owel feeder.

THE ROYAL CANAL. Richard punts the dinghy up the feeder to Lough Owel

THE ROYAL CANAL

MULLINGAR TO THE SHANNON

All the way from Dublin the country through which we passed had been becoming more sparsely populated and less softly pastoral in character, but it was after we had left Mullingar and finally lost sight of the railway at Ballaina Bridge, Habsborough, that we really entered what Cafferty had called 'the wilds'. But these wilds had not the flat monotony of the great bogs which we had seen from the western portion of the Grand Canal, for we were approaching the extreme north-western corner of the central plain and would soon cross the border of Westmeath into Longford where begins that belt of Caledonian granite which geologists call the axis of Newry and which runs diagonally across Ireland to the waters of Strangford Lough. And as is the case in all regions of geological change, the limestone of the plain was beginning to show signs of uneasiness, lifting and folding as the surface of a level lake is flawed by the wind. Thus the engineers of the Royal Canal had a more difficult task than that which confronted the builders of the Grand. A study of the course of the two canals on the map reveals this. With the exception of the short section from Robertstown to Sallins it will be seen that the course of the Grand consists of a series of long straight cuts linked by easy curves, whereas that of the Royal becomes progressively more tortuous as it proceeds westward.

We passed two more gangs of weed cutters in quick succession and as they were evidently working towards each other, we were only troubled with weed in the short level between them. It was nearly three o'clock by the time we had left Mullingar, but by teatime we reached the end of the summit at Coolnahay top lock, and had dropped nine locks before we moored for the night a mile short of the village of Ballynacarrigy.

Unlike their English equivalent, we found that the Irish inch-to-the-mile survey maps, which were our only guide during this voyage, were completely unreliable in their marking of canal locks. Sometimes, very indistinctly, the conventional arrow-head symbol was shown, sometimes the word 'lock' was written, or, more vaguely, 'locks' to denote a flight but with no indication of their number or precise position. Again, some locks were not indicated on the map at all so that their appearance came as a surprise to us. I discovered the inadequacy of the map in this respect soon after we entered the Grand Canal and so made a habit of marking the position of each lock on the map as we came to it. With the aid of a map measurer, this has proved a great help to me in compiling the itinerary at the end of this book.

We thought Ballynacarrigy a strange and desolate place when we passed through its lock under a grey sky the next morning. In the heyday of the canal it had obviously been a centre of some importance, but now the quays were a forsaken wilderness and the cottages and warehouses in ruins; a Robertstown that had died. We dropped three more locks and then crossed the only extensive stretch of bog which we encountered on this canal. My Jamestown boatman friend was to tell me later how, in the days when Guinness was carried on the canal, the boatmen used to stop in lonely places such as this and broach the porter barrels. A small hole would be drilled in the barrel, the jug filled, and the hole stopped with a tiny bung cut from the bog heather and smoothed off so as to be invisible. When a 'dry' boat carrying empties met a loaded one it was the custom to exchange a full jug for an empty one. When next they met the roles were reversed and the debt would be repaid.

Beyond this bog, the canal scenery undergoes a sudden dramatic change. The waterway crosses the broad river Inny by an imposing aqueduct, and having done so makes an acute right-angle turn to follow the river valley through a more sheltered country of trees, little hills and sloping pastures. Here is the hamlet of Abbeysrule where we moored by the quay to have lunch and where we bought two pounds of delicious country butter at the post-office cum general store. As the name denotes, there was once an abbey here, and we walked over the river bridge to look at the extensive ruins. There appeared to be nothing of very remarkable architectural note about them, but there was evidence of more careful preservation than was the case with most of the Irish historical monuments which we saw. Those responsible had let into the wall an inscribed stone which effectually epitomizes the Abbey's story. It read:

'St Mary's Cistercian Abbey of Shruel Mainistir Srothair',
Official Title: De Benedictione Dei.
Founded 1150 by the O'Ferrall of Annally.
Burned 1476 by the English of the Pale.
Rebuilt, but confiscated by Henry VIII.

So even this lonely place did not escape the attentions of this rapacious monarch of ours.

Many English people who have never visited Ireland imagine that the typical Irish cabin is no more than a pig-sty, and that, in fact, pigs do share it with the occupants. This is pure fiction, like the stage Irishman with his bottle-green coat, his bundle, his shillelagh and his frequent 'begorrahs'. Ninety per cent. of the cabins which we saw were neatly thatched, and the walls were fresh with white or colour wash. An occasional bold chicken may perch on the sill of the half-door and then flutter down to peck for crumbs under the table, and why not? - but pigs, no. The row of cabins at Abbeysrule between the canal and the river, however, definitely belonged to that other ten per cent. With their moss-covered, leaky, thatch and windowless ruined walls, they would have made poor shelters for cattle, yet all were occupied. It was a revelation to find, in this twentieth century, people living under conditions which could not have been worse (and were probably a great deal better) in pre-history. Turf smoke was pouring out of the doorway and through the roof of one of them. This, and not a technical fault was responsible for the blur in our photograph.

THE IRISH CABIN AT ITS WORST. Abbeysrule. 'Turf smoke was pouring out of the doorway and through the roof.'

Readers who are in a position to do so will find it of interest to compare this picture with the illustration of the old Welsh cottage at Great Mains, Llaethdy, in Radnorshire which appears in Mr. Iorwerth Peate's interesting book *The Welsh House*. The similarity is striking. All these cottages, in fact, were of great archæological interest whatever a sanitary inspector might have thought about them. Half the roof of the next cottage had collapsed to reveal the interesting construction of the wattle and daub chimney breast, Welsh examples of which are also illustrated in Mr. Peat's book. The end house was remarkable for the fact that its unusually massive walls had a very pronounced batter from ground level to eaves. This may have indicated cruck construction, though no exterior timberwork was apparent. As Mr. Peate remarks in his book, the similarity of early Welsh and Irish domestic architecture reveals the intimacy of the association which once existed between these two Celtic countries.

The canal bore a more and more disused appearance the farther we went westwards, and at Draper's Bridge lock beyond Abbeysrule it was obvious that the chamber was rarely filled. Clumps of yellow musk in full blossom were growing out of chinks in the masonry

THE IRISH CABIN AT ITS WORST. Abbeysrule. 'Half the roof had collapsed to reveal the interesting construction of the wattle and daub chimney breast.'

and looked so beautiful that we were sorry to drown them. The lock-keeper insisted on presenting us with some magnificent new potatoes which he dug from his garden while we were locking through. He refused to accept payment but, noticing Angela's camera, asked if she would take a picture of him with the family. She gladly agreed and took a photograph of 'himself' with his handsome silver-haired wife and two small boys standing before the half-door of the lock-cottage. I hope he was satisfied with the print which we sent him.

I know not for what reason, unless it was that funds began to run out, but from Draper's Bridge onwards the canal is of much more modest section. Water lilies thrust out their floating leaves and blossoms from the margins to leave only a narrow channel of clear water. Moreover, the waterway commenced to wind hither and thither in most tortuous fashion as it followed the contours of the Inny valley. It was a singularly wild and beautiful stretch of water reminiscent in many respects of the older English narrow canals. Away among the trees on the opposite slopes of the valley lay Pallas the earliest home of Goldsmith, and our map, which was so reticent about canal locks, became in this case unusually informative by printing 'Birthplace of Goldsmith' beneath the name. Goldsmith is the only historical personage whose birthplace I have seen commemorated in this way on a survey map, and the distinction is the more singular because it is by no means certain

ROYAL CANAL. Lock-keeper and family. Draper's Bridge Lock.

that the poet was born at Pallas at all. His parents certainly lived at Pallas at this time, but majority opinion now maintains that the child was born prematurely while Mrs. Goldsmith was staying with her widowed mother at Smith Hill near Elphin in the County Roscommon.

A short way beyond the disused wharf which once served the little town of Ballymahon a mile away, the canal, which has hitherto pursued a due westerly course, swings abruptly to the north. At this point it is only three miles from the shores of Lough Ree at the mouth of the Inny River. It is as though the canal surveyors had originally intended to follow the course of the river into the lake, as they might easily have done, instead of which they suddenly changed their minds and carried their waterway another thirteen miles due north and parallel with the Shannon before making the junction at Richmond Harbour. I do not believe, however, that there was really any such change of purpose, but that the curious course of the canal was dictated by the difficult country to the east which precluded a more direct course. Owing to the prevailing winds, any harbour on the east side of Lough Ree would generally be on a lee shore, and goods destined for places on the Shannon might be stormbound there for days before the sailing vessels, or the later steamers, into which they were transhipped, could put out. Furthermore, since trade on the river from Athlone downwards was an obvious monopoly of the Grand Canal Company, the Royal Canal proprietors no doubt planned to capture the river traffic north of Lough Ree and to serve the town of Longford *en route*.

Soon after we turned northward we came to Mullawornia Lock, and this was undoubtedly the scenic high-light of the Royal Canal. We had been travelling through a cutting when, with dramatic abruptness, the bank on our left fell away to disclose a sweep of country below us which stretched away to the waters of the great lake. Just below the lock the canal became a narrow platform of water rounding the bluff of a precipitous escarpment. Obviously this was Cafferty's 'hundred feet of rock' and 'hundred feet of bog', for there, sure enough was the rock rising sheer from the water on the one hand, while upon the other we could look almost vertically down upon the marshy fringes of little Lough Drum, black in the shadow of thick pine woods.

We moored up for the night a few hundred yards from the lonely lock cottage, and it was undoubtedly the most fascinating of our many halting places along this remote and forgotten water road across Ireland. The rock was, unless I am much mistaken, the westernmost outcrop of the Caledonian Axis of Newry, and although it was no great height above sea level the view from the summit was impressive. Under a grey sky, the distant waters of Lough Ree were a sheet of silver, and the horizon of the farther shore was invisible through the rain curtain of a squall which was sweeping swiftly across the surface of the great lake. As I gazed I thought how apt was Spenser's description of the river in the *Faerie Queen* when he called it 'the Spacious Shenan spreading like a sea'.

Shortly after we had left our moorings the next morning we encountered one of the many families of swans which frequent the Royal Canal. As usual, they betrayed great alarm at our approach but behaved with more than usual stupidity. For a while the whole family paddled frantically ahead of us, but the cygnets soon tired whereupon one of the parent birds piloted them close under the bank and we went past them. Not so the remaining bird. Despite every manœuvre on our part it continued to keep ahead of us, alternately swimming and flying, for the best part of three miles until it became completely exhausted and was nearly run down. It is possible, of course, that this arduous performance was undertaken deliberately with the idea of drawing our attention away from the young birds, but somehow I doubt this. We wondered how long it would be before the family were reunited. Just before Mullawornia Lock we had met a pair of wild swans, a rarity at this time of the year, but distinguishable from the semi-domesticated mute swan by the pale bill and the absence of the predominant black knob at the base. They were of slightly lighter and smaller build than the mute swans, and unlike the latter they did not indulge in the usual frantic display of alarm at our approach. On the contrary, they remained apparently unconcerned until we drew quite close to them, when, without the laboured take-off of the mute swan, they suddenly rose from the water simultaneously and flew out of sight in the direction of Lough Ree from whence they had presumably come.

We moored for lunch at Keenagh Harbour which we understood to be usually the western

---

[1] Windlasses are usually left at each lock and are seldom carried on the boats as in England.

terminus of Cafferty's voyages. This meant that for the remainder of our journey to the Shannon we should be travelling over waters disused except for the rare passage of a maintenance boat. We walked the half-mile to the village of Keenagh for stores, for it was a Saturday, and found it a pleasant trim village. Several of the cottages had been freshly painted in that curious convention which decorates the flat surface of the corner stones with lozenge patterns in shades of grey or buff in such a way as to create the illusion (often very effectively) that the surface is not flat but bevelled or rusticated. The effect, though not very beautiful, is unusual and striking. There must be scarcely a town or village in Ireland that cannot boast at least one example of this strange conceit, and I should like to know how it originated. I have never seen anything like it outside Ireland.

Just as we were leaving Keenagh we suffered a mishap. There was a sharp crack and the steering cable parted. The steering had never been very positive in action, largely due to the fact that the cable was of too heavy a gauge for the tortuous course it took round pulleys of very small diameter and through tubes behind the panelling of the aft cabin. We had a cable clip with which we could affect a temporary repair, but because the cable had broken at a point where it passed over a pulley, the clip would foul and we had to re-adjust the cable in such a way that the clip came on a straight and exposed portion. For an hour and a half we laboured, removing portions of the panelling and entangling ourselves like Laocoön in yards of cable which twisted and coiled snake-like, its frayed strands pricking unwary fingers. Eventually, however, the steering functioned again somewhat uncertainly and, order being restored, we continued on our way.

Although the two locks which we passed through showed increasing signs of decrepitude, we travelled well until we reached Cloonsheerin Junction where the short branch to Longford led away on our right. Here it was plain that the fifth and last weed-cutting gang, who had evidently recently cut the length we had just traversed, had gone up the branch before proceeding the rest of the way to the Shannon. The weed was almost as thick as it had been above Decy Lock at Maynooth, but resorting to similar tactics, we battled our way through to the two locks at Killashee. The lock-keeper here was of a somewhat gloomy disposition. Shaking his head he expressed the gravest doubts as to the possibility of our being able to get through the second of the two locks. This was discouraging indeed, but with less, than four miles to go before we reached the Shannon we were certainly not disposed to bring our voyage to an ignominious conclusion without a struggle. We soon discovered the reason for his pessimism.

Canal locks are normally left empty, the small top gates being better able to withstand the pressure of water in the pound above. Consequently, when locks are never used, the timberwork of the lower gates dries out, cracks and opens, so that, when the lock is eventually filled, they leak badly. Most of the lower gates on the Royal leaked for this reason, but in this case not only did the lower gates leak particularly badly, but the beam of one of the top gates had broken off and the two paddle racks were missing. With only two top paddles drawn, the incoming water scarcely equalled the rate of leakage, so that the chamber could not be filled and the top gates could not be opened. However, we managed with some difficulty to lever up the paddles on the broken gate whereupon the level in the lock chamber began slowly, desperately slowly, to rise. We tore up clods of turf from the lock sides and threw them into the water above the bottom gates where, sucked down by the current, they staunched some of the leaks. Anxiously we stood watching the water level creeping up from one joint in the masonry to another. At last we knew that it was now or never and we all put our backs to the beam of the one sound gate. The levels had by no means equalized and for a few tense moments we strained in vain; then we felt the gate give ever so slightly. Encouraged we gave a final united heave and with a swirl of water the gate swung back. There was no necessity to open the broken gate as *Le Coq's* beam was narrow enough to pass through one, and once inside, our troubles were soon over for the lock had begun to empty itself before we had lifted the lower paddles.

We moored for the night a little distance from the tail of this lock, and the next morning Richard walked back to Mass at Killashee so that it was not until afternoon that we resumed our journey. The weather was stormy, so we contented ourselves with a mere two and a half miles to the next lock at Rinn Mount from which we could see Richmond Harbour less than half a mile away. Here the lock cottage was in ruins, and we had been told that the lock windlass was in the charge of the harbour-master [1]. We did not think it fair to call him out on a wet Sunday evening so we remained above the lock till the morning. As the evening drew on, the storm clouds lifted and there occurred one of those dramatic climatic changes so characteristic of Ireland. One moment, it seemed, everything was veiled in driving rain, in the next the atmosphere was crystal clear and there on our left beyond the river was the long ridge of Slieve Bawn, black against a stormy sunset. Angela and I recalled that we had last seen Slieve Bawn as a distant blue hump on the horizon as we tossed about on Lough Ree in a little outboard motor boat. Already that day seemed to have passed into history, so much water had we traversed since then. True, our journey from Athlone to Dublin and back to the Shannon could have been accomplished by car in half a day or by air in an hour or so, but this is mere movement, it is not travel. Travel is not susceptible of measurement. A ten-mile walk can store the mind with memories while a hundred-mile car journey can leave it empty.

We had not known what the Royal Canal had in store for us, and after the doubts expressed at Athlone I had envisaged us struggling with broken-down locks, bow-hauling for miles through dense weed, or fast aground in half-empty pounds. However, apart from trifling difficulties which had only lent a venturesome spice to the journey, our progress had exceeded my highest expectations. However ill-conceived and ill-rewarded the shoemaker's project may have been, his Royal Canal certainly gave us a voyage of unforgettable interest. It was with a delightful sense of achievement that we sailed into Richmond Harbour in the bright morning sunlight, a cool westerly breeze ruffling the water.

The village of Cloondara lives, but not by the grace of the canal, for Richmond Harbour is dead. Apart from the white-washed cottage of the harbour-master and the 'Richmond Bar' where we purchased provisions and celebrated our arrival, all is in ruins. Derelict warehouses and empty cottages tell the story of vanished activity, revealing that this was once the Shannon Harbour of the Royal Canal where the grass grown quays must once have been piled with merchandise and reverberated with the rumble of cartwheels; where the commodious basin must have been filled with boats, unloading at the quay or transhipping into the Shannon steamers. To how great an extent the railway company were responsible for killing this traffic when they acquired the canal I do not know, but this much must be said for them; unlike the English railway companies, they do give courteous and willing assistance to pleasure boat owners wishing to use the waterway, and they do keep the weeds down. Our railways not only display a completely unco-operative attitude to potential users of their waterways, but allow them to become so fouled with weed as to be impassable during the summer months by any boat not fitted with an anti-fouling propeller.

THE ROYAL CANAL. Richmond Harbour. 'Derelict warehouses and empty cottages'.

The 'Richmond Bar' was a great rambling building which had once been a flax mill in the days before flax became a northern Irish monopoly. Why should not flax growing be revived in the Free State?

Across the canal bridge there was a large corn mill which had likewise seen better days but which I was pleased to see was still at work. Moreover it was not, as our few surviving watermills are, relegated by the milling combine to grinding cattle meal. Cloondara Mill was grinding 100 per cent. extraction flour for the village bakeries of the district. As we walked over the bridge a small water-turbine was churning merrily, driving the dynamo which provided electric light for the mill and the miller's house. But the great undershot wheel which drove the mill from the waters of the Fallan River, a tributary of the Shannon, was still and silent. I knew why because, from somewhere in the dim recesses of the rambling stone building I could hear the chip chip of a mill-bill tapping away like some busy woodpecker. This Irish miller, like the English country millers that I have been fortunate enough to meet, was obviously proud of his mill and was delighted by our interest. Having assured himself that the stones which were being dressed were out of gear, he insisted upon opening the sluice for our benefit, setting the giant wheel revolving with a rumble and surge that wakened the mill and which, via a complex of wooden gearing, shafts and pulleys, set screens and sieves shaking and revolving to the very top of the building. It seemed that he must bring his mill to life before he would display it to us.

There were four pairs of stones, two sets of 'Peaks' for meal and two sets of French Burrs for wheat. The runner of one pair of Peaks had been swung off the bedstone, and the dresser sat on a sack, legs astraddle, as he tapped away at the worn furrows with his bill. I had expected to find that the language of the miller's craft was different in Ireland, but this was not so. Thus the stirrup and shoe which feeds the grain into the eye of the runner stone and whose cheerful clink clack contrasts with the rumble of the stones, our miller, like his fellows in England, called the 'damsel'. In an earlier book I described how the miller of Minshull Mill in Cheshire used apple wood to renew the teeth of the wooden mill gearing. Here beech wood was used for this purpose.

Long may the wheels of Cloondara Mill continue to turn. However poor the Irish countryman may be he will be better off than us so long as he can eat country butter on bread made from flour ground honestly in mills such as this. Here, 'the staff of life' has not yet been robbed and adulterated.

The Royal Canal ends at the tail of the Richmond Harbour entrance lock, and here I surrendered to the old harbour-master the pass, crumpled now, and scrawled over with the pencilled signatures of many lock-keepers, which we had carried with us from Spencer Dock. As we emerged from the lock into the River Fallan our improvised steering cable chose this awkward moment to jam and for a moment we were in danger of being carried by the current down towards the mill. By coming hard astern, however, we managed to get back into the slack water by the lock tail where we freed the refractory cable and set out once more. About two hundred yards upstream we turned sharply to the left into the Cloondara Lock Cut which connects the canal with the Shannon. This comes under the jurisdiction of the Shannon authorities who evidently do not take their weed-cutting duties so seriously as the railway company. The cut was choked with a mass of weed so dense that it might well have deterred anyone from approaching the canal from the Shannon. But we were on the last lap and fairly ploughed our way through to the lock.

Cloondara Lock is in the charge of John Bourke, the keeper of Tarmonbarry Lock, who, having been apprised of our approach had come over on his bicycle to meet us. The lock itself was in fair order, but the heavy gates were stiff from long disuse and some haymakers in a neighbouring field came to our assistance. With creaks of complaint, the lower gate swung open and in a few moments we were sailing out onto the broad Shannon, here a quarter of a mile wide. While we crossed the river and entered Tarmonbarry Lock by the farther shore, our lock-keeper was pedalling furiously round by Tarmonbarry Bridge to assist us. The chamber, which seemed vast after the canal locks, was soon filled, and we were presently snugly berthed for the night beside the lock wall above.

CHAPTER ELEVEN

THE UPPER SHANNON
AND THE RIVER BOYLE

The Irish village shop is usually remarkable for the great - sometimes almost grotesque - variety of its stock, but the shop at Tarmonbarry was especially noteworthy in this respect. Not only did groceries, ironmongery, boots and shoes, liquor and haberdashery jostle each other on walls, shelves and floor but a printed notice announced: 'Irish-made Habits and Shrouds Sold Here'. Its proprietor could therefore justly claim to cater for every need from the cradle to the grave.

Tarmonbarry is a somewhat desolate spot, and although we awoke to a morning of lowering cloud and a strong south wind bringing squalls of driving rain, we decided to continue on our way up the river until we reached some more congenial mooring. We passed under Tarmonbarry Bridge and, with the wind dead astern, were soon driving across Lough Forbes at a fine pace, the waves chasing beside us. On our right, the shores of the lake were clothed in the fine woods of the demesne of Castle Forbes.

From the head of the lake, a long straight reach leads to the mouth of the old Roosky Cut and the present Roosky Lock. Having worked our way through the lock, we moored up at Roosky Quay close to the bridge and to the village, a much more pleasant place in bad weather than bleak Tarmonbarry.

Just above Roosky is Lough Bofin which, in turn, leads into Lough Boderg. Our hopes of better weather for the crossing of these lakes were rewarded by a morning of bright sunshine, a fresh westerly breeze and a brilliantly clear atmosphere, conditions which could scarcely have been better or more exhilarating. The breeze only ruffled the sparkling blue waters of the lakes sufficiently to make *Le Coq* feel pleasantly alive, but Richard, fishing energetically but without success from the dinghy, had quite an exciting passage. The channel between the two lakes is narrow and rocky but clearly indicated by buoys and fixed markers, It is overlooked by Derrycarne House, most enviably situated on a wooded headland facing south and with lawns sloping towards the water's edge. As we cleared these narrows and headed out across the sunlit waters of Lough Boderg we caught our first glimpse of the mountains about Lough Allen, twenty miles to the north; the ridge of Arigna Mountain and the peaks of Bencroy and Benbrack blue in the distance.

Lough Boderg is followed by little Lough Tap at the head of which the Dublin-Sligo line crosses the river. At this point it is easy for the stranger, if he is not paying proper attention to his map, to do as we did and take the wrong course. A wide reach stretches invitingly straight ahead, but the course of the navigation turns sharply to the left to enter the Jamestown Lock Cut. This by-passes a great loop which the Shannon makes between the villages of Drumsna and Jamestown. Because this is one of the most attractive reaches of the Upper Shannon, anyone exploring the river by boat would be well advised to follow our example. Before we had gone many hundred yards we discovered our mistake, but as the river was both wide and deep we decided we would attempt to reach Drumsna. A ruined quay obviously marked the limit of navigation just short of the fine old bridge, and here we dropped anchor in midstream, the quay itself being unapproachable owing to fallen masonry. When we rowed ashore and walked up the village street we were greeted by the old blacksmith who emerged from the smallest and most primitive forge I have ever seen and made us the welcome offer of some eggs.

Because there is comparatively little diversity in the use of building materials in Ireland, at a cursory or unobservant glance one village may look very much like any other. Their particular character depends upon detail. Why then did we think that Drumsna, drowsing in the hot bright sunlight of a summer's noon was such an attractive example of an Irish

IRISH VILLAGES. (1) Drumsna, where Trollope once walked.

village? Partly on account of its setting, the trees which sheltered it and the way the short wide street sloped gently down to the old stone bridge with its massive cut-waters. Partly the contrasting colours and textures of paintwork and wall surfaces, gaily painted doors and window frames against dazzling whitewash, primrose coloured plaster or stucco, or the grey of naked stone. Partly well proportioned windows and doorways with simple but effective fanlights. I doubt if this street can have changed substantially since September 1843 when, probably on just such a sunny day as this, two men strolled in leisurely fashion through the village and out to the ruined country house of Headford, just under two miles away. They were Anthony Trollope and his friend John Merivale. The ruins of Headford must have impressed Trollope, for it became the setting for the first chapter of his first book, *The Macdermots of Ballycloran*, which he published with small success in 1847.

Angela and I went shopping in the village, leaving Richard and Marten fishing from the dinghy. While Angela was visiting the victualler I acquired three pennyworth of cheap and vivid sweets, prompted by antiquarian interest rather than by my sweet tooth. They consisted of discs of white, yellow and pink sugar each of which bore an inscription in red letters designed, it would seem, to enable a lover and his lass, each armed with a bag, to conduct a lively courtship. For example, the love-sick swain could proffer his coy mistress a pink heart inscribed 'I Love You' or 'Will you be mine'? whereupon, if she felt that the pace was becoming too hot, she could cool his ardour with a yellow confection of curious shape which retorted, rather incongruously, 'Sez You'. The sweets were, in fact, somewhat debased descendants of those old Victorian 'motto' sweets to which Pigling Bland's girl friend was addicted, and which seem to have long ago disappeared in England.

We returned to the quay to find the dinghy out of sight, but the fishing party presently arrived in a state of great excitement with a pike of three and a quarter pounds which Marten had caught. This was the largest fish taken on the voyage, and its capture was the more remarkable because Richard, who had forgotten to take his landing net, had contrived to haul it aboard in a bucket which fortunately happened to be in the dinghy.

After lunch, fired with this success, we rowed round the loop of the river almost as far as the tail of the Jamestown Weir, but the only result was one small perch. The Shannon hereabouts undergoes a startling transformation. It was hard to believe that this swift and narrow stream, hurrying along in the shadow of dense woods and undergrowth, was the same great river which, above and below this reach, becomes so wide and stately or spreads itself into inland seas.

We made our way back down the river in the late afternoon and turned into Jamestown or, to give it its official title, Albert Lock. The lock was in charge of Michael Bourke, brother to John Bourke of Tarmonbarry. He possessed a great store of conversation and a felicitous turn of phrase which reminded me of Synge's 'Playboy'. Consequently we spent some time sitting on the parapet of Albert Lock. It all began when Angela commenced gutting the famous pike. (Later, fillets of it would be fried with the breakfast bacon, an unusual but excellent combination.) While Michael assisted in this operation he discoursed at length upon the monster fish which, he claimed, lurked in the Shannon, and upon the methods, legitimate and otherwise, of capturing them. Among the latter, he described the deadly 'otter board', a floating board from which depends a fearsome assembly of casts and triple hooks and which is so designed that when towed it does not follow directly in the disturbed wake of the boat but runs out diagonally away from it. From fishing the talk drifted I know not how but in typical Irish fashion to Russian expansionist policy (at that time much in the news) and from thence to some barbarous murder which seemed to have left a deep impression on Michael's mind. Russian policy was easily explained: 'It's no religion they have at all' said he, while his graphic description of the murder was punctuated at intervals by the query: 'And wasn't that a terrible thing now'?

Eventually we bade Michael farewell and moved on through the cut to moor up to the rings of a convenient disused quay situated at the point where the cut rejoins the river just above Jamestown, whither we walked that evening to enjoy an excellent glass of porter. It is a smaller village than Drumsna but equally attractive and of some historical note as the scene of an abortive attempt at Anglo-Irish colonization on the part of James I. He constituted Jamestown a chartered borough with Sovereign, burgesses, free commoners, recorder, town clerk, coroner, and Sergeants-at-Mace, all the dignitaries, in fact, of a Royal Borough. He gave to the 'planter' inhabitants the territory confiscated by Elizabeth from the O'Rourkes, and for their better defence the town was fortified by walls twenty feet high and six feet thick with north and south gates, and by a castle, erected by Sir Charles Coote in 1623. But the project was short lived. The town was successfully attacked by the Irish under Patrick Sarsfield, the hero of Limerick, and the fortifications overthrown with such thoroughness that practically nothing survives above ground to-day and it is therefore difficult to believe the history of this sleepy Shannon-side village. Certainly one massive stone arch still spans the village street, but it is said to be of eighteenth-century date, built over the foundations of the old north gate.

Leaving the Jamestown Cut next morning we soon entered Lough Corry, a stretch of water of no particular note, but memorable for the number of cormorants we saw on it, and for the fact that for a time we could not find our way out of it. Cormorants are among the most ungainly and clownish of birds. They perched on the navigation markers in the most ridiculous attitudes with wing coverts raised as though about to take flight and necks extended in a way which suggested that they were about to vomit. Their wings look scarcely adequate to bear the weight of their bodies, and their rapid motion when in flight suggested frantic effort to remain air-borne. It was noticeable too, that whenever one took off from the top of a marker, furious flapping did not prevent the bird losing height, often dropping to water level.

IRISH VILLAGES. (2) Jamestown, once a Royal Borough.

To anyone looking at the ordnance map of this district, the fact that we circled round and round in this lake peering through binoculars in an effort to find the way out must seem inexplicable. It certainly looks easy enough, but in fact the low island of Inishmucker which forms a bar at the point where the river enters the lake appears to merge its reedy margins with those of the shores in a way that renders the channel invisible. It was some time before we discerned a short black post half hidden by the reeds on the tip of the island and decided rightly, that it must be the broken stump of a marker. We accordingly kept the island to starboard, and before long dropped anchor just below the bridge at Carrick-on-Shannon.

Carrick is the county town of Leitrim and, like Mullingar, we had made it an objective for replenishing stores and fuel and collecting mail. But how different was Carrick from our last port of call! It is a much smaller town than Mullingar, in fact, with a population of only twelve hundred it is the smallest county town in Ireland, yet we found it in every way superior to its larger neighbour in Westmeath. Its shops were well stocked, its people friendly, helpful and hospitable to a degree remarkable even in Ireland. It possesses a good hotel in the Bush, while after we had collected our letters we enjoyed an excellent tea in a cafe which was very different from the dreary and expensive meal which was all we could find at Mullingar.

When I visited the post office, the postmaster, Mr. J. J. Sheerin at once hurried out and proceeded to press upon me, as is his wont with all visitors, a signed copy of his local guide book *Picturesque Carrick-on-Shannon*. This remarkable work, which bears a photograph of the author on the title page, is prefaced by tables of local information which is often so difficult for the stranger to acquire; bus and train time-tables; lists of hotels; of Carrick cattle fairs, and of all annual fixtures; postal information; local mileage tables. There follow twenty-five chapters, some lengthy and some of extreme brevity, which appear to omit no detail of Carrick and district, past or present. For example, chapter fifteen is entitled 'Well Kept Railway Station', and I take the liberty of quoting it in full.

> 'Some time ago the Great Southern Railway Company, in making an effort to improve the condition and appearance of the various stations on their entire system, offered prizes for the best-kept station on each line, and the first prize on the Dublin-Sligo line was won by Carrick-on-Shannon. Mr. Livingstone, a very popular and capable official, was Stationmaster here at that time and he received many congratulations on his well merited success. The general aspect of the station premises, which was enhanced by a profusion of beautiful flowers and evergreens, won the admiration of everybody and was the subject of many favourable comments. Mr. Livingstone has since been transferred on promotion to Cahir, Co. Tipperary. His departure was much regretted, and on leaving, he carried with him the best wishes of all creeds and classes in this district for his future success. It is to be hoped that his successor will continue to emulate the splendid example he has set, and keep up the good name which has been gained for our town in this respect, as all visitors like to see a well kept Railway Station. People from this district, resident in other countries, will be pleased to hear of the distinction which Carrick-on-Shannon Station has achieved, and perhaps, it may also be of interest to prospective visitors to our town.'

The last chapter, which is entitled 'Cleanliness' begins:

> 'Still another attraction which *Carrick-on-Shannon possesses* (and it is one which most visitors appreciate), *is the cleanliness of its streets and the bright, attractive, and inviting appearance presented by its house fronts, particularly those of the hotels and principal shops.* The windows are cleaned regularly, and paint is used freely on the doors and other woodwork when required. This has always been a noticeable characteristic of Leitrim's Capital.'

At a first reading, this sedulous and detailed description of such minutæ as a station platform or the paint on a door may raise a smile. But reflect for a moment. I did not myself visit Carrick station, but is it not true that we all appreciate a well-kept railway station? I certainly do. I can as certainly endorse Mr. Sheerin's comment on the appearance of the town, and who does not appreciate the effect of clean windows and bright paintwork even if he fails consciously to remark upon them? Mr. Sheerin wrote his little book before the war, but the windows are still cleaned regularly and the paint 'used freely when required', while I am sure the railway station is still bright with flowers. The postmaster has given Carrick a reputation which it feels bound to maintain. His book, like the clean windows, the bright paint and the station flowers, is an expression of local pride, a spirit which is very strong in Carrick. In some of the towns and villages of Ireland, this pride seems scarcely to exist and the result is drab and forlorn. In others such as Carrick it is everywhere manifest, being either due to the enthusiasm of some individual, or to some unknown but deep-seated cause. In England, however, such local variations are rapidly being smoothed out to a standard of uniformity imposed from above and which is incapable of reflecting local character. This process saps local pride and gradually destroys all individual initiative. People may grumble at this or that but leave it to officialdom to rectify the source of their grievances. Such passive complaints, if they have any effect at all, produce regimentation and a fresh crop of bureaucratic restrictions. It takes individual initiative actuated by local pride and a sense of personal responsibility to effect any worthwhile improvement. The English country town and village need men with the spirit of J. J. Sheerin and the stationmaster of Carrick.

In old books on the Shannon Navigation, Carrick is called 'Carrick-drum-Rusk' which in its turn is a corruption of its ancient name: Cara-Droma-Ruisg which means 'the Weir of the Ridge of the Swamp'. It is another of the ancient fording places of the Shannon, and is now the most northerly point of commercial navigation. The Grand Canal depot was immediately opposite our anchorage and there were further warehouses beyond the bridge where the *Eclipse Flower* of Limerick discharged her weekly cargo.

We had expected that Richard and Marten would have to leave us at Carrick, if not before, but thanks to our good progress through the Royal Canal there were still a few days to go before their month was up, so they decided to accompany us up the Boyle River to Lough Key. We were favoured with a fine day of almost uninterrupted sunshine which was fortunate because this short passage proved to be the most beautiful of the whole voyage, excepting only Lough Derg which was still to come. The River Boyle enters the Shannon a little over a mile above Carrick Bridge, and here we turned westward into Lough Drumharlow, passing on our starboard side the conical green hump of Inishatirra Island with cattle at graze upon it.

Away beyond the north shore of the lake stand two little hills called Sheemore and Sheebeg, the big and little hills of the fairies. According to tradition there was once a great battle there between the fairies of the two hills in which the army of the little hill was victorious. So overcome with remorse were they, however, that they provided a great and costly funeral for the king of the big hill whom they had slain in battle, and beneath this hill he now lies buried. Like many another legend, I believe that there may be a substratum of truth in this story, and that there may well have been a battle between the people of these hills. I incline to support the theory, for which much fascinating evidence can be produced, that the fairies of legend were not supernatural beings but the remnants of a pastoral people in a neolithic or bronze age stage of culture who continued to survive in the wilder parts of the British Isles for centuries after the introduction of settled agriculture.

There are few Irish place names in whose meaning there does not lurk, as in this case, some link with Irish history or mythology. If I attempted to set down all that I was told and all that I have read of the places we passed on our voyage in this respect, I should fill this book with 'Celtic Twilight'. Liberally sprinkled with unpronounceable names, I must confess with some trepidation that I find these legends rather wearisome when administered in large doses. They have also been fully documented by others more capable and better qualified than I. For this reason I have made this book an account of personal experiences and impressions, leaving the twilight to others except where it contributes very materially to topical associations. When we read the topographical literature of the past we almost invariably skip the history which is the same to-day as it was then, and read with most interest the author's references to the life, customs and institutions of his own day. Frequently we find him infuriatingly reticent on this score because he took for granted as everyday knowledge precisely those things which we are most anxious to learn. Consequently, to reconstruct the life of a particular period and place from contemporary records often involves the most painstaking research. Thus it may be that some of my observations may strike some Irishmen as trivial and obvious. But who knows? Some social historian of the future may unearth a copy of this book in the dim recesses of a second-hand bookshop and find that it fills in a detail or two of his picture of twentieth-century Ireland.

While we were crossing Lough Drumharlow we had a few minutes of great excitement. Angela, who was sitting on the deck of the aft cabin and trailing a spinner in a somewhat desultory fashion suddenly hooked a sizable fish and almost fell overboard in her excitement. From its liveliness and from the flash of silver as it leapt out of the water it was obvious that this was no coarse fish. It would not be easy to land the fish from *Le Coq* owing to her freeboard and the risk of entangling the line in the propeller. Richard solved the problem by seizing the landing net and taking a flying leap into the dinghy, a feat which none of us would have cared to undertake in a more sober moment. Meanwhile I put *Le Coq* astern till she had lost all way, and soon the fish was safely in the net. It proved to be a one and a half pound gillaroo trout whose delicate pink flesh made us a most delicious dinner that evening. The gillaroo is a distinct species peculiar to Ireland, presumably as a result of the prehistoric separation of Ireland from England and the rest of Europe. It frequents the Shannon, Lough Neagh and the lakes of Connemara.

We traversed the narrow and tortuous reach of the Boyle from Drumharlow, passed under the bridge at the village of Cootehall, and crossed Lough Oakport, a lovely little lake set in the wooded demesne of Oakport House. I have traversed few more beautiful stretches of inland waterway than the Boyle from Oakport to Lough Key. Trees grew thickly about the banks, their branches stooping to trail their leaves in the water. Between them flowed the clear still stream, darkly in their shadow or golden in the sunlight. I eased the boat till we were only just making headway against the gentle current, gliding with scarcely a ripple over the smooth surface, and in this way we passed beneath Knockvicar Bridge and so came to the lock and weir above.

Clarendon Lock, Knockvicar, looked very dilapidated. The locksides were overgrown. The gates on one side were chained up, being obviously rotten and unusable, while their opposite numbers looked little better. Because there is no longer any commercial traffic on the Boyle, the Board of Works apparently concern themselves very little with the state of the navigation. It is to be hoped that they will not allow this lock to become unworkable and so prevent boats from entering one of the most beautiful lakes in Ireland.

Mr. Conlon, the lock-keeper occupies a cottage by the bridge and out of sight of the lock. While Angela and Marten prepared lunch and Richard fished from the sill of the weir, I strolled down the path through the trees to advise him of our arrival and to suggest that he come up when his dinner hour was over. It was some time before he put in an appearance; but who cared? Here, certainly, it was a case of 'time enough', for the sun that warmed the beams and the weathered stones of the lock, the soft air and the murmur of the weir soon stilled activity to drowsy content so that I doubt whether we would have concerned ourselves overmuch if Mr. Conlon had not appeared at all that day.

Lough Key shares with Lough Gill, near Sligo, the title of 'the Killarney of the West'. Arthur Young, in his *Tour in Ireland* (1780) seems to have been much impressed by the beauty of

RIVER BOYLE. The weir from the lock tail, Knockvicar.

the lake. 'It is one of the most delicious scenes I ever beheld', he wrote, 'A lake of five miles by four miles, which fills the bottom of a gentle valley of circular form, bounded very boldly by the mountains. Those to the left rise in noble shape; they lower rather in front and let in a view of the Strand Mountain near Sligo, about twenty miles off. To the right you look over a small part of a bog to a large extent of cultivated hill, with the blue mountains beyond.'

As we sailed across the sparkling waters of the lake that afternoon, threading our way between the wooded islets with which it is dotted (an island for every county in Ireland, it is said), I thoroughly endorsed the description of this eighteenth-century traveller. Ahead of us to westward rose the moorland ridge of the Curlieu Mountains. Properly speaking they have not the stature of mountains because they do not reach the 1000 feet contour, but, rising steeply from the lake shore, they certainly have, as Arthur Young put it, a 'noble shape'. Historically, the Curlieus possessed a strategic value despite their modest height, and on August 15, 1599 there was fought a great battle on their slopes between an English army under Sir Conyers Clifford and the Irish under Red Hugh O'Donnell which resulted in a great victory for the latter.

The whole of the southern shore of Lough Key is occupied by the demesne of Rockingham, and as we moved out toward the centre of the lake the view between the islands opened out so that we could see the great grey block of Rockingham House with its terraces falling towards the lake shore. Before we left Knockvicar Lock I had been studying the map of the lake and had decided that the best anchorage would be a bay immediately to the west of the house which looked well sheltered from the south and west by a wooded headland and by Drummans Island which appeared to be linked to the headland by a bridge. Accordingly we left the marked channel across the lake, giving Swallow and Orchard Islands a wide berth to port and keeping a careful look-out for rocks. Most of the submerged rocks in this lake are marked by iron rods which do not project very far above water level and which may be missed, especially if the lake is rough. Moreover the islands should not be approached too closely in anything larger than a rowing boat as their shores are shelving and rocky. We reached our objective without mishap, and finding that the margins of the bay were reed-fringed - a sure sign of a mud bottom - we ventured fairly close in shore before letting go our anchor. Feeling that we were trespassing, our first action was to row ashore and enquire at the house whether we might remain at our anchorage and land on the demesne. We were assured that we might do so.

How can I describe our surroundings? The formal artifice of those who, a century and more ago, had laid out the demesne of Rockingham lay buried amidst a growth of trees, shrubs and flowers of almost tropical luxuriance where native species and strange exotics mingled in equally prodigal growth. The wooded headland which sheltered our bay had been converted into two islets by the construction of canals and these were spanned by graceful stone bridges, one of 'rustic' work, the other more formal with a balustrade. Water lilies floated in the dark, reedy waters of these still canals, and in a clearing by the margin amid bracken, heather and fern there grew tall spires of scarlet-spotted tiger lilies. Farther within the shadow of the wood there was nothing but a brilliant emerald green carpet of moss softer and deeper beneath the tread than any carpet ever made by man. The scene, in its air of unreality resembled nothing so much as some romantic setting for the ballet 'Lac des Cygnes'.

To complete the magic of this fantastic prospect, opposite our mooring and across the bay there rose out of the water a castle, perched upon an islet no larger than the perimeter of its foundations. We rowed across to this castle that evening, and as we neared it, found that what we had taken for windows were merely their semblance painted upon wooden shutters, for the building was but a shell, having been gutted by a fire so fierce that only charred fragments of beams and joists remained. What a strange spectacle this fire must have made. Imagine the castle blazing like a gigantic torch in the midst of this enchanted lake which would mirror the lurid flare of the flames, the black silhouette of the walls and the showers of sparks which must have fallen upon its surface with a hiss of steam. The building that was thus destroyed was actually a 'whimsy', a place of summer residence built by the owners of Rockingham upon the foundations of the ancient fortress of the Macdermots who once held the estates of Rockingham. For their support of Tyrconnel's rebellion and for their victory in the battle of the Curlieus, the Macdermots paid heavily. Their lands were confiscated and awarded by Queen Elizabeth, in 1630, to Sir John King, Muster-Master-General of the Queen's forces, and ancestor of the present owner of Rockingham, Sir Cecil Stafford King-Harman.

On the mainland behind Castle Island we came upon the mouth of another canal and walking up the bank beside it, discovered the ruins of a lock. These canals, we found out later, were not merely ornamental. They once combined beauty with utility by enabling turf to be brought by boat from the neighbouring bogs to a quay on the lakeside immediately below the house. Thence the turf was conveyed to the domestic quarters by means of an inclined subterranean passage beneath the terraces. I have seen private estate railways such as that belonging to the Duke of Westminster at Eaton Hall, but this was the first time I had seen a private canal system constructed for anything other than a purely ornamental purpose.

Rockingham has other unusual features. On the south or landward side of the house there is a semi-circular range of domestic offices sunk below ground level in such a way that the lawn which slopes smoothly to the park is level with their roof ridge, and the view over the park from the ground floor windows is thus unobscured. In the days of its construction, the fact that the domestics were thus relegated to sunless semi-twilight was doubtless considered a negligible price to pay for this amenity. Moreover, in this case, the tradesman's entrance was also underground, access being via a subterranean passage beneath the garden on the east side. When Richard and I had first approached the house to ask permission to moor we had modestly sought this back entrance in vain, and having completed a discreet circuit, gave up the search and approached the imposing west portico.

Rockingham House was built for General Lord Lorton by John Nash in 1805, and subsequently altered by him in 1820. An engraving of Nash's original design shows a two-storeyed facade surmounted by a dome. But it is said that his patron complained that this design did not compete in grandiloquence with another house which the architect was at that time building in the County Tipperary, and the result was the present three-storeyed structure. There can be little doubt that Nash's original longer and lower frontage was better proportioned and certainly better suited to its lake-side site. As constructed, the great grey block towers in a too austere and uncompromising fashion for its romantic situation. Rockingham is an urban mansion set in the wilds of Connaught; it has an arrogance which is incapable of any concession to its surroundings. But having said this, and having been privileged to see its interior, I would be prepared to endorse Sacheverell Sitwell's opinion, expressed in his *British Architects and Craftsmen*, that Rockingham is probably the best example of Nash's country houses.

We returned from our exploration of castle and canal to an excellent dinner consisting of Angela's gillaroo accompanied by a delicious potato dish exotically entitled 'Pomme Anna', and followed by rhubarb and cream. That evening, too, we observed a curious disturbance in the water near the boat, and on going out in the dinghy we found that it was caused by the death throes of an enormous drowning insect. Its body was striped like that of a wasp or hornet, but it was at least twice the size of the latter, in fact, it was the largest insect I have ever seen alive. I am no entomologist, but I hazard the guess that it was a Great Pine Sawfly (Sirex Gigas) which is certainly found in Ireland. Somehow the discovery of this strange monster seemed to contribute a final touch of the bizarre to our surroundings. I should not have been surprised to see vivid humming birds hovering over the tiger lilies or, as dusk fell, great vampire bats come swooping out of the wood. In fact, as darkness came down and the lake fell glassy smooth and still, the sound of a most unearthly uproar echoed over the water. It was as though a number of marauding tom cats had fallen foul of a pack of hounds and were engaged in mortal combat. None of us had heard the like of it before, but we conjectured, how rightly I do not know, that it came from a heronry on one of the wooded islands.

Sunday, July 28th, was the last day of Richard's and Marten's stay, and we spent it in further exploration of Lough Key and its surroundings. We walked through the park to Cloontykilla Castle which stands on a wooded headland overlooking the lake. Like the castle on the island, it proved to be a 'whimsy' consisting simply of a massive castellated curtain wall with towers at the angles enclosing a quadrangle approached through an archway guarded by massive iron gates. Within, was a cottage occupied by the head woodsman of the estate; as remarkable and as gloomy a dwelling place as one could well imagine.

Later in the day we rowed across the lake to Abbey Island, and struggled through dense undergrowth to examine the ruins of the Abbey of the Trinity founded by the White Canons of St. Francis. Here the monastic *Annals of Lough Ce*, now preserved in the library of Trinity College, Dublin, were written, and here, too, Elizabeth's General, Sir Conyers Clifford, lies buried in sight of his defeat on the Curlieus. We could discover no trace of any domestic buildings. Presumably, as was usually the case at these island settlements, the White Canons lavished all their ferried stone upon the building of the Abbey church, living in wattled huts which have long ago vanished without trace.

In the interval between these expeditions, we were taking tea on board when a figure appeared on the jetty below Rockingham House and hailed us through a megaphone. We could not distinguish any words, but we suspected that we might have outstayed our welcome and that we were being warned off by the owner. Accordingly, we rowed to the jetty in a state of some trepidation. The figure proved, in fact, to be Sir Cecil Stafford King-Harman, but so far from warning us off, he inquired whether we would like to come up to the house, have a bath and take dinner afterwards. Thus I can truthfully say that Irish hospitality extends from the cabin to the castle. We gladly accepted the invitation for the following evening. Both suggestions were very welcome for, except in Dublin where it had been impossible, the weather had not been warm enough for bathing and so the prospect of the luxury of a hot bath was most inviting. As events proved, it was to be even more welcome than we anticipated.

We lost no time in getting under way next morning, and were soon heading across the lake in the direction of Boyle. A fresh breeze was whipping the surface of the lake into sizeable waves, and as *Le Coq* dipped her bows into their troughs the spray shot over her quarter and pattered against the windows of the deck house. It became calmer as we drew under the lee of the Curlieu Mountains, and before long we had gained the smooth, narrow waters of the river. From the point where it enters the lake, the River Boyle is navigable as far as Boathouse Ford, one and a half miles from the town. The limit of navigation cannot be missed, for above this point the river at once becomes shallow and rapid and is spanned by a low bridge. Here we made fast and disembarked, a friendly boy with a donkey cart relieving us of the weight of our guests' luggage for part of the distance into the town. After a farewell lunch and a drink at the Royal Hotel by the river bridge, we saw Richard and Marten off by the train to Dublin.

We liked the town of Boyle, not least for its situation. Most of the Irish towns we had so far visited occupied more or less level sites, but Boyle clings to the steep slopes of the narrow valley through which the river hurries in spate from Lough Gara down to Lough Key, falling nearly a hundred feet in a few miles.

Loaded though we were with the stores which we had purchased in the town, on our way back to the boat we did not neglect the opportunity to examine the great Abbey of Boyle. This was the most extensive, and architecturally the richest ecclesiastical building which we saw in Ireland. It was a house of the Cistercian Order, founded by Abbot Maurice O'Duffy in 1161, and sister to the Abbey of Mellifont in County Louth. The style is transitional, the south nave arcade consisting of Norman arches while those on the north side are early Gothic. It was a pleasure to see that here at least was one Irish historical monument that was well cared for. Here was no jungle of nettles and briars, while the north nave arcade, which had subsided to an alarming angle, had been carefully buttressed. In England, our great Cistercian Abbeys, by contrast with the richness of earlier or later work, reflect the austerity of Cistercian rule in their absence of decoration. Their beauty resides solely in the magnificence of their architectural proportions, and we find decoration only in later work such as the Tower of Fountains when opulence had relaxed the rigour of the rule. Yet here, the opposite was true. By contrast with the Abbey of the White Canons on Lough Key and other earlier buildings, Boyle Abbey was richly decorated. Columns, and the corbels supporting the vaulting exhibited carved work of remarkable beauty.

We returned to our anchorage in the bay in an ominous flat grey calm which seemed to have drained all colour and life out of the landscape. The lake, which had been so boisterous that morning, was now a motionless sheet of silver tarnished with islands as black as ink spots. Far astern the flukes of our wake flawed this burnished surface and stirred the reflections of the brooding mountains. But that night the wind rose and *Le Coq* began to swing uneasily, setting the anchor chain rattling in the hawse pipe.

Next morning the wind was blowing strongly from the west, but as its force was broken by the woods of Drummans Island, and as I had the heavy anchor out on a full length of chain, I felt no anxiety. After breakfast we went ashore to explore the magnificent beech avenue that leads from Rockingham towards Boyle. This was an action which nearly led to disaster. As we walked across the park we surprised several hares. These were not the brown hares of England, but, like the gillaroo trout, a species peculiar to Ireland and more closely akin to the variable or Alpine hare of Scotland in that its coat whitens, albeit somewhat irregularly, during a hard winter. It is another example of a species isolated by the disappearance of the land bridges between Ireland, England and the Continent. As a result of this separation, just as England is poorer than the Continent in number and variety of fauna, so is Ireland poorer than England. Most people must know, and many English gardeners and farmers must envy, the fact that the mole is unknown in Ireland. Other absentees, however, are not so widely known and may therefore be worth mentioning here. Though the stoat is common, the weasel and the polecat are unknown, while there are no representatives of the vole family, and of the shrews only the lesser occurs. There are only two of the four British mice and only seven out of the fifteen British species of bats. It is said that St. Patrick, doubtless remembering the fate of Adam and Eve, banished all the reptiles from Holy Ireland. Certainly there are no snakes, but the Saint must have either forgiven or forgotten the little brown lizard. We were to find one of these engaging little creatures sunning himself on a sheltered hedge bank near the shores of Lough Derg. The common frog is abundant, but is said to have been introduced, so that, apart from a single species of newt, the only other reptile to escape Patrick's banishment is the curious natterjack toad of Kerry which, like the spotted slug of the same region, is an isolated survival of the Lusitanian fauna of south-west Europe.

Owing to their command of the air, it is less easy to account for missing species of birds, but the fact remains that the nightingale, the reed warbler and the tawny owl are unknown. It is also said that that wicked marauder the magpie only invaded Ireland in 1864 when a small flock landed near Wexford. On the other hand we saw many hooded crows with their grey plumage, a bird I have never seen in England, while the red-breasted merganser nests in many Irish counties although in Britain and the Continent it confines itself to the far north. I will conclude this brief excursion into natural history with a piece of personal observation. I saw a grey squirrel in a wood near Lough Boderg. Sorry I was to see that this destructive, rat-like little beast had succeeded (who knows how?) in invading Ireland. Presumably, as in England, it will increase and multiply and will ultimately exterminate that most endearing of all small animals, the red squirrel.

Walking in the shelter of the woods we did not realize that the wind had risen to gale force until, emerging into the open park once more, a savage gust almost bowled us over, and the best part of a haycock in a neighbouring field went sailing through the air. With only one thought in our minds, we turned and hurried back to the lake. When we reached the bridge over the first of the canals where we had left the dinghy we looked anxiously towards our anchorage. *Le Coq* had gone. With sinking hearts we jumped into the dinghy and rowed out from the shelter of the canal into waters whipped into a fury of breaking waves It was then that we saw that *Le Coq* had dragged her anchor right across the bay to fetch up, beam on to wind and seas, against the rocks thirty yards or so from the jetty below Rockingham House. A sudden gust must have swept through the narrow gap in the trees left by the second canal which formed Drummans Island and carried her away. It was remarkable that in the whole breadth of the bay her anchor had found no holding ground. We boarded her with difficulty. No damage appeared to have been done as yet, but as the waves lifted her she was pounding horribly upon the rocks. It was obvious that the two of us alone could not hope to get her off in the teeth of such wild weather, so Angela scrambled ashore and ran to the house for help while I tried to hold her off the rocks as best I could. In a very short while she returned accompanied by Sir Cecil and two of his men. If only we could get her clear of the rocks we could start our engine, but to have done so here would have meant a broken propeller blade at the very least. I had drawn up the useless anchor and now linked both anchor chains together. Sir Cecil and his men then managed to put out in the dinghy and, carrying the anchor with them, let it go in deep water at the limit of its chain. But it found no hold in the soft mud bottom for I hauled it in with scarcely any effort. The only alternative now appeared to be to try to haul *Le Coq* up to the head of the jetty. Unfortunately there was insufficient water to come alongside the jetty, while a diving-board projected from the head of it supported by two stakes. However, Sir Cecil assured us that it was never used, and in fact it turned out to be rotten and was soon demolished. This done, by fastening both our chains and mooring lines together we managed to get a line from our bow to the jetty, and while Sir Cecil hauled in, Angela and I and the two men, wading almost waist deep and stumbling over slippery submerged rocks, managed to hold the boat off. In this way we brought her up to the head of the jetty; and then our troubles were soon over. The jetty being very short, it gave us precious little lee-way, and the only remaining risk was that we should be swept back onto the rocks before getting sufficient way on to head into the wind. But in this, fortune favoured us. I swung the helm hard over, put the engine full speed ahead, our helpers cast off, and she came about beautifully. As the gale showed no signs of moderating

LOUGH KEY. Calm after the storm. 'Running into the unruffled water at the mouth of the old canal, we made fast to the bank where the tiger lilies grew.'

I had no wish to trust to our anchor again that night, so we circled round the bay and, running into the unruffled water at the mouth of the old canal, made fast to the bank where the tiger lilies grew. It was indeed a safe harbour and a calm after the storm. Furthermore, to our unbounded relief, a careful inspection revealed that *Le Coq* had sustained no damage and was making no water.

When we had changed out of our dripping clothes into something slightly more presentable, we hurried up to the house. To reach our promised baths we had to climb a magnificent staircase whose ample treads were made for elegant ladies in brocade and be-wigged gentlemen in velvet breeches. Facing us over the first flight hung Lely's portraits of Charles II and of George Villiers, second Duke of Buckingham (the first a copy, the second an original). Their heavy-lidded cynical gaze seemed to be rivetted disdainfully upon my sandals and shapeless flannel trousers.

Rupert Brooke, in his poem *The Great Lover*, includes in his so sensible catalogue of his loves 'the benison of hot water'. Never have I so whole-heartedly agreed with him as upon that evening. As I stretched my legs luxuriously in its warm depths my pleasure was the sweeter for the knowledge that our boat was now snugly berthed and that the wind which buffeted the steamy bathroom window was defeated and impotent. By the time I descended the staircase I felt more than a match for those haughty Caroleans.

The chief splendour of Nash's Rockingham, to my mind, was the suite of three rooms, a long drawing-room, the circular drawing-room and the dining-room, whose windows look out over the lake. In the circular drawing-room which was, as it were, the focal point of the house, there were three pairs of great mahogany doors having curved surfaces to conform with the curvature of the wall. I have seldom seen finer examples of the joiner's craft. Such was the spacious and sophisticated splendour of these rooms that to turn my eyes from them and see the wild beauties of Lough Key beyond the windows instead of the trees of Hyde Park or the squares of Bath, gave me quite a shock of surprise.

Though Nash's great house belongs to the town, the life and the talk within its rooms to-day belongs very definitely to the country. There was no formality. Wearing an old tweed jacket reinforced with leather at the elbows, Sir Cecil talked of farming and of the work of the estate, of the difficulties of saving crops in this humid climate, and of the Proctor system of tripod harvesting which he was at present trying out. In the relationship that existed between him and his men which I had observed when he had come to our rescue that afternoon, and in all that he said and did upon that evening it was apparent to me that the owner of Rockingham lived up to William Cobbett's description of:

> 'the resident native gentry, attached to the soil, known to every farmer and labourer from their childhood, frequently mixing with them in those pursuits where all artificial distinctions are lost,

practising hospitality without ceremony, from habit and not in calculation,'

Probably no country in the world has suffered more than Ireland from the evil of absentee landlordism. Had the great Anglo-Irish landlords of the past looked upon their acres in this way instead of as a source of revenue to be milked by arrogant rack-renting agents such as Captain Boycott, how much misery, bitterness and violence might have been avoided. Great houses, roofless or blackened by fire are everywhere, the symbol of that evil and of the nemesis which fell upon it. Demesnes have been acquired by the Land Board and parcelled out to small tenants or owner occupiers, a process excellent in principle but not so admirable in practice. The average Irish peasant farmer usually lacks the capital necessary to improve his holding, and church dues are a heavy burden which increases if his fortunes improve. Moreover, generations of exploitation and lack of just tenant rights have made him shiftless and unenterprising. The Land Board may act with the best of intentions but it is as impersonal as the largest of the absentee landlords whom it has replaced. The Irish peasant lacks the local guidance, encouragement and example that a good landlord could provide. A lessening of the burden of church dues, an intimate local relationship between landlord and tenant, and a system of tenant right whereby the tenant can nominate his successor and freely reap the benefit of any improvements he might make to his holdings, these things, I believe, would do more than the Land Board has so far accomplished towards building a prosperous rural Ireland.

If the landowners of Ireland had looked upon the health of their land and its people as a personal responsibility and not as a source of exploitation, such a beneficent hierarchy might well have developed. But the sheep have suffered with the goats, and now men of the calibre of the owner of Rockingham are few and far between. Their numbers continue to dwindle, for the wars of our century have taken their toll in Ireland. We in England are too apt to forget this. Thus Sir Cecil's brother was killed in the war of 1914-18, while his only son fell in Normandy in 1944, so who knows what the future holds for Rockingham?

In the past, the great house may have sorely abused its privileges - none know this better than the Irish - but with its passing goes something of grace and stability that no committee or board of bureaucracy however well intentioned can ever replace. As we left Rockingham that night I thought of Yeats' lament for Coole Park:

'A spot whereon the founders lived and died
Seemed once more dear than life; ancestral trees,
Or gardens rich in memory glorified
Marriages, alliances and families,
And every bride's ambition satisfied.
Where fashion or mere fantasy decrees
Man shifts about - all that great glory spent -
Like some poor Arab tribesman and his tent'.

BATTLEBRIDGE

LOUGH ALLEN AND A REGATTA

IT was not without regrets that we left our sheltered mooring at lovely Rockingham, sailing away across the lake and down the Boyle back to Carrick-on-Shannon. We lay that night at anchor below Carrick Bridge, and on the morrow, having laid in a further store of provisions and called for letters, we set off once more to the northward, this time to follow the Shannon to the upper limit of the navigation. For a short distance above the junction of the Boyle, the Shannon was as broad as ever, but thereafter the channel became progressively narrower and deeper with a perceptible current. Like the Boyle it began to wind tortuously. We had covered nearly five miles when we reached the junction of the little river Leitrim. Although there is scanty evidence of the fact remaining to-day, this river, the first few hundred yards of which are navigable up to Leitrim quay, marks the most ill-starred of all the Irish Canal projects. This was no less than a third west-to-east route across the country which linked the Shannon with the waterway system of Northern Ireland. This route comprised the following:

> The Ballynamore and Ballyconnell Navigation from the Shannon at Leitrim to a junction with the River Erne.
> The Ulster Canal from the River Erne to a junction with the Upper Bann Navigation (River Blackwater) at Moy, and with branches to Auchnacloy and Donaghmore.
> The Upper Bann Navigation from Moy to Lough Neagh.
> The Lagan Navigation from Lough Neagh to Belfast.

In addition, this northern complex of waterways afforded access to the sea at three other points. At Ballyshannon on the west via the Erne Navigation; at Coleraine to the north via the Lower Bann Navigation, and at Carlingford Lough below Newry on the east via the Newry Navigation from Lough Neagh through Portadown.

The history of this through route makes a sorry record of failures due to incompetence, and the expenditure of great sums of public money for practically no result, for it is doubtful if any substantial traffic was ever carried from Lough Neagh to the Shannon.

The westernmost link, the Ballynamore and Ballyconnell Navigation was constructed by the Board of Works between 1846 and 1859 at a cost of £228,652. The locks were of generous size being eighty feet six inches long with a breadth of sixteen feet six inches and five feet six inches of water over the cills. But it consisted of a series of lakes linked by cuts, and was therefore useless to the horse-drawn craft of the period. Lord Monk's Commission of 1882 referred to this project in the following melancholy terms:

'The canal is now out of repair and quite unnavigable. The receipts for 5 years ended 1880 were "NIL". The annual expenditure on [1] navigation account, apparently for lock keepers' wages, was about £80. It is alleged that the navigation was originally badly designed, badly made, and passed over to the trustees in an unfit state … The canal was navigable, and no more, when given up to the Commissioners of Public Works and there being no traffic worth mentioning upon it, was allowed to go from bad to worse until it has reached its present condition of absolute uselessness as a navigation. We have been informed by competent engineers that by the expenditure of £7000 or £8000 the canal could again be made navigable, but when it was navigable no use was made of it, and the trustees advertised in vain for persons to establish boats upon it. In 1865, whilst the canal was still in working order, the Grand Jury of the County of Cavan "Expressed their unanimous sense of the utter inutility of the navigation", that it had been in operation for some years and had been fully proved to be totally valueless to the country which had been so heavily taxed for it.'

A private company, formed in 1826, took fifteen years to construct the Ulster Canal at a cost which is said to have been £200,000 but must surely have been more. Opened in 1841, the canal's traffic was unremunerative, and the water supply to the summit inadequate. The Commissioners for Public Works took possession in 1851 and proceeded to lease the canal first to a certain Mr Dargan, and secondly to the Dundalk Steam Packet Company. By the time the latter's lease expired and the waterway was vested in the Board of Works, it had become practically derelict.

The Board decided, however, that defective water supply was the source of the trouble. £20,000 was spent in an effort to overcome this, and the canal re-opened in 1873. But traffic proved trifling, expenses for the year 1878 totalling £1200 and receipts £166. In 1882 the Commission investigating the state of the canal reported as follows:

'Notwithstanding the large sums laid out by the Commissioners of Works on the canal between 1865-73 amounting, as has already been stated, to £22,000, it is now, chiefly owing to leakage, in a very unsatisfactory state, and from want of water navigable only for eight months in the year. The traffic is also restricted, even when the canal is fully supplied with water, by its shallowness and by the smallness of the locks. The boats in use on the Lagan Canal cannot pass along the Ulster Canal, the depth of water in the channel of the latter being only 4 ft., while on the cills of the locks it is only 3 ft. 9 ins. On the Lagan Canal vessels can generally be loaded so as to draw 5 ft. 6 ins. The locks on the Lagan Canal are 16 ft. wide. Those on the Ulster 12 ft. 2 ins. Evidence has been submitted to us that by a further expenditure of £10,000 on the Ulster Canal it may be deepened to 5 ft., both in the channel and in the locks, additional water supplied, and all the leaks staunched. Many witnesses expressed their confidence that if this were done a large traffic would spring up, and the canal would become a remunerative concern.'

In 1890, the Ulster Canal was transferred to the Lagan Navigation proprietors who proceeded to spend £12,700 in deepening the waterway. Yet the original lack of water supply on the summit still remained and in 1902 it was reported that:

[1] One wonders how many lock-keepers there were to share this princely annual sum.

'No attempt having been made to increase the size of the storage reservoir or to remove an obstruction which exists in this portion of the canal, the waterway above Monaghan is still impassible by boats during a portion of almost every summer, and in dry seasons stoppage of traffic is complete for considerable periods'.

From all this it would seem that the blunders perpetrated in the construction of the Royal Canal were as nothing to those which marred this ill-fated northern route. A great part of the route including the whole of the Ballynamore and Ballyconnell Navigation was constructed for land drainage purposes as well as for navigation. Though traffic over it might never have been heavy or remunerative, the waterway might be serving this dual purpose to-day if a standard broad gauge of lock had been adopted throughout and if an adequate water supply had been assured. The fact that so recently as the last decade of the nineteenth century the Lagan Navigation should have spent so much money in deepening the Ulster Canal while they did nothing to improve a water supply which had been proved long before to be inadequate for the canal even in its previous shallow state, is surely astonishing.

From the junction of this abandoned waterway it was but a brief journey to Battlebridge where the Shannon becomes a shallow stream brawling over boulder strewn rapids under

RIVER SHANNON. Battlebridge, the present upper limit of navigation, 'where the Shannon becomes a shallow stream'.

the arches of the fine old bridge. Here, in the last few yards of deep water, we came about to moor to two trees beside the bank at the tail of the ruined entrance lock of the Lough Allen Canal. It was a delightful mooring, secure, secluded and sheltered, the country round being undulating and well-wooded, for we had now left the levels of the plain for the fringe of the broken, lake-studded country of central Leitrim. For this reason we could no longer see the mountains about Lough Allen though we could sense that they were close at hand.

The Lough Allen Canal, as its name denotes, formed the most northerly section of the Shannon Navigation. Through it, boats used to trade to quays on the lake with grain, and load back with sand or with coal from the Arigna mines. The fate of the canal was sealed when Lough Allen became a storage reservoir for the great hydro-electric station at Ardnacrusha. To increase its capacity, the level of the lake was raised to a height above the canal banks, and on this account a dam was built across the channel at Rose Lodge where it enters the lake. Still the capacity of the lake proved to be inadequate to meet the needs of Ardnacrusha so the rocky natural cill of the Shannon outfall at Ballintra was blasted away to allow more water to be released from Lough Allen in a dry season. At such times the lake now falls so low that acres of the lake bottom appear, islands are linked to the mainland, and the old canal debouches on dry land. This lowering does not improve the beauty of Lough Allen, but it resulted in the interesting discovery of the remains of a colony of crannoges - ancient lake dwellings built upon artificial islands which were constructed of timber rafts loaded with stones until they sank to the lake bottom, in a similar manner to the Celtic lake village of Glastonbury.

No doubt Ardnacrusha's needs outweighed the value of the Lough Allen Canal, but now that shrinking coal imports have enhanced the importance of the Arigna mines this water communication would surely have been a great asset. Aerial ropeways down the mountain could have loaded coal directly from the mines into the boats at the lakeside, whereas present transport facilities consist only of a light railway supplemented by road vehicles.

The last trading boat left the Lough Allen Canal in 1927, while the last pleasure craft battled its way through the weeds in 1932. The lock-keeper, young Sean Nangle, still lived in the neat, freshly white-washed cottage beside the ruined entrance lock, but his duties were confined to bank ranging on the reach of the river below. *Le Coq* was the first craft to visit Battlebridge for seven years, so that our arrival was a minor sensation, and it was with a sense of newly discovered importance that Sean signed his name on our pass.

That evening Sean accompanied us to the inn which stood by the road side just across the old bridge, and a grand friendly house it proved to be. Nowhere in rural Ireland did we find any lack of kindness, hospitality and friendship, but in these respects this little inn at Battlebridge is particularly memorable. For this, credit must go to the Beirne family,

LOUGH ALLEN CANAL. 'Young Sean Nangle still lived in the neat, freshly whitewashed cottage beside the ruined entrance lock'.

mother, daughter and son. I will not attempt to characterize them; they speak for themselves in their photograph. Leaning against the counter in the bare whitewashed bar we enjoyed the best glass of 'single' porter that we found on our travels, while intruding chickens pecked unconcerned about our feet. Through an open doorway a turf fire glowed in a wide open hearth equipped with crane and ratchet-hook. Upon the fire reposed a squat, black pot-oven with more smouldering turf upon its lid. The talk itself had a particular local flavour for it was of smuggling over the mountains and across the border round Swanlinbar, and of certain lorries which were said to leave the Arigna mines in the dead of the night. I will not be more explicit. Conversation was interrupted when a drove of bullocks passed by with a soft patter of hooves. Everyone crowded to the door to comment and criticize and to speculate where they had come from and whither they were bound, an argument which was settled when the drover himself stepped in for a glass.

Mrs. Beirne presently disappeared into the inner room and soon emerged with a flat round soda 'cake' fresh and hot from the pot-oven which, with typical generosity, she placed in Angela's hands. It is in the interest of the English milling monopoly to encourage the habit of dismissing those of us who inveigh against the adulteration of 'the staff of life' as harmless cranks. Yet this is one of those cases where economic sense, or rather nonsense,

IRISH INN 'The Beirne family…speak for themselves in their photograph'.

defies and derides plain reason as any unprejudiced person who has ever eaten an Irish pot-oven cake made from honest flour must admit. Most of the rural population of Ireland make their own bread in this way, using two pot-ovens, one for the baking and the other for boiling such staple dishes as bacon and cabbage. But the bought bread, both soda and yeast leavened, of the towns is generally little inferior. The proof of the pudding is in the eating; we demolished our Irish bread to the last crumb, whereas in England, despite ministerial adjurations to economize, many were the uneatable, brick-like loaf ends we threw away. Moreover, we both experienced a quite unmistakable improvement in digestion during this Irish voyage, partly, perhaps, due to fresh food, but mainly, I am convinced, to honest bread. The English 'Battle for Bread' should begin with the loaf itself.

What we could no longer accomplish by boat we determined to do on foot, so the next morning we set out to walk to Lough Allen along the towing path of the old canal, gathering and eating as we went the late wild strawberries which we found growing on the hedge banks. Beyond the ruined lock at Drumleague, brambles had made the towing path impassable, so we struck across a field to join a country lane which ran parallel with the canal. Here we came upon a party of tinkers encamped on the wide grass verge beside the road. It was an encounter of mutual surprise, but with typical ready opportunism the

IRISH TINKERS. 'The McGinleys had a gaily painted wagon of the Leeds Type'.

woman who was mending the camp fire offered to tell our fortunes. We forthwith struck a bargain that if she told our fortunes, we should take their photographs. There were two families, the Byrnes who occupied a low pitched tent, and the McGinleys who had a gaily painted waggon of the Leeds type, that is to say with a barrel roof. The men-folk and the horses were away, leaving the camp to the two women, their numerous offspring, whose ages appeared to range between two and sixteen, and a lean greyhound which, chained to a wheel of the waggon, whined and padded to and fro. One of the children, a dark girl of sixteen or so with cropped hair and dressed in man's clothes had a fine pair of bold grey eyes and could have been a beauty with a little encouragement. Fortune telling, photography and an inspection of the neat interior of the McGinley's waggon occupied some time, while there was much talk. Mrs. Byrne seemed to be the more widely travelled, not only in Ireland but in England. She spoke intimately of the circus folk, and maintained that England was the easier country for the nomad, a view which surprised me. We were still talking when a clatter of hooves round the bend of the lane announced the arrival of the men and horses. Byrne was a gypsy-like fellow, tough and swarthy, while 'Barney' McGinley was a typical Irish tinker with his engaging grin and shock of red hair. We had to take their picture too before we said good-bye and tramped off down the road, having promised to send copies of their photographs to the post office at Cavan to be called for.

The Irish tinkers should not be confused with gypsies. Though they are allied, and though there may occasionally be an infusion of gypsy blood, the English gypsies have never invaded Ireland in any numbers, and the Irish tinkers are a race, a very ancient race, apart.

IRISH TINKERS 'Byrne was a gypsy-like fellow, tough and swarthy, while Barney McGinley was a typical Irish tinker with his engaging grin and shock of red hair'.

In Shelta they have their own secret language, though it seems doubtful whether this tongue is still used in its pure form but only in an admixture of cant, Romani, Gaelic back-slang or that other secret language of the masons, the ancient Gaelic of Bearlagair na Saer. Mr. Brian Vesey-FitzGerald in his *Gypsies of Britain* gives a fascinating account of the discovery of Shelta, unknown until 1808, from the brief vocabulary of Edward Fitzgerald of Youghal to the intrepid researches, carried out at great personal risk, of John Sampson in the nineteenth-century slums of Liverpool's Irish quarter. Smiths, horse-dealers and fortune-tellers, most Irish towns have, like Athlone, a small resident tinker colony, but the majority are nomadic, travelling the round of the great fairs of Ireland. One of their chief rallying points in the west is the great sheep fair at Ballinasloe where they are accustomed to elect their 'king'. Such gatherings frequently end in bloody combat, for they have their own code of honour and the punishment for its transgression is summary. One family will help another financially if it is down on its luck upon the pledge that the debt is repaid when the two meet again at a certain fair. Woe betide the debtor if he ventures to appear without being prepared to honour his pledge! Debtor and creditor are soon involved in a free-for-all in which all the tinkers, usually enlivened by porter, join with a will. The result is a pitched battle such as took place at Portumna Fair a few years ago when, in the words of our informant 'the blood was running in the gutters, and that's the truth I'm telling you.'

When we reached the dammed up mouth of the old canal at Rose Lodge, we saw that the level of Lough Allen was very low. Navigation markers, black and red, which had once indicated the course of the channel from the lake, now stood, forlorn and ridiculous, high above water level. Skirting round the lake we tramped on until we reached the Shannon outfall at the huge sluice gates of Ballintra. Here we sat upon the bank and ate a somewhat belated picnic lunch.

Luke Doyle has charge of the Ballintra sluice, regulating it according to the instructions which he received from the engineers at Ardnacrusha a hundred and thirty miles downstream. The wooded bulk of O'Reilly's Island somewhat obscured our view across the lake, so Luke Doyle very generously lent us his boat. O'Reilly's Island has become a promontory of the mainland, and the receding waters have uncovered bronze swords, dug-out canoes and the foundations of an ancient bridge linking it to the land. Once we had rounded this one time island we could see the whole expanse of the lake, and a fine sight it was on this clear day of fitful sunshine and fleeting showers. On our right the majestic mass of Benbrack rose almost sheer from the eastern shore while opposite the mountains walled in the valley of the Arigna River. Beyond them, across the water, lay ridge beyond ridge, some sunlit, some shadowed, but all coloured by the magic of the limpid atmosphere with every hue from palest blue to a purple that was almost black. Of the Arigna coalfield, surely the strangest in the British Isles, there was little evidence at this distance. We could see small buildings set high on mountain sides pocked in places by spoil banks, and at one point the pylons of an aerial conveyor marched over the top of the ridge, but that was all. There are no headgears, for the coal is got by means of horizontal drifts in the face of the mountain. I should have taken them for slate quarries had I not known otherwise.

Lough Allen is virtually encircled by mountains with the exception of the narrow southern end by which we had approached it, and it has a reputation for treacherous eddies and sudden squalls which brought disaster to more than one trading vessel in the past.

Glad to be able to claim that we had navigated at least a small portion of the waters of Lough Allen, we gratefully returned the boat to its owner. Then began the long tramp home on which we were buoyed up by the prospect of a good dinner on board followed by another glass of Mrs. Bierne's excellent porter.

The next day, Sunday, August 4th, was the eve of Carrick-on-Shannon's red-letter day - the Regatta, held annually on the first Monday in August. We got up late and spent most of the day quietly at our moorings. For part of the time I occupied myself with the boat, removing some of her travel stains and touching up her hull here and there with white paint. Then at four p.m. we slipped quietly away down the river. When we reached the mouth of the Boyle we remembered Angela's gillaroo, and turning off our course, cruised round Lough Drumharlow hoping that her success would be repeated. Alas, this time no gleaming fish responded, and at length we returned to Carrick empty handed. Coming about below the bridge we anchored close in to the shore opposite the quay, a position well clear of the fairway but with a grandstand view of the finish of the regatta course.

All the next morning the crowd on the quay and upon the bridge steadily thickened. Bunting, fluttered bravely over both bridge and quay, so to add our small contribution to this gay display, we unfurled at the stern a large Irish tricolour which we found stowed in one of the lockers. At noon, a heavy shower cleared the crowds with remarkable speed and brought a sudden rush of trade to the Carrick bars. But the storm soon passed, and the sun came out bringing with it the crowds and the crews. One by one the eights and fours came by manned by the clubs of Dublin, Galway, Athlone and Carrick and stalwarts from Bann, Portadown and Drogheda in Northern Ireland.

The day resulted in a series of victories for the Bann Rowing Club which became monotonous, but the Carrick crew won the Maiden Eights amidst tremendous applause, while we cheered lustily as the Athlone 'A' crew rowed to victory in the Maiden Fours. But the events which interested us most and provoked the most intense excitement were the pleasure boat races in which local crews from Cleaheen, Ballindoon and Lough Arrow competed. These craft are beautiful examples of the art of the Athlone boatbuilders; feather-light four-oared rowing boats over thirty feet long with a beam of three feet ten inches. Unlike the outrigger races, these events started and finished at the quay the crews rounding a mark down the river. When the starting gun went the boats fairly shot away amid a roar of excitement, their crews rowing an unbelievably rapid stroke with clockwork precision. Lough Arrow won both open and junior events, and I have never seen a more impressive exhibition of powerful, tireless and perfectly concerted action than that provided by their 'A' team.

The jollifications of the previous year's victory days in England were still fresh in our memories, but for sheer riotous enjoyment and gusto they could not compare with regatta night in Carrick. There can be no doubt that the Celt has a far greater capacity for spontaneous enjoyment than the stolid Saxon whose reserve takes a deal of breaking down. I believe we inherit this reserve (which has good qualities as well as bad) from our Puritan ancestors. I do not think that the frank expressions of joy or sorrow in which the less sophisticated Celtic or Latin peoples indulge, and which we tend to find embarrassing, would have appeared at all unusual in the England of Elizabeth. Certainly the exuberance of this scene in Carrick had an Elizabethan quality. It seemed as if the whole population of the surrounding countryside for miles around had converged upon the streets of this one small town. Crowds surged to and fro, while the bright lit, densely-packed bars resounded with strumming pianos and choruses of song. When closing time came the reinforced guards attempted to clear the bars, but so often as they persuaded one convivial gathering to depart through one door, another would enter through the next. Everybody hailed everybody else as though he were a long lost brother. Everywhere there was argument and good natured banter, while as the evening wore on a fair proportion of the throng exhibited a certain unsteadiness in the legs. Yet nowhere on that evening did we see any ill-humour. At length, except around the dance hall where the Regatta Ball was in progress, the crowd began imperceptibly to melt away, though lighted windows and the sound of singing told of private parties still in full swing. We made our way back to the coolness, the dark and the quiet of the river. It was a fine night, still and clear, and before turning in I sat on the deck for a few moments smoking a last cigarette. Already the great river, gently but eternally flowing down to the western ocean, seemed to have forgotten the little craft which a few hours ago had been sporting on its surface like so many water-boatmen. Not a sound or ripple betrayed its motion, but in the wide reach below, the water was faintly luminous, for although it was midnight there was still the lightening of an afterglow in the west. The footsteps of some late reveller echoed from the bridge. As though to emphasize that another Regatta Day was over, the bunting which had fluttered so bravely now hung motionless, colourless and damp with dew. Even our flag had furled itself around its pole.

Yet the spirit aroused by Carrick's annual saturnalia dies hard. We spent the next night at the quay near Jamestown where we had moored on our way up the river, and on the following morning we rowed down to the village to buy a loaf of bread, expecting to return within the hour. But the practice of purveying porter with provisions has its pitfalls; within, we found a small but jovial company engaged in sampling the hair of the dog that had bitten them at Carrick. One was the ex-boatman of the Royal Canal whose tales I have already recounted. Another was a 'spoiled priest', still wearing his suit of sober black, a dark lean-visaged fellow with a sardonic wit and a wry smile. The term 'spoiled priest', which is popularly used to describe a man who has entered for the priesthood but has failed to take orders, is an ungenerous one. The very fact that such men have the courage to decide that the vocation is not for them indicates that they must possess integrity and scruples which many ordained priests may well lack.

In the intervals of tale-telling, each member of the company contributed at least one song, usually a 'come-all-you' in which all could join the chorus. Repression in the past, and the ubiquitous canned music of the present have between them silenced the voice of the average Englishman. He feels self-conscious, and when he can be persuaded to lift up his voice, it is all too often a painfully tuneless performance. But the Irish countryman still creates his own amusement and will burst into song on the slightest provocation, the result being usually pleasant to listen to. Nor does he necessarily have to be merry with porter before he will do so. I recall one memorable evening in a crowded cafe in Athlone when, on the strength of nothing more potent than a cup of tea, a young Irishman at a neighbouring table began to sing that song of the 'troubles', 'The Foggy Dew'. His plaintive tenor voice had that particular quality which is the very sound of sorrow and which plucks at the heartstrings. The buzz of conversation ceased abruptly and everyone was silent while he sang his song through. When he had done there was applause and calls for more, but the singer walked out, appearing to be scarcely aware of his audience.

The song which most appealed to us on this occasion at Jamestown was a ballad which we afterwards searched for in vain in Angela's books of Irish songs. Subsequent enquiries in Athlone still failed to elicit either words or music, and it was not until we reached Lough Derg that we ran it to earth. We were dining with hospitable friends at their house by the lake shore when we happened to mention it, whereupon our host appealed to the little servant girl who was waiting at table. 'Wait now, I think I have it, sir' said she, and slipped away to return presently with a crudely printed slip of paper. This in itself was a curiosity to me, for it was no less than a broadsheet of the type once purveyed in England by strolling players at the country fairs and which, acquiring local glosses with the passage of years, was the source of many of our traditional songs. This was the song, and I reproduce the spelling of the broadsheet:

THE WILD COLONIAL BOY

There was a wild Colonial Boy, Jack Dubbin was his name,
He was born and bred in Ireland in a place called Castlemane.
He was his father's only pride, his mother's only joy,
And dearly did his parents love the wild Colonial boy.

At the early age of sixteen years he left his native home,
And to Australia's sunny shore he was inclined to roam.
He robbed the wealthy squires, all arms he did destroy
Of all who dared for to combat with the wild Colonial boy.

At the youthful age of eighteen years he began his wild career,
Upon a horse he knew, no danger and a spirit that knew no fear.
He robbed the rich and helped the poor, he stabbed James McAvoy,
A terror to Australia was this wild Colonial boy.

One morning on the praire as Jack rode along,
Listening to the mocking birds singing their mocking song,
Out sprang three mounted police, Kelly, Davis and Fitzroy,
They all set out to capture him, the wild Colonial boy.

Surrender now Jack Dubbin, you see there are three to one,
Surrender in the Queen's name, for you are a plundring son.

Jack drew two pistols from his belt and proudly waved them high
'I'll fight, I'll not surrender!' said the wild Colonial boy.

He Fired a shot at Kelly which brought him to the ground,
And turning then to Davis he received a fatal wound,
A bullet pierced his proud young heart from the pistol of Fitzroy,
And that is how he captured him, the wild Colonial boy.

Such is the story of the melancholy fate of an Irish Robin Hood which we first heard related in song at Jamestown. Instead of mid-day, it was four o'clock in the afternoon before we returned to the boat. Things like this are apt to happen in Ireland where time is of less account. And why not? We are all bound upon a journey from which no traveller returns and whither we may carry no worldly goods. Why should not the journey be sweet, with singing by the way?

AN INTERLUDE ASHORE

DRUMSHAMBO AND SLIGO

Ever since my earliest childhood, my interest in railways has been second only to my interest in canals. In fact, upon reflection, I think that the former was originally dominant and was only deposed for the reason that the most ardent railway enthusiast must either construct his own railway or be content to take his ticket like any other passenger. He cannot acquire a locomotive and a first-class saloon and set out to explore the railway system on his own account, stopping wherever the mood takes him. In the canals, I found a transport system which also had its tunnels and bridges, its main and branch lines, but where I could do just this.

Sleepy branch railways such as the Golden Valley line of the Great Western on the Herefordshire Marches (now, alas, closed to passenger traffic) have especially fascinated me. So have narrow gauge lines in which Wales was once so rich. Many of these over which I have travelled are now no more than a memory like the Welsh Highland or the Glyn Valley Tramway. From this it will be gathered that I was unlikely to spend three months in Ireland without travelling on at least one of the Irish narrow gauge railways. Whereas in England only two gauges, four feet eight and a half inches and seven feet, struggled for supremacy, the period of Irish railway construction began in a positive riot of gauges, and it is said that order was only restored by the Solomon-like mediation of Sir Charles Pasley, Inspector General of Railways, who persuaded the rival promoters to accept a standard determined by calculating the average gauge of all the projects. The result was the Irish broad gauge of five feet three inches. But between 1873 and 1909 a considerable mileage of three feet narrow gauge lines was laid down in Ireland to serve the more remote rural districts. These were mostly constructed either under a grant or guarantee from the Government or, more usually, under the system known as 'baronial guarantee' whereby the interest on portions of the capital charged on the local rates was guaranteed. Yet in some cases the traffic returns of the lines so constructed did not even cover the limited working expenses of a light railway, while the wind of road competition was soon felt. As a result, several lines such as the Clogher Valley or the Cork, Blackrock and Passage have already disappeared, while, with the exception of the Donegal Railway, the remainder survive precariously as branch lines (some used only for goods traffic) of Coras Iompair Eireann. By this large concern they are regarded as an archaic nuisance. Not only does the break of gauge involve transhipment, but owing to the closing of local repair shops, when any of the narrow gauge locomotives need extensive repair they must be loaded on special transport waggons in order to reach the works at Inchicore. In spite of their absorption in one large system, however, these little railways each retain their individual characteristics, their curious locomotives and rolling stock, so that whatever economists may think of them, their charm for the railway archæologist is undeniable.

The obvious choice for our excursion on the narrow gauge was the Cavan and Leitrim Light Railway which runs from Dromod on Lough Bofin to Belturbet in County Cavan (where it joins the Great Northern Railway) with a branch from Ballinamore to Drumshambo and Arigna. But a study of time-tables revealed that there was only one passenger train a day each way, and that the running times might have been especially designed to thwart our project. However, I eventually evolved an itinerary which included two nights in Drumshambo and a journey by bus to Sligo on the intervening day. Dromod was the obvious starting point, but Dromod Harbour had looked disused and inhospitable as we came up the lake, so, as we were anxious to leave the boat in safe custody, we decided to moor her under the eye of our friend Michael Bourke at Albert Lock.

When we returned from our convivial party at Jamestown we accordingly moved down the cut to the lock, and the next morning caught a train to Dromod from Drumsna Station which was within sight of our mooring. Our train from Dromod was not due to leave until early afternoon as it waited for a Dublin connection, so we occupied ourselves in a walk through the woods of Derrycarne. Soon after our return, the train backed in, and I saw that we were to be hauled by No. 2L, one of the original 4-4-0 tank engines built for the opening of the line by Robert Stephenson of Darlington. All these engines were originally named - this one was once 'Kathleen' - but now only No. 1L, 'Isabel', which we later saw at Ballinamore, retains her plate. How needlessly utilitarian is this removal of locomotive name-plates!

The train consisted of a number of goods waggons and two of the original eight-wheeled coaches built for the line by the Metropolitan Carriage and Waggon Works of Birmingham. These had clerestory roofs and open 'observation' ends which, combined with the cowcatcher on the locomotive, gave the train a curiously transatlantic appearance. Seating was longitudinal, and by means of gates in the railing of the observation platform and hinged footplates over the central buffers, the guard could make a somewhat precarious passage through the train. I noticed that the legend 'C.L. & R.R.' cast on the axle-boxes remained to remind the observant traveller that this railway, like so many Irish projects, was never completed. The original intention of 'The Cavan, Leitrim and Roscommon Light Railway and Tramway Company' was to extend their line southwards to Roosky where it would connect with the Shannon passenger steamers which then plied to Athlone and Killaloe, and that it should there cross the river to proceed to Strokestown and Roscommon. This in turn recalls the fact that the line once formed a link in a far more grandiose scheme which never matured. This was the Ulster and Connaught Light Railway project which, launched in 1899, was one of the most ambitious light railway schemes ever proposed. Using portions of the Clogher Valley and Cavan and Leitrim lines, it was intended to connect, by a somewhat circuitous route, Newry on the east coast with Galway and Clifden in the west. Had the plan been realized, the main line from Newry to Clifden would have been 234 miles long, a prospect which sets the railway enthusiast dreaming of such fabulous treats as dining or even sleeping car 'expresses' on the three feet gauge.

I had imagined that we might make our journey in almost solitary state, but when the Dublin train came in a number of passengers changed to the narrow gauge, and we pulled out with the train quite full. The quality of the running was far smoother and steadier than I had expected. The track was enclosed, but there were numerous level crossings protected by gates, and, in response to our urgent whistle, women, or sometimes small children, ran out from the gate-keepers' cottages to open them for us. In this connection it is curious to note in passing that there is a railway not very far from London where no such crossing service is provided, with the consequence that the guard has to open the gates and close them again behind the train, a proceeding scarcely conducive to rapid travel.

IRISH NARROW GAUGE. The Cavan and Leitrim Railway Dromod train at Ballinamore, 2-4-2T locomotive No. 3c, ex Cork, Blackrock and Passage Railway.

At the small town of Mohill I had time to stretch my legs and admire the station with its bright flowers and closely-mown lawns while our train performed some desultory shunting operations. The line between Dromod and Ballinamore traverses a wild tract of undulating, broken country scarred with outcropping limestone and pitted with innumerable small lakes. Consequently, since earthworks were reduced to a minimum, the line has a switchback character and the journey consisted of an alternation of swift, free-running descents and slow, panting climbs.

Ballinamore Junction, where we changed for the Arigna branch, proved to be the largest narrow gauge station I have so far seen. Besides two main line platforms and a branch bay, there were extensive goods yards and the locomotive sheds of the line. Thanks to the increased importance of the Arigna coal traffic, it also presented a scene of great activity. On the strength of this improvement in the fortunes of the Cavan and Leitrim, locomotives from other less fortunate light railways have found a new home at Ballinamore shed. Thus a six-coupled engine which sported a large bell on the top of her firebox had migrated from the Tralee and Dingle in the farthest west, while the wheels of a large 2-4-2 tank engine remembered the vanished metals of the defunct Cork, Blackrock and Passage.

Unlike the main line, the Arigna Branch is a tramway. For the first three miles to Ballyduff it has its own right of way, but thereafter it runs beside the public road except for a short deviation at Drumshambo. Riding was by no means so smooth as on the main line, and in true light railway style the train, consisting of one composite coach, a guards van and a number of waggons drawn by another of the Stephenson engines, rattled and rocked at what seemed a most exhilarating speed down the long incline from Ballinamore. The scenery hereabouts was attractive, the line weaving along the slopes of a narrow valley and affording us views of the old Ballinamore and Ballyconnell Navigation with its ruined locks, gateless but massive.

The road to Drumshambo is winding and undulating, and as the line followed it closely our progress resembled that of a switchback railway, the wheel flanges occasionally squealing in protest as we swung round the sharp curves. At one point, to the accompaniment of prolonged whistling, we shot from one side of the road to the other and back again by unprotected crossings. The Cavan and Leitrim has at least two unique distinctions. One is that it was once the only railway in the British Isles to be operated by a limited liability company, and the other is that one of its drivers was recently summoned and fined under the Road Traffic Act for failing to give adequate warning of approach at one of these crossings on the Arigna line. This remarkable case was heard at Carrick in 1944.

As on most Irish roads, horse and donkey-drawn traffic easily outnumbered the cars and lorries that we met. The donkeys minced along unperturbed, only acknowledging our passage by a disapproving movement of their long ears. But the horses in this neighbourhood did not appear to have become railway minded. Almost without exception our approach made them quite panic-stricken, and our progress was marked by a succession of scenes reminiscent of some early nineteenth-century engraving entitled 'The Coming of the Iron Horse' as drivers leapt from their carts to hold the heads of their struggling steeds. Despite its driver's frantic efforts, one horse backed across the road towards us with the result that the tail of the cart only missed the rear of the train by what seemed a hair's breadth. Occasionally we halted at stations which consisted merely of a name-board in the hedge at the roadside, but soon the now familiar peaks of Benbrack and Bencroy loomed near at hand and, leaving the road, we descended a long incline to draw up at Drumshambo Station. It had been a stirring journey.

Drumshambo is a pleasant little town to which the boom in Arigna coal has brought a prosperity which was reflected in the shop windows. There is also a jam factory whose products rejoice in the brand name of 'Breffni Blossom' to remind the visitor that this was once the ancient kingdom of Breffni. We had arranged to stay at Flanagan's Hotel, and here, after an excellent glass of brown sherry, we enjoyed a substantial meal. This was the 'high tea' of the Irish small town hotel which usually consists of a generous meat course followed by unlimited supplies of yeast bread, soda cake, butter and jam. Where the small hotel offers dinner as an alternative (this one did not) the stranger would do well to choose the 'high tea' which is the custom of the country. Dinner is a concession to strangers which, except in a few of the larger hotels, often turns out to be less substantial and more expensive. We had heard gloomy reports of Irish hotels, yet wherever we had occasion to stay ashore during this voyage we fared excellently well. Though it may occasionally be irksome to the proprietor, there can be no doubt that the registration and periodical inspection of hotels by the Tourist Board authorized by the Tourist Traffic Act of 1939 has raised the standard of Irish hotels. Moreover the complete list of hotels with details of all charges, which the Board issues, is a boon to the stranger. By English standards, Drumshambo was no more than a large village. I cannot think of an English village of equivalent size and character where, at the present time, we would have fared so well as we did at Flanagan's Hotel.

After our meal we walked out of the town by a lane which led along the lower slopes of Benbrack high above the eastern shore of Lough Allen. In the westering sunlight of a stormy evening the view over the water to the mountains on the farther shore was magnificent, exceeding in its atmospheric effects our previous view from the water. On our way back we met a peasant farmer coming towards us on his donkey with a load of hay in the wicker creels. Except on our brief visit to Connemara we did not see the creel in general use outside this Lough Allen district. Sometimes reins and creel harness consisted of hay or straw rope, presumably made with the hay-bond twister which has become a museum bygone in England.

IRISH PEASANT FARMER. 'We met him coming towards us on his donkey with a load of hay in the wicker creels'.

Next morning we caught the Sligo bus from the square. The prospect of this long road journey did not particularly appeal to us, but we were determined not to leave Ireland without paying at least a brief visit to the home of W. B. Yeats. Irish bus timings appear to be as strenuous as train timings are easy, for although on this, as on other occasions, we roared along the narrow winding roads at what seemed a death defying velocity, our driver was unable to maintain his schedule. The chief trouble seems to be that insufficient allowance is made for stops along the route, Irish bus stops do not merely involve the picking up and setting down of passengers. There are bicycles and bulky packages and luggage to be either raised onto or lowered from the roof, a job requiring the assistance of the driver and the disturbance of the billowing tarpaulin which protects this roof-top miscellany. Then again the conductor will sometimes disappear on some mysterious errand while the driver pushes his cap onto the back of his head, leans over his steering wheel and puffs resignedly at a cigarette.

The standard of bus driving, however, impressed me as highly competent, which is more than I can say for the two occasions when we travelled by private car. Both these journeys would, I am sure, have been fraught with fatal consequences on the more crowded roads of England. Our first driver drove continuously in top gear at a speed which never exceeded twenty miles per hour, a proceeding which caused both engine and transmission to protest audibly. Yet even to the non-mechanically minded this sedate progress was not conducive to peace of mind, for we held firmly to the wrong side of the road except when an approaching vehicle forced a change of course. As our driver frequently turned to wave and nod to acquaintances at the roadside, or to point out objects of interest, such changes of direction were only affected when collision appeared imminent. Our second driver performed in the Italian manner with considerable skill and verve, the only controls which really mattered to him being the accelerator pedal and the horn button. The former was held firmly down to the floor-boards, while the latter was used for negotiating cross-roads and other hazards, for which purpose a tumbler switch rather than a push button would have been more convenient.

I must confess that I was disappointed in Sligo town. In my view it has not the quality and character of Galway. Perhaps Sligo is unfairly handicapped, for it is doubtful whether any town, however beautiful, could successfully live up to the magnificence of Sligo's setting between sea and mountain. We walked along the quays to the extremity of the harbour and, leaning on the sun-warmed stones of the breastwork, looked out across the sparkling blue waters of the bay towards Rosses Point. On our left rose the green conical crown of Knocknarea; opposite, a beetling brow followed by a superb sweep to the sea, rose the majestic Ben Bulben, names which will be familiar to any readers of the poetry of W. B. Yeats.

In England, we sometimes tend to carry our veneration for our literary immortals to the length of commercial exploitation, but that is a less grievous fault than their consignment to oblivion. Though Yeats was not born here, it is with Sligo that his name will forever be associated. Yet surely there was never a poet of European stature who so lacked honour in this his own country which he has immortalized. I searched the town in vain for any copy of his works or any mention of his name. The only direct association with the poet I discovered was a brass plate on an office door which bore the name of Pollexfen. Yeats, in his *Reveries over Childhood and Youth*, gives us a grand portrait of that old buccaneering shipowner, his maternal grandfather, William Pollexfen:

'We knew that he had been in many parts of the world, for there was a great scar on his hand made by a whaling hook, and in the dining room was a cabinet with bits of coral in it and a jar of water from the Jordan for the baptizing of his children and Chinese pictures upon rice paper and an ivory walking stick from India that came to me after his death. He had great physical strength and had the reputation of never ordering a man to do anything he would not do himself. He owned many sailing ships and once, when a captain just come to anchor at Rosses Point reported something wrong with the rudder, had sent a messenger to say "send a man down to find out what's wrong". "The crew all refuse" was the answer, and to that my grandfather answered, "Go down yourself", and not being obeyed, he dived from the main deck, all the neighbourhood lined along the pebbles of the shore. He came up with his skin torn but well informed about the rudder. He had a violent temper and kept a hatchet at his bedside for burglars and would knock a man down instead of going to law, and I once saw him hunt a party of men with a horsewhip. He had no relation for he was an only child and, being solitary and silent, he had few friends ... yet he was so looked up to and admired that when he returned from taking the waters at Bath his men would light bonfires along the railway line for miles.'

.   .   .   .

'Under bare Ben Bulben's head
In Drumcliff churchyard Yeats is laid.
An ancestor was rector there
Long years ago, a church stands near,
By the road an ancient cross.
No marble, no conventional phrase;
On limestone quarried near the spot
By his command these words are cut:

Cast a cold eye
On life, on death.
Horseman, pass by!'

Yet at the time I write eight years have passed since that January day when the poet died at Cap Martin, and he has not yet come back to lic, as he wished, under Ben Bulben. 'When', I asked, 'Will Yeats be brought back to Drumcliff'? no one seemed to know or to care. [1] If the resurgence of Irish Catholicism has had anything to do with this obscuration of greatness in its own place, and I confess I suspect that it has, then indeed that movement has much to answer for and little deserves to be called Catholic.

.   .   .   .

The daily train from Drumshambo back to Ballinamore left at the premature hour of 6.58 a.m., so I suggested to our hospitable host at Flanagan's Hotel that night that I should pay our reckoning, and that he should make us up a packed breakfast so that we could let ourselves out in the morning. He positively refused to entertain this suggestion, declaring that he had never yet failed to speed a guest, suitably breakfasted, at the appointed hour. Professional pride was obviously at stake in this so we dropped the matter and had another glass of port together.

Possessing that queer gift, a sub-conscious alarm clock which wakens a sleeper at a predetermined hour, I woke up at 6 a.m. and lay for a while listening for any sound of movement in the house. It was as still as the grave. At length we got up and dressed. By the aid of the Tourist Board List I reckoned up our score as best I could and left the money, with a note bearing our Athlone address, on the visitors' book. Then we let ourselves out of the still silent house.

---

[1] It is gratifying to record that the poet has now been brought back to Ireland to lie, as he wished, in Drumcliff churchyard.

The beauty and the tonic freshness of a brilliant early morning compensated for our lack of breakfast. The only cloud in the sky was a white fleece perched like a woolly nightcap on the peak of Bencroy. I stood on the rear observation platform of our single coach looking out at the splendid panorama of mountain, lake and bog, bright and sparkling with dew like a world new made, and watching the string of little coal waggons which rattled along behind us, writhing and undulating like a snake along the tortuous track. It was an exhilarating experience.

At Dromod, as we knew, there was no broad gauge connection to take us back to Drumsna, so we set out on foot beside the railway track. This was an irregular proceeding, and it proved to be rough and tiring going, for the Irish lines, laid with flatbottomed Vignoles metals, are not regularly patrolled by gangers like our keyed bull-head rails, and consequently there was no continuous beaten path beside them. But to have followed the road would have entailed a long detour in order to cross the Shannon, so we plodded on, crunching through the loose ballast or walking with unnatural stride on the sleepers. It was noon by the time we reached the boat, so I need hardly add that we very soon prepared a belated and substantial 'brunch'.

DOWN RIVER

JAMESTOWN TO PORTUMNA

When we had finished our much-needed meal, we lost no time in getting under way. The day was a Saturday, and I was anxious that we should clear Roosky and Tarmonbarry Locks before nightfall. The Shannon Locks will be opened at an extra charge on Sundays if the lock-keepers are available, but there was no point in incurring expense, trouble and possible delay if it could be avoided.

The weather still held beautifully clear and fine, and all along our course we saw whole families at work 'saving' hay in the meadows by the waterside. After a delightful passage through Loughs Boderg and Bofin we made a brief halt at Roosky Quay to lay in provisions to tide us over the week-end. In Roosky Lock we found the Shannon Navigation maintenance boat *Fox*. Her cheerful skipper lives aboard and leads a roving life repairing locks or re-painting or replacing buoys and markers on nearly 200 miles of river and

RIVER SHANNON. 'In Roosky lock we found the Shannon Navigation maintenance boat *Fox*.'

estuary. The *Fox*, which carried a crane, was loaded with a miscellaneous collection of gear; baulks of timber, sheer legs, buoys and barrels of tar. She also included a diving suit in her stores, and her captain told us that one of his last jobs had been to take up the buoy anchorages at the old seaplane base at Foynes, made obsolete by the opening of Rineanna. He paid tribute to the work of the masons who had laid the massive stonework of the Shannon Locks which, after a century, was as sound as ever and had never needed repair. The admirably designed paddle gearing, too, protected from the weather by an iron casing, was practically fool-proof and trouble free. He also explained how the weight of the massive gates did not depend upon the equipoise of the balance beams (Athlone and Meelick lock-gates have no beams, being moved by winches), but was taken by rollers, adjustable from above, which moved over traverse plates on the lock sills. If the navigation of the Shannon is not all it might be, especially as regards the maintenance of the buoys and markers, this reflects no discredit upon the crew of the *Fox*. The job is too big for one maintenance gang to tackle effectually, and responsibility for the deterioration of the navigation in recent years must rest with the Electricity Supply Board who now dominate the Shannon in the interests of Ardnacrusha, and to whom the requirements of traffic on the river are of very minor concern.

We spent some time talking to our interesting friend at Roosky, with the result that by the time we had crossed Lough Forbes and sighted Tarmonbarry Bridge the light was beginning to fail. Tying up at the head of the lock, I walked back to John Bourke's cottage to be told by his old mother that he was still out in the fields saving his hay. I had not long returned to the boat, however, before John came down the track to the lock on his bicycle, and we had soon locked through and made fast to the quay below. While Angela prepared our supper I stood on the quayside talking to John. It was a grand night, clear and windless, the west still bright with the afterglow but the first star glimmering in the eastern sky. 'Do you think the weather's going to hold'? said I, thinking of the crossing of Lough Ree on the morrow. John, who was staring across the river in the direction of Cloondara, shook his head, 'Look there now', he directed, pointing. Following his gaze I saw a great cloud of rooks come wheeling and sweeping across the darkening sky. When they reached the tall trees of their rookery by the village they circled and soared above them with such a clamorous chorus of cawing and croaking as could be heard clearly even at this distance. 'If those birds did be coming home one by one now', said he, 'Then its grand fine weather we'd be having. But,' he went on, shaking his head again, 'that's a terrible bad sign you see now, terrible bad and that's the truth, certain sure it is'.

We were not sorry to climb into our comfortable bunks that night, for it had been a long day. Before I lay down I glanced through the port-hole and saw a glinting pathway of moonlight stretching across the broad Shannon towards the mouth of the Cloondara Cut. I felt quite certain that John was wrong about the weather.

The morning appeared to vindicate my judgement, for although a fresh breeze had arisen, the white fleecy clouds that were blowing out of the west looked harmless enough, and the sun shone bravely. We had a leisurely breakfast and then got under way. There was nothing particularly remarkable about the reach of the river between Tarmonbarry and Lanesborough. My most memorable recollection is of a lonely cabin which we sighted dead ahead of us close by the water's edge on the outside of a loop of the river. It was trimly thatched and newly whitewashed. Though a wisp of blue turf smoke drifted from the chimney, the place was very quiet, and I think the family must have gone to Mass. A few chickens scuffled in the dust before the half-door, while a donkey, head drooping and ears laid back, drowsed in the sunlight against the bright white wall. In the foreground, sparkling blue water, tall reeds and emerald green turf; in the middle distance a sweep of russet brown bogland; beyond, the long purple ridge of Slieve Bawn. The elements of the composition were simple enough in themselves, but together they composed a picture that could be seen nowhere else in the world.

We reached Lanesborough at 12.30 p.m. and moored up for lunch at the quay beside the Grand Canal Company's depot. I found that I had to come hard astern in order to bring *Le Coq* in to the quay wall, for at this point, where it falls into Lough Ree, the Shannon narrows and the current is swifter than at any other point on the river south of Carrick. After lunch I carefully checked over our engine, replenished fuel and oil, and then, not without a slight feeling of trepidation, for the wind appeared to be freshening, we set out to make the crossing of the great lake. Soon the banks began to recede and we found ourselves pitching into the waves of a waste of waters.

To those who know the Shannon intimately, the marking of the navigation is no doubt sufficient, but to the stranger crossing Lough Ree or Derg, particularly the former, it is very far from adequate. A good pair of binoculars is essential, and even with these it is often difficult to pick up the next buoy, still less determine its colour. Red buoys are often so discoloured that their identity only becomes apparent at close range. Despite the fact that the lake is comparatively narrow thereabouts, and that we had been given advice as to our course, we found the first three miles out of Lanesborough particularly confusing. To the accompaniment of much pointing and peering through the glasses, we headed across the lake toward the west bank, turned due south, passed between Ferrinch and Incharmadermot Islands, and then returned toward the eastern shore to leave Goat, Bushy and Little islands and the green hump of Inchenagh with its farmhouse to starboard. I still do not know whether we were correct in passing between the first two islands, but the passage between Incharmadermot and the east bank looked treacherous. We were certain, however, that we were right now in keeping to the east shore, and after we had left the island of Clawinch also to starboard, we picked up a red buoy off Inchcleraun. That is the spelling of this island according to my Ordnance Survey Map. Its correct ancient name, I believe, is Inisclothrann, the Island of Clothra, sister of the celebrated Queen Maeve of

Connaught who, according to one legend, is said to have met her death on the island. But because a certain Mr. Fairbrother, a Quaker, acquired the island a century ago, it is generally known locally as Quaker Island. It is also called variously Holy Island, Saint's Island, or Iniscleraun which is a good illustration of the problems with which Irish nomenclature bedevils the conscientious topographer. Whichever name he chooses he is bound to rouse some Irishman to disputation. In this book I have generally followed the Ordnance Survey versions, right or wrong.

As we approached Inchcleraun there was a most extraordinary change in the weather. The wind died so suddenly that it was as though some draughty doorway had been abruptly closed, and a flat calm fell upon the lake. At the same time the sun disappeared and we noticed that the fleecy clouds had gone, leaving a uniform silvery film which enveloped the sky from horizon to horizon. We were reminded of our passage across Lough Key from Boyle to Rockingham before the gale which had so nearly brought us to disaster. Once again all colour seemed suddenly to have ebbed from the distant landscape to leave only a chiaroscuro of black and silver. It was so clear that we could now see two useful landmarks ahead, the aerial masts of Athlone radio station and the spire of St. Mary's Church, eleven miles away. By a strange optical illusion these objects and the black brushstroke of the distant coastline appeared like a mirage, suspended in the air, so indistinguishable were burnished water and burnished sky.

We returned from this Irish voyage with a store of many imperishable memories, but if I were to be asked which of these is the least likely to become blurred by time, then I think I would choose this passage of Lough Ree, 'the Lake of the King', in the ominous brooding stillness of this extraordinary afternoon. When we had visited the lake before in the outboard motor boat, we had seen it in its normal mood, its surface alive and sparkling, whipped into wavelets by the wind. It was impressive but there was no mystery about it, and the expression 'inland sea' sufficed to describe it. Yet now it had become a dead sea, and the effect was uncanny and indescribable. Imagine the feeling of loneliness, of littleness and isolation which those who put out to sea in small boats experience, but add to this the fantasy of an ocean, waveless and flawless, distant landscape, ethereal as the world of a dream, shifting and disintegrating with our movement as islands appeared to float away from the shore or recede into its background.

It is said that in the days of Queen Maeve and her sister Clothra, Inchcleraun was a place of Druidism and magic, but in accordance with the wise policy of the Celtic Church this old centre of faith was not suppressed so much as absorbed by the subsequent Christian settlement founded in this instance by St. Diarmid. There are six churches on the island, the oldest of which is believed to be the original oratory of the saint. We had thought of effecting a landing on the island, but I mistrusted the weather. Irish ruins of this sort are apt to be unrewarding, while I could see through the glasses as we passed fairly close

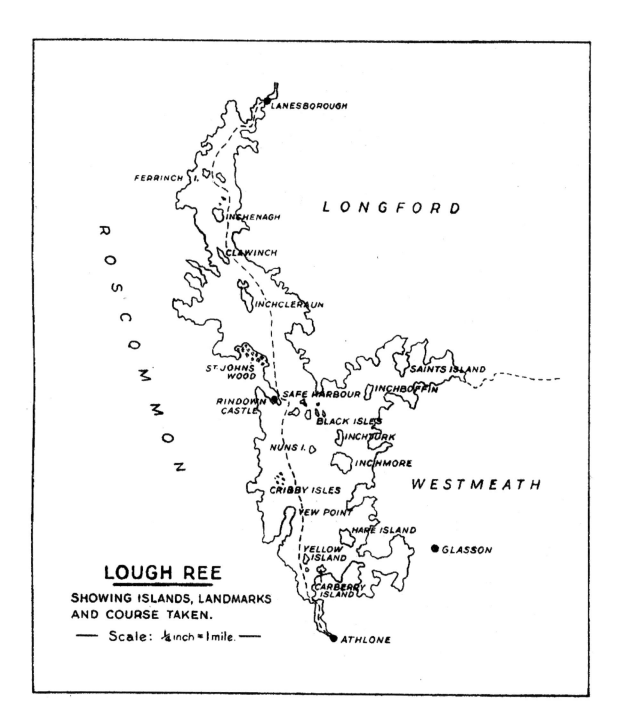

LANESBOROUGH

FERRINCH I.

LONGFORD

INCHENAGH

CLAWINCH

ROSCOMMON

INCHCLERAUN

ST JOHNS WOOD

SAINTS ISLAND

SAFE HARBOUR

INCHBOFFIN

RINDOWN CASTLE

BLACK ISLES

INCHTURK

NUNS I.

INCHMORE

CRIBBY ISLES

WESTMEATH

YEW POINT

HARE ISLAND

YELLOW ISLAND

GLASSON

CARBERY ISLAND

LOUGH REE

SHOWING ISLANDS, LANDMARKS
AND COURSE TAKEN.

—— Scale: ¼ inch = 1 mile. ——

ATHLONE

inshore that these were much overgrown.

The low reef of Cow Island opposite was crowded with birds, swans, gulls and cormorants. The dazzling white plumage of the former, reflected in the water, had been visible to us from a considerable distance with mystifying effect which even the binoculars did not resolve until we approached them quite closely. These birds seemed to have been influenced by the stillness, for they perched motionless, and even our passing occasioned no commotion among them.

When he has cleared Cornahinch Point, the southerly tip of Inchcleraun, the navigator must bear away to starboard towards the west shore. This is a point on the lake where the stranger can easily be led astray if he cannot, with the aid of good glasses, pick up the distant buoy. A map of the lake is deceptive for it looks as if it is only necessary to keep going straight ahead. In practice, however, such a course would in all probability lead into the cul-de-sac of Elfeet Bay, not to mention a possible encounter with rocks. By thus inclining towards the Roscommon shore in what appears to be a westerly direction, a due southerly course will in fact be kept, and this was the first occasion on the voyage when our compass came in useful. Soon, landmarks noted on the map began to appear, first the woods of St. John's and then the ruins of Rindown Castle on Warren Point with a red buoy offshore. Just beneath the castle ruins is a small inlet which is called Safe Harbour because it is practically the only point on the sixteen mile passage of the lake which provides a reasonable anchorage, sheltered from the south-west. Here the Grand Canal boats occasionally make for shelter if they are caught by sudden storms. Immediately opposite this headland lay the archipelago of the Black Islands which had looked true to their name from a distance but which now appeared as whale-backs of emerald green. Upon the largest of this group, King's Island, dwell two families, the Hanleys and the O'Haras, who for generations have lived by netting trout and setting eel lines on the lake. On several occasions while we lay at our Athlone moorings we had watched them come rowing down the river to land their boxes of eels for despatch, by rail. As one would expect, they are consummate watermen, both men and women being virtually unchallengeable in 'pleasure boat' events at Athlone Regatta. Even their cows have become semi-aquatic, swimming from green islet to green islet in quest of fresh pasture. Yet at the time of which I write these sturdy independent people were in imminent danger of being deprived of the vocation which their ancestors have followed for generations, a loss which would inevitably bring about the abandonment of their island life. The Hanleys and O'Haras are (or were, for by the time this book sees the light the case may have gone against them) the only professional fishing folk on the Shannon to survive the monopoly created by the Electricity Supply Board. The bribery of cash 'compensation' has been tried but sturdily refused. Force has also been tried. We were told of a party of E.S.B. bailiffs and officials who set out in a boat for the Black Islands, and how the islandmen came out, armed and grimly resolute, to meet them. Fortunately a fog came down, blotting out the lake, and the bailiffs turned back, otherwise there might well have been murder done.

The same arguments are put forward by the E.S.B. to justify their monopoly as were advanced by those who prohibited net fishing on some of our English rivers, and they are open to the same counter argument. They maintain that the fish population has been depleted as a result of indiscriminate and unregulated net or line fishing. If this were so, since the Black Island folk and their like have been net and line fishing for generations, the fish should by now be extinct. Even if the contention can be upheld, it is merely an argument for regulation, not for abolition. Most important of all, the feeling of resentment which such a display of arbitrary authority breeds, particularly among the independent Irish, leads to a great increase of a far more damaging practice - poaching in the tributary streams where the fish spawn. There could be no keener incentive to the spread of this mischievous practice than the spectacle of the fish weirs, at Athlone for instance, which the E.S.B. control. According to regulation a gap must be left in the frame of the weir where the nets are hung, through which the fish can pass freely, thus ensuring that the weir shall not take undue toll. As anyone may see, powerful electric lights have been fixed and trained upon this gap, and at night these are illuminated in order to deter fish from using it and so to divert them into the nets. Below, and guarded by, the weir bailiff's hut is a large tank where the netted fish are stored alive to be despatched in accordance with the state of the market. In my view the proper task of the Electricity Supply Board is to supply electricity, not to catch fish or to prohibit others from doing so. Though his harvest comes from the water and not from the land, the fisherman is as much a small property holder as the peasant farmer. That such a situation should ever have arisen in a country which purports to champion the cause of the small proprietor is surely astonishing.

From this the reader may gather that we were anxious to visit these intrepid lake dwellers in their island fastness. Because we did not know how closely we could approach the islands without running foul of rocks, nor where we could find anchorage, we planned to anchor for the night in Safe Harbour and row over to King's Island in our dinghy. We accordingly edged slowly into the harbour and dropped anchor about fifty yards from the shore. We first of all landed from the dinghy to inspect the ivy-covered ruins of the castle which frowned down upon our anchorage. As the name indicates (Rinndun, 'the Point of the Fort') there has been a stronghold here since ancient Celtic times but the present structure was built in 1227 by Marisco the Justiciary, presumably for the purpose of dominating the navigation of Lough Ree, a task which it must have performed very effectually. Even in its advanced stage of ruination, the fortress was still impressive in size and in the immense thickness of its walls, while it was made doubly secure by an equally massive wall, now likewise ruinous, which crossed the neck of the headland and so guarded the only landward approach. Passing through the archway with its portcullis grooves into what had once been the courtyard, we were surprised to find a small cabin sheltering within the ancient walls. At this moment a sudden shower of rain came on and a woman appeared, framed in the open half-door, and bade us come in out of the wet. We did so gratefully. No more simple interior could be imagined. It was living reduced to the barest essentials: an earth floor, bare whitewashed walls, blackened rafters and thatch overhead, an open turf fire with the familiar crane and pot oven, simple wooden chairs, table and cupboard. The master of the house sat by the chimney corner, a frail old man white of hair and beard, his gnarled hands clasping a stick and a dog at his feet. He acknowledged our entry only by a courteous inclination of the head. 'It's not well he is at all', his wife explained in a whisper. He spoke no word, in fact he seemed to be scarcely aware of our presence, and his old eyes had in them a strange dreaming, childlike quality. They seemed to be gazing upon something far beyond the confines of the bare little room. Was he looking into the long past of his memories or did he believe he saw the future beyond death? We tried to make conversation with the woman, but we were unresponsive guests because of the tragic presence that seemed scarcely to belong any more to this world. We were glad when the rain stopped and we left this sorrowful house.

As we rowed back to *Le Coq* we observed that while there was still a dead calm, the sky had become greyer and still more lowering. We put the kettle on and made tea. Meanwhile inclination was battling with discretion. We both dearly wished to visit the Black Islands, but for the visit to be worth while it would mean remaining in Safe Harbour for the night, and I no longer had faith in the ability of our anchors to hold us in a high wind. The leaden sky and the unnatural calm were certainly ominous, and suggested that John Bourke's prophecy might be fulfilled after all. Suddenly, the lightest catspaw of wind from the north-east ruffled the water for a moment and *Le Coq* swung idly to her anchor. It had gone as soon as it had come, but it settled matters. Though the prospect seemed unlikely at this season, if there should come a hard blow from that quarter, Safe Harbour would be very far from safe for any craft. The decision was made without further hesitation; the Black Island project must be abandoned; we would make for Athlone without further delay. The evening was drawing on and there was still some way to go. We hauled up our anchor and were soon heading out across the lake once more.

This is the widest part of the lake, and here again it is easy for the stranger to lose his bearings. This time our inclination was to steer too far over to the west in the direction of the Cribby Islands which should be left well to starboard. In fact, improbable though this may appear from the map, for a moment we confused the bunched Cribbys with Nuns Island which must be left to port. This error might have had disastrous consequences, but, by holding a compass course due south, the Cribbys soon revealed themselves as an archipelago of little black humped shapes, while other recognizable landmarks began to appear. The long promontory of Yew Point was the mark we were looking for, and once we had identified this everything was plain sailing. Beyond this point we soon found ourselves in familiar waters. There, across the lake, was Hare Island, and here was the little bay where we had landed from the outboard and had our lunch. As we passed the

Yellow Islands I could see through the glasses the friendly black marker on its cairn of stone that guarded the mouth of the river, and soon we were slipping gently down the river to Athlone. We came about in the river just above the familiar railway bridge, and while I headed *Le Coq* very slowly into the current, Angela picked up the float of our permanent mooring with a boathook. There was something very reassuring about that heavy chain and the knowledge that it was secured to an old ship's anchor. We had covered twenty-seven miles that day, and felt we had earned a good dinner and a sound sleep.

We had not long gone to bed before the storm broke, a deluge of rain accompanied by a violent north-easterly gale. When morning came it was still raging with unabated fury; the dinghy was wallowing about half full of rainwater, the river was in flood, and even in this sheltered place, sizeable waves set *Le Coq* pitching and straining at her moorings while the wind screamed overhead. Had we remained at Safe Harbour we should undoubtedly have been driven ashore and smashed to pieces by so violent a storm from such a quarter.

After I had bailed out the dinghy with a bucket, we managed to struggle to the shore and went round to the Beahans' house to collect our mail. Already we felt as though we were re-visiting friends whom we had known for a lifetime, and it was a great welcome they gave us. Having warned them by letter from Carrick that we were coming, they were relieved to hear that *Le Coq* was safe and sound at her moorings. Dolly invited us to a sumptuous tea that evening, after which, accompanied by her nephew Sean, we continued our reunion party with drink and song. Sean, who sang in the choir at St. Peters, had a fine tenor voice, and to him must go the chief credit for teaching us most of the Irish songs which we were able to add to our repertoire. A Gaelic speaker, he was also able, with much patience, to teach us a few - very few - words of the Gaelic. One difficulty appears to be that there is not one Gaelic but several, so far as the spoken word is concerned. The Gaelic of Connemara with which Sean was familiar seems to be a very different thing from the Gaelic of Mayo or West Kerry. Upon one occasion, Sean's lesson was interrupted by a Kerryman with the result that the two soon became involved in an abtruse philological argument which travelled far beyond our reach.

This Kerryman was something of a poet, and he assured me most emphatically that the Gaelic equips the poet with a far more subtle and supple vocabulary than does the English tongue. Although I am myself no linguist, I am prepared to believe this, in fact it confirmed my own conjectures. A so-called 'primitive' language coined by a rural people is necessarily rich in phrases of natural and realistic imagery and in onomatopoeic words, all of which are the very stuff of poetry. As J. M. Synge discovered, this Gaelic richness echoes in the English of Western Ireland to restore to our tongue something of that Elizabethan felicity of phrase that we have long lost in the mire of hideous urban abstractions, but which was once turned to immortal purpose in the plays of Shakespeare. It is safe to say that the language of a people changes with their way of life and is thus a sensitive barometer of social values. Our own language to-day reflects the abstract values of a materialistic civilization based upon machines which has lost contact with the realities of human nature and of the natural world. Therefore it has lost its poetry and grown sterile.

In Wales, physically and politically so closely associated with England, the national language continues to flourish. Yet in Ireland, despite the defensive moat of the Irish Sea and centuries of passionate resurgent nationalism, the language must needs receive artificial respiration in the attempt to prevent it dying out. This is a mystery which continually puzzles me. I can evolve no theory to explain it. Those who sponsor the Gaelic revival in Ireland might study the phenomenon with advantage, because I believe that artificial aids cannot, in the long run, deflect those strange forces which determine whether a language shall live or die. To the dispassionate observer there is something slightly absurd about the self-conscious and earnest Irish endeavour to restore the national language. The majority of the generation educated in Gaelic appear to forget it as soon as they have passed their examinations. Hardly any of the people we met knew more than a few words. Sean knew it, not as a result of education, but because he served in an Irish-speaking (Connemara) battalion of the Irish army during the 'emergency'. A great sum of money must be spent in producing bi-lingual signs for public buildings and unwieldy bi-lingual Government forms. One cannot help wondering what proportion of the population ever looks at the Irish half. There is, I fear, some truth in that unkind parody of the words of the patriotic song 'Galway Bay': 'The people on the uplands digging praties, speak a language that the Irish do not know'.

.   .   .   .

The wind moderated during that day, and the night was clear and moonlit. We read in the Irish Press of the havoc which the great storm had wrought, of flooded roads and flattened crops, of vessels lost at sea and many small boats sunk in Dun Laoghaire Harbour. The morning of the storm had been August 12, the day when duckshooting opens on the Shannon. When we had arrived at Athlone we had seen several sportsmen preparing their craft for an expedition to Lough Ree, but although the shooting of the first duck on the twelfth is an event to which great importance is attached, conditions on the lake deterred even the most intrepid. I should imagine that even the duck took shelter.

On the morning of the next day, conditions looked more promising. We moved down to the quay and, having spent the morning shopping in the town, passed through the lock soon after noon bound once more for Clonmacnoise and Shannon Harbour, but this time under our own power. The weather held until we had passed Shannon Bridge when a fine but very wetting rain began to fall. However, it was still and much warmer, for the wind had left the north-east for the prevailing south-westerly quarter. It was what the Irish call a 'soft' day. The river looked broader than before, as indeed it was, for it was eighteen inches above normal summer level and had invaded some of the lower callows. The great levels of lonely water and bogland pocked and veiled with rain were a desolate prospect which turned our thoughts back to the friendly warmth and hospitality which we had enjoyed at Athlone the previous night. We enlivened the journey by rehearsing some of the songs, notably, 'Galway Bay' and 'Kevin Barry' that Sean had taught us. While I sang, Angela played an accompaniment on her flute. The effect of this musical progress must have been rather remarkable, but only the birds could appreciate it, for except for one undaunted party of duck shooters in an outboard motor boat we never saw a soul between Athlone and Shannon Harbour.

We had resolved to moor for the night in the same berth at the mouth of the Grand Canal, but when we reached this point, we hardly recognized our little island, so much had it shrunken. The waters of the swollen River Brosna were rushing like a millrace in a brown, foaming spate through the narrow channel which they share with the canal. Nevertheless, we breasted the torrent and made fast to the familiar tree. We had covered a good many miles since our previous visit, and our old friend at the cottage opposite was surprised at our unexpected re-appearance. I myself had little thought that we should revisit Shannon Harbour, for much as we had looked forward to seeing Lough Derg, I had originally dismissed the idea regretfully as impracticable. But our good progress, coupled with fuel economies in the first stages of the voyage and an extra allowance for August, had left us with time and petrol in hand.

Before we left the next morning, we walked up beside the canal to see how the work of enlarging the Shannon Harbour Locks was proceeding. We found great activity. The two locks and the pound between them had been drained and the gates removed. Portable air-compressors roared away beside the locks, while from the chambers came the deafening clamour of pneumatic drills. It had been found that the new boats which the company had acquired were not only too long but also too wide for the locks, so the men were engaged in shaving away the sidewalls, a formidable undertaking. I noticed that the great inscribed block commemorating the completion of the extension of the canal from Tullamore had been broken in half in the process of removal. I hoped that it would be repaired and replaced and not wantonly destroyed.

We saw another scene of activity as we sailed past Banagher Quay where a number of boats were loading the cargoes transhipped by road from the canal-bound craft at Shannon Harbour. A mile below Banagher Bridge the Shannon is split into two streams by the large island called Inishee, the navigation following the left-hand channel going downstream. At the point where these divergent channels reunite, the gardens and trees of the demesne of Shannon Grove come down to the water's edge in pleasant contrast to the somewhat bleak levels around Banagher. This improvement persists all the way to Meelick Lock, the trees lining the banks interspersed here and there by attractive riverside cottages and farmsteads. We saw that all the sluices were drawn at Meelick Weir, so we gave it a wide berth as we entered the Meelick Lock Cut.

Below the lock the river flows once more through open callows, but these were no longer veiled with rain, they were coloured and patterned by the sunlight and shadows of a bright day which was only marred by a few April-like showers. Twice in the length of this reach the river again divides to encircle islands, the navigation taking first the left-hand channel and then the right. At the first of these partings, at Ballymacegan Island, the red marker on the tip of the island was so faded and obscured that we had already entered the wrong channel before we distinguished it. Doubtless with our shallow draught we could have continued without mishap, but we decided to take no chances and came about.

Where the channels reunited below the second island, the river approached a low ridge of wooded hills on the east, or Tipperary shore. Here we presently sighted Portumna Bridge. This is an iron bridge of comparatively recent date, and built so low over the water that at first sight it appears to present an impassable obstruction to the navigation. Mystified, we peered at it through the binoculars, and it was only upon closer approach that the swinging span by the Galway shore came into view. We made fast to the Grand Canal Quay just above the bridge, but later the span was swung for us and we passed through to lie snugly in a convenient little cut just below.

It was not long before we visited the little town which lies a mile away from the river. Portumna vies with Carrick-on-Shannon for the distinction of being the brightest, neatest, most hospitable and generally most attractive town on the river. We found the houses freshly colour washed and brightly painted, while miniature trees in gaily coloured wooden tubs stood upon the pavement flanking the doorways. Part of the market square near the Catholic Church had been transformed into a garden where, between smoothly shaven grass walks, roses bloomed in profusion. This in itself was an unusual sight for, unlike the English, the Irish are not as a rule great flower gardeners. In the bright sunlight of the following morning all this festive gaiety combined to give Portumna a Continental air. One half expected, on rounding a corner, to come upon the local inhabitants drinking their *aperitifs* at the umbrella shaded tables of some open air cafe.

Unlike Carrick, there is no mystery about the source of the local pride which Portumna reflects. It draws its inspiration from the boundless enthusiasm, energy and leadership of one man, the parish priest, the Right Reverend Monsignor Joyce, V.G. A man of his abilities might, there can be little doubt, have risen to a position of great eminence in the hierarchy of the church. Instead, he has chosen to devote that ability throughout a long lifetime to the welfare and betterment of his native place. I believe that he was right in so doing, and that the result is a finer and more durable reward and memorial than a Cardinal's hat. I had previously seen the Monsignor's name mentioned in the Press as founder and president of the Shannon Development Association whose aims are to advocate the development and improvement of all the amenities of the river including the restoration of the steamer service which operated regularly until the 1914-18 war. This, only one of the Monsignor's many activities, was a project after my own heart, so I had already written to Monsignor Joyce expressing my wish to meet him when we visited the town. No sooner had we arrived than we were welcomed by Mr. Flynn, Grand Canal agent in Portumna and Secretary of the Association to whom I am indebted for much of the useful information about the river which has found its way into the pages of this book. It was he who introduced us to Monsignor Joyce.

Our talk in that quiet study was by no means confined to the aims of the Shannon Development Association. The Monsignor's mind was a treasure house of local history and archæology. This in itself was not remarkable; the country priest or parson usually turns out to be the village antiquary. But for Monsignor Joyce Portumna's past was not merely a subject for academic study, a hobby which provided a convenient escape from everyday affairs; it was indissolubly associated in his mind with Portumna's present and future. This became apparent as he spoke of the small collection of Portumna's 'by-gones' which he had assembled, of the welfare of its people, of schemes for vocational education, and efforts to establish local industries suited to the neighbourhood. Nowadays when we tend either to cling desperately to the past as to a raft, or to allow ourselves to be swept away on the torrent of scientific 'progress', we are sorely in need of more minds with this vision of the present as a synthesis of past and future. It is the essence of wisdom. Here was a man whose alert and vigorous mind belied his white hairs and who, withal, possessed a natural dignity and courtesy which, alas, is nowadays termed 'old fashioned'. Here, too, was a priest who had sought to exemplify the word Catholic not merely in the doctrinal but also in the general sense of that word which, according to my dictionary definition means: 'Universal; of interest or use to all men; all-embracing, of wide sympathies, broad-minded, tolerant'. Under such a man, the patriarchal system of Irish Catholicism works, but unfortunately, men of this calibre are rare in any society and at any time. They are born, they cannot be manufactured wholesale by Maynooth or by any other institution. When their Monsignor passes from them, the people of Portumna may never see his like again. [1]

The Monsignor's window looked out upon the coloured quiet of the garden which he had made, but beyond this there was a scene of great bustle and activity for it was a fair day. We left the peace of that room, which is virtually the hub of Portumna's little world, to walk between the lines of horses and cattle, and the close-packed pens of sheep which crowded the square and its adjacent streets, listening to the bargaining of the intent, excited crowd. The horses were a motley collection; the cattle mostly shorthorns with a sprinkling

[1] Soon after writing these words I learned with great sorrow of the death of Monsignor Joyce in February, 1947.

of those black cattle common to the Irish peasantry which are said to be a cross between the small native Irish black and the Dexter breed. Sheep predominated, for it is at the fairs in the towns along the Shannon border country that the breeders of Connaught sell their stores to graziers from the richer lands of the eastern, midland and southern counties. In this respect the great sheep fairs of Banagher and Ballinasloe are the Irish equivalent of those which are held along the Welsh marches at Craven Arms or Clun. Here the sheep were mostly white-faced Roscommons. It is said that this breed was originally evolved by crossing the native Irish sheep with the Leicester. Arthur Young, describing a visit which he made to the farm of a Mr. Mahon of Strokestown, Roscommon, in 1776, lends support to this belief when he writes: 'Mr. Mahon's breed, both cattle and sheep, are improved by a bull and a tup which he bought from Mr. Bakewell, and has bred from them with great success'. It was Robert Bakewell who first developed the Leicester. The Roscommon is a large bold animal with a proud patrician face. It is long in the body and high on the leg like the Border Leicester, but is not gaunt looking, and the white, close, silky fleece somewhat resembles that of our Welsh Border breeds, the Kerry, Clun or Radnor, being midway between the mountain and the shortwool downland types.

The tinkers, we noticed, were present in force. Their vividly painted carts and waggons, the scarlet or yellow neckerchiefs of the men and the glinting ornaments of the younger women contributed a barbaric note to the scene. Happily, on this occasion they appeared to be on good terms with each other for we saw no repetition, even upon a small scale, of the notorious 'battle of Portumna'.

At the end of one of Portumna's streets stand the lodge and entrance to Portumna Castle, once the seat of the Clanricardes, who were the largest landowners in Ireland, and now the property of the Earl of Harewood. Of the original mediæval fortress of the Norman Richard de Burgh no trace remains, while the great seventeenth-century house of the Clanricardes which succeeded it was accidentally burnt out in 1818. Close beside it stand the ruins of the thirteenth-century Cistercian (later Dominican) Abbey. It is singularly unfortunate that the Earl's present agent will not admit visitors to the estate at any time with the result that these two notable monuments of Portumna's past are usually inaccessible. We were fortunate, however, thanks to the indefatigable Monsignor Joyce who provided us with a note which, when we presented it to the gatekeeper, acted like a miraculous 'open sesame'.

Though it is no more than a gaunt shell, the Castle still retains an air of grandeur. The main entrance is in the north front, and is approached via another gateway and a gatehouse leading into a walled forecourt which has become a wilderness of thistles. Our photograph shows the south front, the small central semi-circular bay forming what was once, no doubt, the garden entrance. Beneath the mullioned window in this bay we came upon a tablet bearing the following inscription:

IRISH CASTLES. (3) Portumna. 'No more than a gaunt shell, the castle still retains an air of grandeur.'

> This stone is erected to the Memory
> of a much lamented Animal
> Who with a beauteous form possessed
> Those qualities which are esteemed
> most valuable in the Human Species:
>   Fidelity and Gratitude.
> And Dying April 20th 1797 Aged 11 years
>   Was interred near this place.
>   Alas! poor Fury.
> She was a Dog take her for All in All
> Eye shall not look upon her like again.

Of all the proud house of Clanricarde, only their pet dog has still a memorial at Portumna Castle. A Victorian topographer would doubtless have found this an excellent text for a lengthy soliloquy upon the transience of human vanity.

After we had examined the Castle we turned our attention to the Abbey, a proceeding which involved literally hacking our way through dense undergrowth. At the cost of a severe nettling and numerous scratches from thistles and briars we managed to secure a photograph of the only notable surviving feature, the east window with its remarkably beautiful tracery. Through it may be seen the windows of the Garden House where the present owners of the Castle stayed on the occasion of their last visit to the estate.

After this prickly venture we decided that we had explored enough for one day, so we returned to the boat for tea. The fair was beginning to break up, and down the road to the river straggled a procession of flocks and herds interspersed with horse and donkey carts. There were animated scenes at the bridge. Because the swinging span rung hollow under the hoof, many of the animals refused stubbornly, and the utmost persuasion, loudly voiced, was required before they could be induced to cross. Once, the column was temporarily halted when the bridge was opened for the passage of the *St. James*, a fine craft which the Grand Canal Company operate on the river service between Shannon Harbour and Limerick. The bridge was manually operated, and the bridge-keeper, red of face and slightly 'market peart', as we would say in England, wound manfully at the large handwheel. He has the distinction of being the only Irishman I met who used the word 'begorrah' as an expletive, thus confounding my belief that it was pure music hall Irish.

IRISH ABBEY. Portumna. 'The east window with its remarkably beautiful tracery.'

On the slopes overlooking the river directly opposite our mooring was the demesne of Belle Isle. It was a guest house until the war, but now the place stands empty. For all followers of motor racing, Belle Isle is noteworthy as the birth-place of Sir Henry Segrave who lost his life in his ill-fated water speed record attempt on Lake Windermere. 'Och! I remember him well now, surely' said the old bridge-keeper, 'And him putting the fear of the Lord into us with the old motor bike that he had then'. With the exception of the late Parry Thomas, I doubt whether any more lovable personality has ever graced the sport. Segrave, like Thomas, was an Elizabethan born out of his time, and because he could find no better outlet for his restless energy and unquenchable spirit he sacrificed his life in the pursuit of speed.

Portumna is far from rail communication, but a little to the north of Belle Isle may be seen a cutting through the ridge spanned by an overbridge. This is a relic of the projected branch line from Birr which was intended, not only to serve Portumna, but to connect with the Shannon steamer service at a riverside quay. According to the story I was told, the line soon got into financial difficulties, whereupon the local inhabitants tore up the rails and removed the sleepers for firing or building material. Whether this story is true or not, the line is always referred to locally as 'Portumna's Stolen Railway'.

RIVER SHANNON. 'Portumna bridge was opened for the passage of the *St James.'*

LOUGH DERG

PORTUMNA TO KILLALOE

Lough Derg is the largest of the Shannon lakes, the passage from Portumna to Killaloe being twenty-two miles. Longer and narrower than Lough Ree, however, it is not so easy for the stranger to lose his bearings. On the other hand, the mountains which encircle the southern portion of the lake make it very subject to sudden treacherous squalls. This is particularly true of that portion of Lough Derg where the deep inlets of Killaloe, Scarriff and Youghal Bays unite. Here, especially between Parker Point and Scilly Island at the entrance to Killaloe Bay, a squall will quickly raise a raging sea often accompanied, if the blow comes from the south west, by a vicious 'box wave' caused by seas converging from Killaloe and Scarriff. Only a short while after our departure from Ireland we read in the Irish Press of a tragic disaster at this very point. The Grand Canal Company's boat M 45, bound for Limerick and in tow behind the *St. James*, was engulfed, broke her towing lines and sank. Only one of her crew of three reached the shore. The master of the *St. James* was powerless to aid them for the waves were running twenty feet high and to have attempted to put about would have meant certain destruction.

The sea-faring man is apt to look upon all inland navigation with some contempt, and frequently refers to devotees of the pastime as 'ditch-crawlers.' But no navigator, however experienced he may be, can afford to take too many chances on Lough Derg. The very narrowness of the lake adds to the hazard since it affords little sea room. Consequently, in the event of engine failure or other difficulty, the unfortunate navigator invariably finds himself caught on a lee-shore.

I emphasize these points in case the Shannon Development Association, in their laudable campaign to popularize the river, should convey the erroneous impression that cruising on the Irish Shannon is as safe and simple as navigating the English Thames. There should assuredly be more traffic on the river, and I am certain that there would be if the cruising facilities which the Shannon offers were more widely known to boat owners in this country. But to encourage those without any previous experience to hire craft and take them out on the lakes would be folly. My own view is that, if the Shannon is to become a more popular cruising ground, the existing navigation markers and buoys should be better maintained and their numbers increased on the lake crossings. Also that unmarked danger points situated off the main course through the lakes but *en route* to lake harbours or anchorages should be buoyed. It would also be of great assistance if charts of Loughs Ree and Derg were available to intending cruisers. The lakes were last charted by Commander

James Wolfe for the Admiralty in 1839, and I was lucky to be presented by a friend with a photostat copy of the original Lough Derg chart which is unobtainable. Owing to the passage of time and the effect of the Shannon scheme, the soundings are no longer accurate, but we found it a great help nevertheless, and, failing another survey, a reprint would be most useful.

From this it will be appreciated that when we slipped into our bunks that night at Portumna it was with fervent hopes of fair weather for our passage down the lake on the morrow. We had been told that the Lough Derg Yacht Club were holding their annual regatta week at their club house in Dromineer Bay, so we had decided to make this our first port of call. Our hopes were rewarded. We awoke early to find ourselves enveloped in a thick white ground mist which hung over the level sallies between the river and Portumna. It was cold and damp, but by the time the breakfast bacon was sizzling in the pan, the mist had turned from white to gold, and through its thinning veil we could catch glimpses of a sky of cloudless blue.

Angela had some shopping to do in Portumna, and when we eventually cast off soon after noon the weather could not have been better. The sun shone brilliantly, and as we entered the lake a mile below our mooring it sparkled on the wide expanse of blue water, ruffled by the lightest of breezes, between Terryglass and Portumna Bays. For a few moments we were uncertain of our course, but we sighted a red buoy, passed through the narrows off Drominagh Point, and presently picked up with the binoculars the prominent black marker on its cairn of stone which is situated on the tip of Goat Island. This is a useful mark, visible from a great distance in either direction, but it should be given a wide berth. As we approached it we saw an insignificant iron rod projecting out of the water between us and the marker. Had we not been keeping a good look out we might easily have failed to see it. We learnt afterwards that this rod marks the Goat Reef, a submerged shelf of rock which extends for some distance into the channel from the point of the island where the marker stands. This is a good example of the way in which, a stranger might easily come to disaster as a result of inadequate navigation marks.

I am glad that our first passage through Lough Derg was made in the southerly direction because it is much the better from the scenic point of view to approach the mountains which gradually converge upon the southern half of the lake. Already the heather-purpled moorlands of the Slieve Aughty Mountains were marching beside us along the Galway shore. Beyond, blue in the summer air, we could see the mountains guarding the approach to Killaloe, Slieve Bernagh - The Gapped Mountain - in the County Clare beyond Scarriff Bay, and opposite, in Tipperary, majestic Tountinna, highest point of the Arra Mountains, with the Silvermines and Keeper Hill, highest of them all, closing the far horizon. This splendid amphitheatre of mountains looming ahead made a fitting climax to our voyage and made us realize what we should have missed had we been unable to visit Lough Derg.

We passed Illaunmore, largest of the lake islands, on our port side and saw the flash of white sails beyond the wooded archipelago of the Corrikeens. Evidently a race was in progress. Through the glasses we watched the little Shannon class sailing boats round a mark and then run swiftly before the westerly breeze back into Dromineer Bay. We altered course, leaving the main line of navigation and passing between the Corrikeens and the Tipperary shore with the ruined keep of Dromineer Castle dead ahead. In the remote distance beyond the bay there now appeared the familiar gap of the Devil's Bit which we had last seen from the summit of Slieve Bloom.

We heard the crack of a gun as the winner of the race sailed between the finishing marks, and drifted along slowly until the last straggler had crossed the line. Then we speeded up to find a mooring before craft should appear for the next race. As we drew nearer we saw that there was quite a concourse of people on the smooth green turf beneath the castle keep and before the club house, while a number of cruisers of varying size were moored in the lee of the little Goose Island just off shore. We became acutely conscious that many critical eyes were turned upon us. Finding a berth in a completely strange place beset by who knows what unknown hazards is always a somewhat anxious proceeding, but doubly so when the luckless navigator has to perform his manœuvres before an audience. It would be just our luck, I thought, if we were to run firmly and ignominiously aground, or if our engine stalled and we ran down some other craft while frantically endeavouring to re-start. However, to our great relief, all went well. We passed slowly down the line of moored craft until we saw a convenient berth beside a floating staging which was secured to the island. We ran alongside and made fast in a manner which, I hope, appeared sufficiently competent.

Two perfect strangers butting into the middle of the proceedings, we felt very diffident, and wondered what sort of reception we would receive. We need not have worried. So far from being reserved or exclusive, the Lough Derg Yacht Club proved to be as friendly and hospitable as any other Irish institution. We had hardly secured our lines before we were boarded by a boatload of enthusiastic boys who politely but eagerly enquired whether they might examine *Le Coq*. As they did so they plied me with questions which betrayed a much greater knowledge of boats than I could boast when I was their age. Their elders were little slower in making our acquaintance, and before we had been at Dromineer an hour we were taking tea on the verandah of the clubhouse, and had both been invited to sail as crew in the next race.

So far as I was concerned this offer was particularly generous, for I know nothing of the sailing game and was therefore so much super-cargo. My activities were confined to raising or lowering the centre board promptly when instructed to do so, and to shifting my weight when the little craft heeled over. But because my ignorance was due, not to disinclination but to lack of opportunity in the past, I soon fell under the spell of the elemental fascination

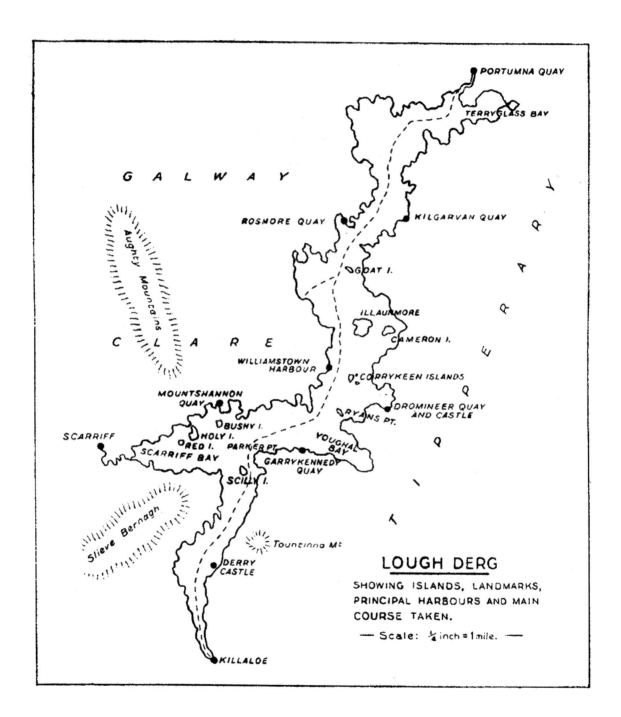

PORTUMNA QUAY

TERRYGLASS BAY

G A L W A Y

Aughty Mountains

ROSMORE QUAY

KILGARVAN QUAY

GOAT I.

ILLAUNMORE

CAMERON I.

C L A R E

WILLIAMSTOWN HARBOUR

CORRYKEEN ISLANDS

MOUNTSHANNON QUAY

DROMINEER QUAY AND CASTLE

BUSHY I.

RYANS PT.

SCARRIFF

HOLY I.

RED I.

PARKER PT.

YOUGHAL BAY

SCARRIFF BAY

GARRYKENNEDY QUAY

SCILLY I.

Slieve Bernagh

Tountinna Mt

DERRY CASTLE

LOUGH DERG

SHOWING ISLANDS, LANDMARKS,
PRINCIPAL HARBOURS AND MAIN
COURSE TAKEN.

— Scale: ¼ inch = 1 mile. —

KILLALOE

and splendour of sail. I felt as excited as anybody as we sped home to finish a close second, the white wing of straining canvas overhead driving the little hull, a lovely example of Athlone craftsmanship, with effortless and thrilling speed across the blue waters.

When it was suggested that we should stay and take part in the races on the next and last day of the regatta, we did not need much persuading. And when the last race was over, the conclusion of a successful week was suitably celebrated at Mr. Flynn's hotel which was conveniently situated within a stone's throw of the clubhouse. Here we bitterly lamented the fact that the time left to us in Ireland was now so short. For these hospitable folk showered invitations upon us, and as many of them occupied beautiful houses upon the lake shore, we might easily have spent a delightful month in cruising from one to another.

In these lakeside families we encountered a new stratum of Irish society, that of the Protestant Anglo-Irish or, as they are sometimes called, 'the old ascendancy'. Many of them had been resident in the district since Cromwellian times, and they represented an example, interesting to the social historian, of a community, originally colonial, which has contrived to outlive the parent stock from which it sprung. Farming, riding, fishing, shooting, or sailing, despite all the troubles with which Ireland has been rent, these people continue to follow a way of life which can have changed very little in two hundred years, but which has virtually disappeared from England as a result of our bloodless but far-reaching social revolution. In a remote and sparsely populated countryside, hospitality has not been strained by abuse as is the case in our overcrowded island; consequently their doors seem to be ever open to the traveller. To cross their thresholds was for me a bitter-sweet experience, unlocking forgotten stores of the nostalgic recollections of a childhood when vestiges of such a life still lingered in England and then seemed to me stable and assured. Spacious rooms were rich with the lovely, gracious possessions of past generations, yet there was nothing oppressive or self-conscious about them; they were no museums of a vanished past. Everything was worn and well, almost carelessly, used. Dogs padded about or slumbered before the hearth. Passages and lobbies were perhaps the most eloquent with their clutter of guns and fishing rods, oilskins, sou'westers, riding crops, old tweed hats bristling with flies, gardening baskets and perhaps a spare suit of sails or an outboard motor for the boat that rode in the little harbour at the foot of the smoothly sloping lawn. Here, too, there was 'honey still for tea', and as like as not laden espaliers of figs, nectarines or peaches in the warm shelter of a walled garden. Like Sir Henry Segrave, the menfolk of these houses have a certain Elizabethan energy and gusto about them, and it is they rather than the native Irish who are responsible for the English legend of the hard-riding, devil-may-care 'wild Irishman'. They take delight in braving Lough Derg in her stormy moods in the frailest of craft, and on a particular occasion one of them, trained in this hard school, sailed away single-handed down the Shannon estuary and was next heard of in the Canary Islands. Another story which we heard is a typical illustration of their quality. A certain gentleman had purchased a large craft for use on the lake and was bringing her up from Limerick. When he reached Killaloe he offered the local inhabitants a trip on the lake for a nominal sum. The invitation was accepted with alacrity, a large number crowding on board, but when they had passed under Killaloe Bridge and travelled a few hundred yards to the pier head the owner hoped that they had had a pleasant trip and proposed putting them ashore. It then dawned upon them that they had merely acted as a very convenient form of ballast to enable the boat to pass under the low arch of the bridge. Whether the owner succeeded in discharging his profitable and useful cargo or whether he was forced to undertake the promised excursion is not recorded.

On the Sunday following the last day of the regatta we had planned to leave for Scarriff, but the fickle Irish weather changed overnight and the day dawned wet with the wind blowing half a gale. We therefore remained in the sheltering lee of Goose Island. With one exception our neighbours had sailed away the previous evening and we missed their friendly companionship. We were sitting in the cabin that evening listening to the rain pattering on the deck and the wind whistling mournfully through the reeds when we heard the sound of an outboard motor boat and a voice hailing us. It turned out to be one of our friends of the previous day. Clad in glistening black oilskins, he had braved the storm to invite us to a bath and dinner at his lovely house across the bay, having seen through his telescope that we were still at our moorings. Thus at one generous stroke a damp and depressing evening became a memorable occasion.

By morning the rain had ceased, but though the wind had moved to the north it was still blowing strongly. We were impatient to be off for there was much that we wished to do in the short time that remained, and once again, as at Safe Harbour on Lough Ree, there was a battle between inclination and discretion. This time inclination won, and, when the wind showed signs of moderating about noon, we cast off. Had *Le Coq* possessed a really reliable marine engine, and had she been in seaworthy trim I would have felt no qualms about putting out in rough weather. But the old Morris, while it had served us faithfully, was subject to minor fits of temperament such as oiling plugs or shedding water-pump chains which, while they could be quickly rectified, could be quite enough to spell disaster under certain circumstances. Moreover, the high wheelhouse, combined with the lack of ballast which had been such an advantage on the Royal Canal made *Le Coq* an uneasy, or, as the Irish put it, a 'giddy' boat in broken water. Dromineer Bay was comparatively sheltered from the north, but in order to reach Scarriff Bay we had to cross that most treacherous part of the lake, and I knew that we should make heavy weather of it as soon as we cleared the northern arm of the bay. The great thing seemed to be to keep the weather off our beam, so instead of taking a direct course I decided to head north-west to the Corrikeens, come about in the lee of these islands, and then run before the wind until we entered Scarriff Bay when we should get a certain amount of shelter from the north shore. Although the open lake turned out to be even rougher than we had expected, this plan worked admirably except for one thing which we had failed to consider - the dinghy. If some more experienced yachtsman can tell me how to control a towed dinghy in rough weather I should be eternally grateful. We duly came about off the Corrikeens and commenced to run before the wind in fine style, but the dinghy evidently resented this proceeding and began forcibly to demonstrate the fact. Poising itself on the crest of a wave, it would hurtle down upon us and strike our rudder a resounding blow. It would then retreat rapidly to the length of its painter and presently make another assault. Crawling out onto the stern, Angela tried the effect of lengthening or shortening the tow but all to no purpose. When we reached the vicious looking reef called Ryan's Point we saw the encouraging sight of a cruiser, wrecked a week or two earlier, being pounded to pieces on the rocks. Her back was broken, and a flotsam of splintered planks was drifting and surging round her. It was at this moment that Angela suddenly shouted 'The dinghy's gone.' Sure enough, her painter had parted under the strain, and I looked over my shoulder to see her drifting away towards the reef, alternately tossed on to the crest of a wave or disappearing out of sight in the trough. There was only one thing to be done. We must put about at once and try to retrieve her before she had drifted onto the rocks. It seemed a desperate undertaking with only a forlorn hope of success, but we could not face the prospect of losing Jack's dinghy without making some effort. Wind and sea were almost too much for *Le Coq*, and for a time we wallowed broadside on. We seemed to be rolling to forty-five degrees though it may have been less in fact, and although we had made everything reasonably secure in anticipation of a rough passage, for a few moments the interior of the boat resembled a violent manifestation of poltergeist phenomena as hitherto inanimate objects suddenly sprang to life. To make matters worse our improvized steering cable stretched, produced an inordinate amount of play in the steering gear, and threatened to jam altogether. It was a bad moment. Slowly and reluctantly, however, with engine full ahead and racing intermittently as the propeller came out of the water, *Le Coq* came about, and more by luck than judgement we bore directly down upon the dinghy. Angela clinging to the wheelhouse handrails accomplished the seemingly impossible feat of grappling it with the boathook and we began to bear away from the reef which by this time seemed perilously near.

Our difficulties were by no means over, however, for Angela's hold on the dinghy was precarious, while I could not leave the wheel for more than a moment at a time. Somehow or other we managed to detach the old tyre which we were using as a fender, and to attach the line which had secured it to the dinghy in such a way that Angela was able to relinquish the boathook and cling instead to the tyre. The line was not long enough to make fast to the stern cleats, while the wheelhouse handrail to which the fender had been secured would undoubtedly have carried away under the strain. There was nothing for it but for Angela to hold on grimly while I made for the nearest shelter. I always kept the relevant sheet of the Ordnance Survey before me on the shelf above the wheel, and a quick glance at this showed me that the little harbour of Mountshannon, sheltered by the high north shore of Scarriff Bay which we were now entering, was obviously the best place to make for. There is a string of islands off this part of the coast, Inishparran, the Cribby Islands, Bushy Island, Young's Island, Holy Island or Inis Cealtra, and Red Island. At first, these effectually hid Mountshannon, but eventually the channels between the islands opened out and enabled me to distinguish through the binoculars the quay wall, as it appeared between the Cribbys and Bushy Island. I altered course accordingly, and as we passed between the islands we entered calmer waters to Angela's great relief. Soon we had rounded the massive sheltering arm of the breakwater and were making fast to the iron rings of the quay.

For several days afterwards Angela's arms and shoulders ached and displayed red weals which told their own story, but apart from this neither crew nor craft appeared to have suffered in our little adventure. Even our crockery and other breakable articles had survived in spite of the alarming sounds which had accompanied our dinghy-saving manœuvre. But my first jobs on arrival were to make another and stronger painter for the dinghy and to make a better and more trustworthy job of the steering gear. When this was done we sat down to a substantial and very welcome tea.

Comparisons of scenery are bound to be invidious, so much depends upon weather, season and individual taste. But upon reflection, if I were asked which were our best moorings in this respect on the whole voyage I think I would choose Mullawornia Lock for the canals and the harbour of Mountshannon for the river and its lakes.

While we were having tea there was a sudden change in the weather, and we stepped from the wheelhouse onto the quay to find this fickle lake transformed. Though there had been no rain, the skies had hitherto been grey with hurrying clouds and the waters leaden. Now the clouds had parted, the sun was shining brightly and the wind had dropped. Lough Derg, having played us one of its capricious pranks, now lay placid, basking in the sunlight as innocent and innocuous as a village duckpond. Leaning on the weathered grey limestone of the harbour wall and gazing across to the noble shape of Tountinna Mountain I now found it impossible to believe that this same stretch of smiling, sparkling water could become a raging sea capable of battering down breakwaters and engulfing a canal boat. It was indeed a lovely prospect whichever way the eye turned. Farther to the west across the bay and beyond the grey finger of the round tower on Holy Island rose Caher Mountain and Knocknagower, foothills of Slieve Bernagh, their green lower slopes dotted with cabins and small farm-steads, while looking landwards the southern escarpment of the Aughty Mountains, purple with heather, lifted its long ridge above the lakeside trees.

We had now left the ubiquitous limestone of the plain, for the mountains which cluster about Killaloe are of old red sandstone and slate formations, and on the lower levels by the lake, accumulations of detritus yield fertile sandy loams. A 'soft' climate, sheltering mountains and rich soil combine to produce a more luxuriant growth than we had seen

LOUGH DERG. The harbour of Mountshannon. 'I leaned on the weathered grey limestone of the harbour wall and gazed across to the noble shape of Tountinna Mountain.'

elsewhere on the Shannon, and this richness, by contrast, enhanced the beauty of the mountain scenery. Thus the narrow high banked road which climbed steeply from the quay to Mountshannon was reminiscent of a Herefordshire lane, while the village - itself, a single broad street of brightly colour-washed houses poised between lake and mountain, was deeply bowered in trees. That evening we took the dinghy out and rowed across to Holy Island. The religious settlement on the island is traditionally associated with St. Colum and St. Caimin, but it is most probably another Christianized Druidic centre, and its origin is therefore lost in that misty dawn of Christianity in the west. It is said that St. Caimin, his brother Guaire, and another anchorite named Cuimmine once discussed what, if they had their wish, they would have their little church filled with that would be of most service to their fellow men. Guaire suggested silver to give to the poor, Cuimmine proposed books for his students, but St. Caimin wished to bear the ills of mankind by filling the church with disease. It was probably as a result of this legend that miraculous healing powers were attributed to the church of St. Michael on the island, the sick being carried thither until quite recent times. The island was also the subject of an annual pilgrimage for many years.

The most unique archæological feature on the island is the Saints' Graveyard with memorial stones inscribed with Greek, Celtic and Latin crosses and ranging in date from the eighth to the twelfth centuries still intact. Alas! as at Clonmacnoise, the Saints have not been permitted to sleep sound on their lonely island. The place is still used for burial, and on this account the slumber of centuries has been rudely and wantonly disturbed. Already the unique quality of this ancient burial place has been seriously impaired and will soon be utterly destroyed. As Holy Island is the second largest on the lake, with an area of forty-nine acres, there is plenty of room to consecrate fresh ground so that this iconoclasm need never have occurred.

St. Brigid's Church, south of the round tower, possesses a fine Hiberno-Romanesque doorway, while in the church of St. Mary we found an altar bearing a carving of the crucifixion on its stone frontal. This last looked as if removed thither from some other site. The carving was of a type which would probably be unwittingly described as 'primitive' for the reason that we can no longer fathom the mind and motive of the sculptor. His purpose surely was symbolic and impressionistic; hence there was no attempt at verisimilitude. The result is not 'lifelike', and consequently our so-called Age of Reason calls it primitive because it has lost the vision which is above reason. The workmanship was certainly crude, yet this time and weather worn stone picture in this lonely place still conveyed an eloquence of meaning utterly lacking in the plaster effigies of modern Catholicism which are 'primitive' in the worst sense of the word.

LOUGH DERG. Holy Island. 'The island glowed like a brilliant emerald and the round tower became a shaft of gold against the darkness of the eastern sky.'

Clouds had once more obscured the westering sun and the light was failing. We were just about to abandon the hope of a photograph of the island and return to the dinghy when a narrow shaft of sunlight suddenly gleamed through a rift in the clouds to shine directly upon the island. It was as though some great spotlight had been trained especially for our benefit, and the effect was most dramatic. The island glowed like a brilliant emerald and the round tower became a shaft of gold against the darkness of the eastern sky.

This evening stormlight seemed to bode little good for the morrow, but contrary to all expectations we awoke to a brilliant cloudless morning. While the breakfast bacon sizzled appetizingly in the pan I strolled upon the quay, whose stones were already warmed by the sun, and thought I had never seen so fair a prospect as this symphony of lake and mountain resplendent in all the freshness and glory of the morning. Had I been born by this lake shore I would carry such a memory of it to the ends of the earth.

While we were breakfasting, the now familiar *St. James* appeared at the head of the quay, dropped some barrels of porter and sailed away again. It is impossible to travel far on Lough Derg without encountering her. Many of the older folk in the lakeside villages indiscriminately refer to her, or to the smaller canal boats, as 'steamers'. 'There's a steamer by the quay', they will say, thus perpetuating the memory of the vanished Shannon steamer service.

Soon after the *St. James* had disappeared from sight in the direction of Killaloe, the little stone quay was deserted for we had cast off and were setting out to complete our interrupted journey to Scarriff. This second stage was as languorous and idyllic as the first had been adventurous and tempest-tossed. Passing out of Mountshannon Bay between Young's Island and Holy Island, with engine idling we drifted slowly and with scarcely perceptible motion across the blue waters of the great bay of Scarriff until searching ahead with binoculars, I picked up the navigation markers by the mouth of the little river Scarriff. The town of Scarriff lies some little distance inland from the lake, and for the one and a half tortuous miles from Lough Derg to Scarriff quay the river has been canalized. It was a curious and fascinating transition to pass suddenly from the wide levels of the lake into this narrow channel which twisted bewilderingly through a bed of tall reeds, a dense swamp bordered by a belt of dark woodland.

We soon left the marsh for rich pastures and water-meadows, while at one turn we passed the disused Tuamgraney quay. The meanderings of the little river were such that it was difficult to keep a sense of direction, and as I spun *Le Coq's* wheel this way and that I was glad that I had effectively righted her steering gear. It must be as much as a loaded canal boat can do to negotiate some of these turns, and I should doubt whether the larger craft which the Grand Canal Company propose to run on the Shannon service will be able to call at Scarriff.

It was just after noon when we came in sight of Scarriff quay and Grand Canal depot at the end of a short cut which branched away from the river on our left hand. We moored against the quay wall and had our lunch before walking up to explore the town which we could see standing upon high ground about half a mile away.

Scarriff is an attractive place, curiously sited after the manner of Gloucestershire's Stow-on-the-Wold; that is to say, instead of seeking shelter as most country towns and villages do, it seems to invite the winds to do their worst. Its centre consists of a wide square perched upon a knoll to which all the radiating streets must climb. At the foot of the steep street by which we ascended we crossed a high stone bridge over a typical mountain torrent which brawled noisily in its swift descent between boulders and over shelving rocks. Looking down over the parapet it was hard to believe that this was the Scarriff River and that only a few hundred yards below this point it became navigable by boats of forty-five tons.

We found that there were some good shops in Scarriff, and after a thorough exploration we returned to the boat laden with purchases which included two pounds of most delicious butter and a pair of shoes which I am wearing as I write. We had decided that after tea we would return to our lovely berth at Mountshannon. We proposed to travel to Killaloe on the morrow and considered it advisable to take full advantage of the fair weather by returning in that direction. As there was little time left to us we could no longer afford to be unduly delayed by storms. We knew now how swiftly Lough Derg can change her moods.

While we were having tea a curious incident occurred which might well have turned to tragedy had we not chanced to be there. Three youths drove onto the quay in a small motor van which they proceeded to wash down with water drawn up from the canal. When they had completed this task they began to amuse themselves with the wharf crane, one of them hanging onto the hook while his companions swung the crane round and round. We were not paying any particular attention to this stupid pastime until we heard a splash and looking up, saw that the youth had lost his hold and had fallen into the canal. Horse-play had met with its just deserts, and our first reaction was one of amusement. Suddenly, however, the incredible fact dawned upon us that an active fellow of eighteen or so was actually drowning within a yard or two of the quay. He made little commotion, and his head alternately appeared and disappeared. Meanwhile his two companions simply watched him, being apparently petrified with fear. It did not even dawn upon them to lower off the crane until the hook came within his grasp which would have been a simple matter. So soon as we realized what was happening we seized a spare line, ran up the quay, threw it to him, and in a few seconds had hauled him, white and dripping, over the parapet. Almost too unnerved and shaken to thank us, a very chastened trio clambered into their van and made off. I do not think they will play any more games with the Grand

190

Canal Company's cranes.

The weather was still clear and fine as the sun set that night at Mountshannon, but wind galls in the sky suggested a possible change by morning. We had found by previous experience that the wind often rose with the sun, so we decided that we would make a really early start next morning, brew a cup of tea as we went along, and have a late breakfast when we reached Killaloe. When we awoke it certainly seemed as if our decision was a wise one for the weather could scarcely have looked more threatening. Grey clouds hung over the mountain peaks while the eastern sky flamed with the proverbial shepherd's warning. There was no wind, however; the lake lay in a flat calm, and so we lost no time in getting under way, heading for the black tree-clad shape of Scilly Island under the cloud capped dome of Tountinna. Soon we had rounded the island, leaving it to starboard (the channel west of the island is beset with rocks) and were heading down Killaloe Bay. The great walls of the mountains now rose almost sheer from the water's edge with most impressive effect, but we had not proceeded very far before we noticed that the clouds were creeping inexorably down their steep sides. Already our view ahead had become vague and blurred in outline, and in a few minutes everything was blotted out as the white blanket of mist, chilling and damp, swept down to water level. This was doubly unfortunate for it not only obscured the grand scenery of the approach to Killaloe, but it also made navigation difficult. With a comforting, steaming cup of tea beside me on the ledge above the wheel, I peered ahead, but the lenses of the binoculars might have been made of frosted glass for all the use they were. Had we been in wider waters we might easily have gyrated in circles, but fortunately Killaloe Bay narrows like a tundish towards its southern end so that whenever we deviated from our course we could discern the faint loom of the land upon one side or the other.

It was a strange experience, this groping through these still waters, silent, mist-shrouded and colourless. Lough Derg had certainly provided for us an astonishing variety of weather conditions. Though the encircling mountains were invisible we could somehow sense their presence, this opaque curtain being so much a part of them. The mist played us one odd trick. Dimly there appeared ahead what I took to be a red navigation marker upon a blackened cairn of stone. If it was indeed a red marker we were well off our course for it was far over on our port side whereas we should leave it to starboard. We both peered at it anxiously, and as we did so we suddenly realized that this curious mark was moving towards us. It presently revealed itself as a Grand Canal boat coming up from Killaloe. What we had taken for a marker was the bright red flash on her bow upon which her number was painted. We heard the steady beat of her Bolinder engine and caught a glimpse of the solitary muffled figure at the tiller as she slid by and was soon lost to sight astern.

Soon after this I was able to distinguish a ruined keep perched upon an islet off the Tipperary shore. On referring to the map, I decided that this could only be Derry Castle which meant that we were fast approaching the narrows which lead to Killaloe. The mist was thinning, both shores were now in view, and we picked up without difficulty the markers which indicate the channel out of the lake. Sailing down a wide river reach we presently saw on our right the entrance to Killaloe Lock Cut at the pier head. We swung into this and found a fine mooring beside the wall which, for most of its length, is all that divides the cut from the river. It was a quarter-to-ten, and as may be imagined we lost no time in preparing a substantial breakfast.

RIVER SHANNON. Killaloe. 'We found a fine mooring beside the wall that divides the cut from the river.'

KILLALOE AND LIMERICK

Killaloe, with its smaller township of Ballina just across the river bridge, occupies a magnificent situation in this narrow gorge which the Shannon has carved through the mountains. The waterfront facing the fine bridge is attractive; so is the narrow and steep main street at the foot of which stands the stately twelfth century cathedral of St. Lua. Yet there seemed to me to be a slightly drab and dejected air about Killaloe for which I suspect that Ardnacrusha is at least partly responsible. For Killaloe, like O'Briensbridge and the even more celebrated Castleconnell, was a great resort of fishermen until the advent of the Shannon scheme. 'The dam' at Parteen which diverts the river into the great headrace, or Ardnacrusha Canal as it is usually called, ruined rod fishing by altering the river levels. Upstream of the dam the level has been raised to such an extent that the Shannon spreads into a lake below Killaloe. The rapids above the bridge have ceased to exist and boats need no longer use the cut where the water makes a level at the lock. While Killaloe has too much water from the fisherman's point of view, O'Briensbridge and Castleconnell have too little, for, except in time of high flood, practically the whole flow is diverted at Parteen. Only a mere trickle is released to flow down the famous falls of Doonnass over which the mighty river once thundered like a gigantic mountain stream. It is this prodigal display of power which has now been harnessed at Ardnacrusha. By means of the Parteen dam and the titanic headrace, a fall of a hundred and ten feet has been obtained at the power station, and the water rushes down four penstocks twenty feet in diameter, each of which drives a 40,000 H.P. turbine. However much one may regret the virtual destruction of this beautiful reach of the river, or the conversion of Lough Allen into a reservoir, one must admit that, by modern standards, Ireland has paid an astonishingly small price for so much power. The waters of the river are not polluted or heated; the source of power is inexhaustible and does not therefore involve any squandering of natural capital resources and consequently none of the ugliness which such exploitation involves. No miners toil in their dim galleries, no headgears spin or spoil heaps spread to feed the turbines, while at the power station itself there is no smoke, no tall chimneys or cooling towers; only a lofty building filled with the surge of turbines as the Shannon thunders down the penstocks at the rate of four hundred tons a second.

It is the geological structure of Ireland which, by forming a natural dam at Killaloe, has made the Shannon scheme practicable, and there are probably few places in Europe, and certainly none in England, where as much water power could be harnessed for no greater expenditure of labour. Looking at a relief map of Ireland it appears incredible that the Shannon should furrow this gorge through the mountains when, by turning westwards it could fall by an easy course into Galway Bay. The answer is that when the Shannon first formed its course to the sea there was no mountain barrier because the limestone plain was then a high tableland. In the course of ages the limestone has eroded away leaving the harder Silurian and Devonian formations to form the mountains of Killaloe, the Slieve Blooms, and the Curlieus. Throughout this age-long process of change the Shannon has continued to pursue its original course, but as the levels of the limestone plain dropped, so the Silurian dam at Killaloe gradually formed the Shannon's chain of lakes.

The first church at Killaloe is said to have been founded in the sixth century by St. Lua, the first bishop, and the present cathedral, which is believed to occupy the same site, is attributed to Donal O'Brien, king of Munster. The cruciform exterior, though pleasing in its texture and proportions, lacks any especial feature worthy of note. The chief glory of the cathedral is the beautiful interior doorway in the south wall. Now converted into a window, it is of Hiberno-Romanesque architecture and consists of four orders of intricate and beautiful workmanship, some of it alas, sadly weathered and mutilated. Close beside it is preserved a curious stone, presumably the stump of a cross, which was discovered in 1916, built into the churchyard wall. It is the only stone so far discovered in Ireland which bears a Runic inscription, and the only one in existence which possesses an Ogham inscription also. Both have been deciphered. The Runic reads: 'Thorgrimr carved this Cross' and the Ogham: 'A blessing upon Thorgrimr'. The stone is believed to date from the eleventh century.

Apart from these two treasures, the interior contains little of note, in fact it presents as horrid an example of misguided restoration as I have seen. To make matters worse, the nave and the transepts have been screened off from the crossing, a process which has most effectually dismembered the church and made it quite impossible to appreciate its proportions. We persevered, however, and in examining the memorial tablets on the north wall of the chancel we were rewarded by the following interesting epitaph:

Sacred to the memory of
JOHN GRANTHAM
Civil Engineer.
Formerly of the 11th Light Dragoons
who died in Limerick
on the 23rd of February 1833
aged 58 years.
This monument was erected
by a few of his friends
in testimony of their esteem
for his private worth
and as a memorial of his
having made the first survey
of the RIVER SHANNON

with a view of improving it
and of his having been
the first who introduced
STEAM NAVIGATION
on its waters in the year 1825.

This John Grantham, I have subsequently discovered, was John Rennie's assistant, and it was in this capacity that he undertook the Shannon survey and also a number of other canal and railway projects in Ireland and England. His steam vessels plied not only upon the Shannon, but also on the Grand Canal for they are spoken of as trading between Dublin and Limerick. His system was taken up by the City of Dublin Steam Packet Company and was continued until rail competition diverted the traffic. In this work he was assisted by his son John Grantham II (1809-1874). [1] I would dearly like to know more details of these early steam vessels.

Beside the cathedral stands a small stone church attributed to the seventh century St. Flannan, but which is almost certainly of later date. It has an overcroft, reached through an opening at the west end, set in the steeply pitched stone roof, and by a stone roof I do not mean stone slates or tiles, but a roof of jointed masonry of immense strength and in perfect preservation. A similar though smaller church stands in the precincts of the Catholic church at the top of the hill. This is the oratory of St. Lua which originally stood upon Friars Island in the Shannon a few miles below Killaloe. Before this island was submerged by the Shannon scheme the chapel was dismantled and re-erected on its present site, a proceeding which demonstrates a respect for historical monuments which seems to be all too rare in Ireland.

A great wealth of history, myth and legend which I will not attempt to detail, is associated with the neighbourhood of Killaloe. Much of it deals with the great palace of Kincora where the celebrated Brian Boru once held court in great state. On a spur of glacial drift which commands the once fordable point where the Shannon leaves Lough Derg there is a fort with inner and outer fosse and vallum which is often said to be Kincora, though informed opinion seems to be that the palace stood on the top of the hill near the present Catholic church.

Oh, where, Kincora, is Brian the Great?
And where is the beauty that once was thine?
Oh, where are the princes and nobles that sate
At the feast in thy halls and drank the red wine?
Where, oh, Kincora?

Thus runs Brian's chief bard's lament for the king and his palace as translated by that unhappy, tragic poet James Clarence Mangan.

[1] Institute of Civil Engineers, *Proceedings*, vol. xxxix, p. 266.

Upon the shoulder of Tountinna opposite there is a mound and a row of slate slabs. These are attributed to the Bronze Age, but they are known as The Graves of the Leinster Men in commemoration of the ambush of the King of Leinster and his men, at the instigation of the wife of Brian Boru, as the king was on his way to Kincora to sue for the hand of Brian's daughter.

The mountain is also associated with another and far older legend which is of much greater and wider interest being no less than a Celtic version of that flood myth which is woven into the folklore of the world. This story, which is related in *Lebor Cabala Erenn* - 'The Book of the Taking of Ireland' - tells how Cessair the daughter of Bith ('Life'), and Fintan the Deathless, the son of Bochna ('Ocean') were warned of the coming of the flood and told that only in Ireland would they escape destruction. In company with others they sailed from the Island of Meroe on the Nile and after many protracted vicissitudes landed in Ireland from one of the three ships which put out. But when the flood came all were drowned except Fintan who had found refuge on the summit of Tountinna.

It may well be that beneath the irrelevant and misleading accretions of unnumbered centuries there lies in this story a hard core of historical truth. For the Diffusionists have amassed a formidable body of evidence which suggests that civilization did not appear spontaneously in different lands, but that it originated from a common source in the Mediterranean basin. At the same time geologists tell us that the Mediterranean Sea was formed by the inundation of a fertile basin, while ethnologists assert that the Celt is of Mediterranean stock.

After the bleak levels of the plain, the luxuriance of this sheltered gorge of Killaloe was very striking. Great bushes of hydrangeas laden with blossom grew beside the old lock on the cut, and when we walked up a narrow valley in the Slieve Bernagh mountains on the day after our arrival we found fuchsias and gladioli flourishing amidst the bracken and bell heather high up on the mountain sides. They were obviously escapes from the gardens of the ruined crofts which, alas, were all too numerous on the higher levels.

On our way back from this walk we passed along the steep flank of Crag Mountain which rises sheer from the lake, and in so doing passed by Greenanlaghua or Greenaun. This is by repute a Sidh or Fairy Fort, and according to the annals of Lough Ce it was the home of Aeibhill, banshee of Brian Boru and his Dalcassian ancestors. From the highest point of our walk, Lough Derg had been invisible, lost in the deep gorge, and we had had a magnificent view of range beyond range of mountains, the Silvermines, Keeper Hill, Mother Mountain, Slieve Felim, and far, away towards the skyline, cloud capped Galtymore. Now the more distant peaks had vanished, but as we came to Greenaun the lake suddenly came into view far below with the noble shape of Tountinna rising beyond. So steep was the declivity that it looked as though we could lob a pebble into the lake, yet

RIVER SHANNON, Killaloe. 'Great bushes of hydrangeas laden with blossom grew beside the old lock on the cut.'

such was the scale of the landscape that a Grand Canal boat, heading down the lake towards Killaloe, was dwarfed into insignificance. It resembled a minute black slug crawling slowly over a smooth surface of frosted glass and leaving in its wake a long trail of silver.

The branch railway line to Killaloe, which extends to a lakeside quay, has been dosed. When we walked along the rust-reddened rails down to the quay, a donkey was dozing, head a-droop, on the platform of the forlorn little station which, incidentally, is situated in Ballina on the Tipperary shore and not in Killaloe at all. For this reason we had perforce to take a bus when we decided to visit Limerick.

Even had time allowed, we had not planned to extend our voyage any further south than Killaloe, and on our road journey to Limerick we saw nothing to make us regret this decision. We obtained several good views of the Ardnacrusha Canal as well as of the power station itself. The canal is certainly a work of impressive magnitude but from the point of view of the water traveller it makes a very dull highway, an aquatic equivalent of an arterial road. From the average cruiser it would obviously be impossible to see anything of the surrounding countryside owing to the height of the banks. Unless, therefore, the water traveller has some particular reason for calling at Limerick, or wishes to explore the Shannon estuary beyond, he would be well advised to follow our example.

There are two Limericks. The traveller passing through the town in course of a journey as we had done on our arrival sees the spacious Georgian city of O'Connell Street and its neighbours, streets which boast of many houses that rival those of the Dublin squares in their elegant proportions and beautiful doorways. But on this occasion we were able to go further afield, and thus we saw Limerick of the slums. After that, even O'Connell Street seemed to have changed for the worse. Our perspective of the city had altered, and Georgian Limerick now resembled a thin fancy crust on a very unsavoury pie. There may be slums as bad or worse in Dublin, but if there are we did not see them even though we did penetrate into some mean quarters of that city. It is only fair to add that we saw evidence that much slum clearance work has already been done in Limerick, and doubtless much more would have been accomplished had it not been for the 'emergency'. In this matter of slum clearance, Ireland would seem to be about a quarter of a century behind England, for I have childhood recollections of slums in our cities as bad as those in Limerick to-day.

Materially, we have now virtually eliminated such slums in England, and this overdue reform must undoubtedly have improved the physical health of our urban population. But what our earnest reformers have failed to take into account is that the slum is a portent of spiritual as well as physical degradation. Rehousing, proper drainage, running water, health clinics and such-like improvements, estimable though they may be, are no cure-all. They are powerless to solve the problem of the spiritual impoverishment of urban man in this twentieth century. On the contrary they may even aggravate it. Though much could be said against these Limerick slums, as we walked through them we were bound to admit that they positively teemed with life, rich, abundant and full of character for all its squalor. Just as the body's vital forces muster to fight disease germs, so, perhaps, this is nature's reaction to bad living conditions. By comparison, the workers' flats and housing estates with which we have replaced our slums have no such character or vitality. In our sincere effort to make them physically sterile we have made them spiritually sterile also. This is not an argument in favour of slums, it is a statement of a problem which must be solved. If it is not, the urban 'worker' will become a mechanized moron without a soul. It remains to be seen whether Ireland will succeed in solving the problem more effectually than we have done. The answer, I believe, does not lie in the new housing estates which are growing round Dublin and Limerick. It is more fundamental. It is to be found in the ruined crofts which we had seen the day before, submerged in a creeping tide of bracken, on the shoulders of Slieve Bernagh.

In the course of our perambulation we stood upon Limerick's fine bridge and looked down at the waters of the noble Shannon now restored to their rightful bed. We walked the quays, fascinated, as always, by the shipping and the inevitable sights, sounds and smells associated with a seaport. We visited the Cathedral of St. Mary with its great Norman doorway, and thought that the nave with its massive rectangular columns was the most impressive church interior which we had seen in Ireland. We also admired the finely carved misericords of the choir stalls, the only examples in the country. But it was when we visited the Grand Canal depot that we saw the most interesting thing that we encountered that day. The depot is situated at the end of the old canal, and now that the canal is no longer used, craft enter and leave via the lock into the river. Yet as we stood upon the lockside, we saw, coming down the canal, a small boat which appeared to be heavily laden, being very low in the water. As it approached us we saw that it was a primitive type of dredger. It carried a long dredging 'spoon' consisting of stout sacking rigged on a metal frame at the end of a long shaft which could be slung from a simple wooden jib mounted amidships. Except for the small size of the boat and the curious construction of the spoon, the outfit was similar to the old spoon dredging boats of our canals. One man stood in the boat steering with a sweep over the stern, while a second, walking barefoot with his trouser rolled to his knees, was bow-hauling along the towing path. Why, I thought, should they be dredging a disused canal? When the men tied up at the head of the lock I looked down and saw that the boat was loaded, not with mud as I had expected, but with clean sand. The bow-haulier was now resting from his labours, and as may be imagined we were soon talking to him.

They worked their boat along the old canal and onto the Shannon below the falls at Plassy. At this point the waters of the river, stilled after their rapid descent, have deposited a great bed of sand which, being ready washed, finds a good sale to the building trade. Our informant's name was Frawley, and for three hundred years, he maintained proudly, the Frawley family had been engaged in this singular trade of delving in their submarine sand-pit. In all those years, he declared, they had had no cause to change their equipment, and looking at his craft with its load of eight tons, I could well believe him. Had he been at the job all his working life? No, sometimes he went to sea for a spell - most of his family did that - but like them he always came back to the old job. He assured us with great emphasis that it was a very healthy occupation. Almost always he went barefoot and, said he, shaking a shapely foot, he never suffered from corns.

Thus did Limerick make notable contribution to our collection of queer trades. It remains to be seen whether Ardnacrusha, by reducing the flow down the falls will so diminish the rate or deposition that the sand will eventually be worked out. I hope this does not happen. All such curious and distinctive local trades make their contribution to the local scene and their passing is always a loss.

CHAPTER SEVENTEEN

BACK TO ATHLONE

On the evening of the day after our visit to Limerick we regretfully set sail from Killaloe with our old moorings off Goose Island in Dromineer Bay as our objective. In exactly a week's time we were due back at Athlone, and we wished to see more of Lough Derg and to accept the pressing invitation of some friends whom we had met at the regatta.

A golden evening made ample recompense for our mist-shrouded arrival, and as we sailed up Killaloe Bay the mountains looked magnificent. The steep flank of Tountinna glowed in the westering sunlight which left the opposite slope of Crag Mountain with its fairy fort wrapped in deep shadow, a shade which extended over the water.

It was sheltered in this deep defile, but when we emerged from the lee of Scilly Island we discovered that a fresh west wind was blowing down the length of Scarriff Bay and *Le Coq* was soon rolling heavily with the weather on her beam. We met the inevitable *St. James* with a loaded canal boat in tow. The *St. James* was travelling well, and her tow appeared to me to have perilously little freeboard even for these comparatively calm conditions. She was wallowing along, the water foaming and boiling over her bluff bows as she seemed scarcely to respond at all to these short steep seas but to buffet her way through them. Having studied the behaviour of this boat through the binoculars I can feel little surprise at the disastrous loss of the M 45. It struck me at the time that in rough weather on the lakes the standard type of Irish canal boat would have a perilously low safety factor, when loaded.

Once we were well clear of Parker Point we were able to alter course and run easily and swiftly before the wind across the wide mouth of Youghal Bay and into Dromineer. Once again we made fast at the little floating stage by the island, and after dinner rowed ashore to renew our acquaintance with Mr. Flynn of the hospitable Dromineer Hotel.

The next morning broke fair and so warm that I indulged in a bathe in the lake before breakfast. We decided to take advantage of the good weather by doing some exploring, and it was not long before we were heading across the bay and past the Cribby Islands in the direction of Illaunmore. As we cautiously approached the southern shore of the island we could see the island farmer's black, swim-ended, flat-bottomed boat or 'cot' lying in his little harbour, but the entrance proved to be so narrow and beset with rocks that we put about, dropped anchor fifty yards off shore, and entered the harbour in the dinghy. We found no rowing boat there. It being a Sunday, the farmer and his family had

200

presumably gone to Mass on the mainland for the whole place lay silent and deserted. Sheltered among trees close by the harbour, the little farm drowsed in the bright sunshine. Over the wall of the neighbouring paddock a fine young short-horn bull gazed at us inquisitively. Judging from the well-filled barn, all the hay crop had been saved in good condition (no mean achievement that uncertain summer) and we noticed that the farm had its own grinding mill. Walking out of the farm-yard into the fields we saw a fine flock of Roscommons at pasture, a good field of oats, and the best and cleanest field of wheat that I saw in Ireland. I was not surprised later when I was told that Illaunmore was reputed to be some of the best land in the district, and that the island farmer 'bulled his own cows', which is the Irish way of saying that he was a 'strong' farmer. With his lands set like a green and amber jewel in the heart of this great lake, he is certainly lord of all he surveys in his own little kingdom.

LOUGH DERG. Illaunmore. 'Sheltered among the trees the little farm drowsed in the bright sunshine.'

When we left Illaunmore, we ran into Castletown Bay with the idea of mooring for lunch at Luska Quay. When we had passed Buggane Island at the mouth of the bay, we came up fairly close in to the south shore, for our chart told us that the centre of the bay was shallow and beset with submerged rocks and shoals. Luska Quay would appear to be disused, for we could not pick up any channel through the reeds which seemed to grow right across the end of the bay. Twice we cruised up and down peering through our glasses and then, as a westerly breeze was getting up and was tending to blow us onto the shore, we put about. Heading straight across the lake, we ran into the harbour of Williamstown on the Galway shore, and moored alongside the stone pier. Williamstown is the finest and most sheltered harbour on the lake. Not only is there a splendid anchorage within the long protecting arm of the pier, but there is also a commodious, tree-surrounded inner basin where craft can lie up securely in the worst of weather. How bad that weather can be the pier bore witness, for on the weather side the massive masonry had been torn apart so savagely that the wall will soon be breached if nothing is done. Situated close to the main line of navigation down the lake, Williamstown is a favourite place of refuge in times of sudden storm. Because it is a private harbour, however, the crews of storm-bound Grand Canal boats are not permitted to land but must needs make their craft fast to a rectangular framework of piling set out in the anchorage from which, as they carry no dinghy, they are unable to get ashore. As this framework has no staging they cannot even step off their boats. How a boat's crew are expected to obtain sufficient food if a protracted blow should strand them at Williamstown for any length of time is not clear. I fear that this is typical of the attitude of the lake-side residents towards the working boatmen who, without dinghys, anchors or any other safeguards, must ply over these treacherous waters at every season. I should doubt whether any inland navigators in the British Isles undertake such hazardous work and get so little credit for it as do these Grand Canal men who operate the lake service. I will admit that many of them are rough diamonds, and while we found them unfailingly helpful and kindly, we heard several stories of their depredations which I do not disbelieve. But to treat them as 'untouchables' is the better calculated to provoke rather than to amend such behaviour.

We felt disinclined to leave Williamstown that afternoon. We sprawled upon cushions on the deck in the bright sunshine soothed to somnolence by the sound of lake water lapping gently against the breakwater. The stones of the pier were carpeted with wild thyme; honey-heavy bees droned about it, and the warm air was aromatic with its fragrance. But this languorous afternoon was not without incident. An empty canal boat suddenly appeared and made fast to the piling. She was one of the bye-traders which carry turf from the quay at Garry Kennedy, and we wondered what she could be doing here on this fine Sunday afternoon. We were not left long in doubt, for presently a rowing boat put out from the shore heavily laden with the ample matrons of some neighbouring village who were assisted into the canal boat to the accompaniment of much laughter and badinage. Time and again the sweating oarsman returned to the shore for a further load until the hold was quite full; the parish priest, who was apparently superintending the loading, hopping about on the deck plating like some lank black crow. When all were safely on board, the boat put out across the lake. One of the few menfolk present had brought his 'music', with him, and as they moved away the company burst into song. When the boat had become a small black speck in the blue, the sound of their voices, punctuated by the popping of the engine still carried faintly across the water. I thought what a pleasant form of outing it was, and wondered why in England we so seldom used our canal boats for such a purpose.

Scarcely had the canal boat disappeared when we saw white sails bearing towards us and soon recognized the *Tyg-na-Mara* which had lain beside us off Goose Island during the regatta. She was a large and curious craft which had begun life as a patent steel lifeboat which was supposed to be mounted on the deck of a steamer and to float off if the ship went down. She was of such a size that the project struck me as quite fantastic, and I was not surprised to hear that it proved a failure. Though of shallow draught, she had a large centre board, and when she was brought over from England in bad weather she proved herself an excellent sea boat. Though for her original purpose she may have proved a failure, rigged for sail and with twin auxiliary engines, she made an admirable and very

LOUGH DERG. 'The Tyg-na-Mara looked a fine sight as she came towards us, her white sails gleaming in the sunshine.'

roomy cruiser particularly suited to the lake on account of her shallow draught. She looked a fine sight as she came towards us, her white sails gleaming in the sunshine. Anchoring some little distance off the pierhead, her crew came ashore and were surprised to find *Le Coq* which had hitherto been hidden from them by the pier wall. We had a drink together to celebrate our unexpected meeting, and in return we were generously invited to dinner on the *Tyg-na-Mara* at her moorings off Riskaheen. We accordingly followed them back across the lake, and when they had anchored we came up and made fast to the stern of the larger boat.

Tyg-na-Mara seemed a veritable luxury liner after our cramped quarters, and we were so hospitably entertained on board that it was pitch dark by the time we eventually took our leave. We found our way back to our Goose Island mooring in the pale starlight after a most enjoyable day.

We had been invited to come for a sail in *Tyg-na-Mara* next day, and in return we had undertaken to convey a bicycle from Dromineer to Riskaheen. Having duly collected the machine in the dinghy and lashed it on top of the wheelhouse we set out. A fresh west wind had raised with quite a swell, but the task of coming alongside *Tyg-na-Mara* and transferring the bicycle was accomplished without untoward incident. Not trusting our anchor after our previous experience, we then manœuvred *Le Coq*·into the little private harbour at Riskaheen, rowed back to *Tyg-na-Mara* and presently set sail. It was grand to watch the sails fill and to feel the boat come alive and glide smoothly across the water. Once out of the lee of the land we travelled splendidly, the big hull riding easily, swinging along with an almost lazy motion through waters which would have made our little cockle shell bob about like a cork. Tackle creaked and strained, sunlight sparkled on the spray flung from the bow, the tonic west wind sang through the rigging and, an added fascination not to be found at sea, the eye was often drawn to the splendid panorama of the encircling mountains which stood clear and blue in the evening light.

We came about off Williamstown, but by this time the sun was setting, the wind had dropped, and on our return journey we found ourselves almost becalmed - another example of the sudden vagaries of Lough Derg weather. *Tyg-na-Mara's* engines were not started, however, and eventually the light evening airs wafted her slowly but surely back to her anchorage. Here we said farewell to her friendly company, and moving *Le Coq* out of the harbour, sailed back across the lake that was now calm and golden in the reflected sunset light to Williamstown where we had decided to lie for the night.

The good weather still held next morning when we left Williamstown and moved up the lake, bound for the Long Quay at Kilgarvan where lived yet another of our regatta friends who had pressed us to call on him on our return journey. Travelling well before a light south wind, it was not long before we spotted Kilgarvan through the glasses. Leaving the main line of navigation and heading for the quay, we were soon near enough to see the familiar figure of our friend moving his own boat (a Galway Pookawn which he had converted himself) and waving to us from the end of the breakwater.

It was a grand hospitable welcome that he and his wife gave us, and a fine dinner that we had that night in their lovely house that looked out over the lake from among the trees by the shore. A great talk we had too, so that it was late when we took the path through the wood back to the Long Quay. It was pitch dark and there was not a star to be seen. A great wind was roaring through the branches overhead, and as we heard the sound of the waves beating upon the shore we were glad to think we had found so snug a berth. Soon after we had slipped into our bunks it began to rain heavily, but the wind showed no sign of abating.

It was still blowing half a gale the next morning and, though the rain had ceased, a tattered wrack of low flying clouds was sweeping across the sky from the south-west. Waves were thundering against the weather side of the quay and sending clouds of fine spray flying over the wall, while white and amber coloured flecks of foam lay quivering or blew about like cotton wool on the stones beside the boat. It was obviously impossible for us to leave until the wind moderated.

That afternoon our friend and I walked into the nearby village of Ballinderry where we visited Dick Stanley the local baker and proprietor of the village shop. At this point I must confess that I had formed the conclusion during our tour that the Irishman has little talent for craftsmanship of any high order. While I had seen much solid honest workmanship, I had also seen much rather shiftless bodging. My list of the examples of fine craftsmanship which we had seen was a short one: the tweeds of Connemara and Donegal which we had seen at Galway and Sligo; the boats of Athlone; the carts of a wheelwright at Roosky; neat thatch in some of the villages. Upon this conclusion I had built a theory that not only lack of mineral resources but the Irish lack of the Saxon's patient skill accounts for the fact that Ireland has not been industrialized. For surely it was very largely the Saxon genius in the manual arts which made possible the industrial revolution and which thus enabled him to create a monster which has now robbed him of his own genius. I do not know whether there is any truth in this theory or not, but I do know that Dick Stanley undermined it for me and made me think again.

In the intervals of baking bread and minding his shop, Dick Stanley makes violins. His art is entirely self taught, he uses the crudest of tools, and he finds and seasons his own materials. He showed us one instrument which he had recently completed and another which was in the course of construction. Though my companion had already told me something of his activities I had expected something which, though praiseworthy enough, bore all the evidence of amateur workmanship. Consequently, even if I had been told nothing I could scarcely have shown more surprise when Dick Stanley placed in my hands the beautiful, perfectly finished violin that he had made. Had I not seen the same fine craftsmanship exhibited in the other instrument which was under construction, I doubt if I should have believed that he really had made it. The sound-board was cut from a pinewood beam salvaged from a ruined mill nearby, the body was of sycamore, the pegs of holly wood, while the bridge and frets were of black bog oak dug from the neighbouring bog. None of the instruments he had so far made were exactly the same. He had begun by copying an old fiddle, but he had discovered the improvement and differences in tone which were produced by subtly varying the shape and depth of the sound-box or the thickness of the sound-board. No doubt these critical dimensions are well known and have been standardized by commercial makers but Dick Stanley took nothing for granted. Like all true craftsmen he strove for perfection and expressed a dissatisfaction with his violins which was not false modesty. He admitted, however, that each instrument he had made had a better tone than its predecessor, and his latest one certainly sounded the mellow soul of sweetness as he ran the bow over it. Unfortunately, however, he could not give us an adequate idea of its capabilities because, strange to relate, he was no performer on the violin. He played the flute, using an old finger-stopped instrument with which he often obliged at local gatherings and it was his son who played his fiddles.

When we had taken our leave of this accomplished craftsman we adjourned to John Tierney's Bar close by, where, to the accompaniment of much village gossip and racy badinage, we fortified ourselves against our walk through the rough weather with pints of porter. Then back to Kilgarvan where we were once more royally entertained despite our protestations that we had surely outstayed our welcome. Never were stormbound travellers so fortunate in their haven.

All that night and all the next day the storm continued. No sign of a break appeared in the grey clouds and the leaden waters of the lake were whipped into a fury of swift white horses. This was Thursday, and we were due back at Athlone on Saturday. We began to be alarmed lest the continuance of the storm should wreck our carefully arranged time-table of departure. That evening, however, the wind showed some slight signs of moderating, and we decided if it proved at all practicable we would repeat the tactics we had adopted at Mountshannon, slipping away at sunrise the next morning. We therefore said farewell to our long-suffering host and hostess and went early to bed. We were in luck, for when we awoke a pallid sunrise was visible, and though the lake still heaved uneasily the wind had dropped to a light but searchingly cold breeze. It would probably rise with the sun, so we got under way without delay.

This was our farewell to Lough Derg the beautiful and treacherous. The great lake looked very cold and lonely that raw morning; a vast expanse of rolling leaden waters touched here and there with a pale golden light from the fitful uncertain sun low in the east. The Irish are not notably early risers, and we saw not a sign of life on lake or shore. We felt very much alone and yet in some strange way exhilarated as *Le Coq* steadily forged her way northwards to Portumna. No untoward incident occurred. At a quarter to nine we passed between the buoys that mark the mouth of the river, and in a few minutes more we were preparing breakfast at our mooring below Portumna Bridge. As the day wore on the sky brightened, but as we had anticipated, the wind freshened. That, however, was now a matter of small concern. We replenished out stores in Portumna and after lunch continued on this the last lap of our journey. The bridge swung open for us, while Monsignor Joyce and the ever helpful Mr. Flynn waved us good-bye from the bank.

Little more, alas, remains to be said of our water journey. We lay at Banagher Quay that night, and at six o'clock on the following evening, having run exactly to schedule, we entered the lock at Athlone. It was one of those queer little ironical tricks of fate that we had just passed under Athlone railway bridge, and were within twenty yards of our permanent moorings when our old engine, which had driven us so bravely round Lough Derg where a falter might have spelt disaster, suddenly stalled. I checked the petrol, found there was plenty left and wound the starting handle fruitlessly. We began to drift slowly back towards the bridge. Hauling the dinghy alongside, we, towed Le Coq those last few yards up to her mooring. I then investigated, and soon discovered a short circuit in the earthing wire to the magneto. When the contact-breaker cover was removed, the old engine sprang to life as cheerfully as ever. It was a trivial fault for which, in other circumstances, we might have paid dearly before I had had time to trace it.

Most of the last few days which remained to us were devoted to the somewhat melancholy tasks of clearing up, packing, making *Le Coq* ship-shape after her long voyage, and completing the arrangements for our return to England. On one evening we entertained Jack and Dolly Beahan, and on the next, our last in Athlone, we came at their invitation to a farewell party at their friendly and now familiar little house. It was an evening that I shall never forget. Sean was there to sing in his sweet tenor voice, Jack played the clarinet, a friend of his had brought his fiddle, Angela her flute, and together we played and sang again all the old tunes, 'Galway Bay', 'Kevin Barry', 'I'll Take You Home Kathleen' and many more. Our fiddler, who played entirely by ear, knew the air of 'The Wild Colonial Boy' and as we now had the words we were able to sing this old ballad also. But the tune that lingers most hauntingly in my mind and which I shall always associate with our farewell to Ireland was a song that Sean sang for us. It was a lament for a tragedy of the time of the 'Black and Tans' and he called it 'The Woods of Drumbo'. But I suspect that, like most of the songs of this period, the air to which it was sung was far older. As is usually the case with these old tunes, in each verse the first and fourth lines and the second and third lines were sung to the same refrain. But despite this simplicity, this air, in the plaintive melancholy of its cadences, seemed to express that tragic sense, the sorrow and heartache, which is a part of the soul of the Gael and which seems to lurk even in the midst of his laughter. I am not of Irish blood, yet even to my mind, as Sean sang, there came images - I cannot call them memories for they were too intangible - of 'old unhappy far-off things'. These were the words of the song that he sang:

> 'T'was the eve of Saint Patrick at the dawn of the day,
> The hills of Tyrconnell lay slumbering grey,

The first light of morning illumined the sky
As four Irish soldiers were led forth to die.

They were Enwright, O'Donnell and Daly by name,
From the Counties of Cork and Kerry they came,
While the gallant Stan Larkin from the banks of the Rowe
Completes the four martyrs shot dead at Drumbo.

Four Irish soldiers were dragged from their cell;
For months they had suffered the torments of hell.
No mercy they asked from their merciless foe,
And no mercy was shown by the Tans at Drumbo.

Three left their homesteads in Munster's green vale,
And one came from Derry to fight for the Gael,
But instead of true friendship they met traitor and foe.
Now they lie in their coffins at the woods of Drumbo.·

Church bells were ringing in the cool morning air
To bring forth the faithful in penance and prayer,
When a shot from the wild wood brought terror and woe,
'T'was the death knell of Daly, shot dead at Drumbo.

Let Tyrconnell not boast of her honour and fame;
All the waters that flow will not wash out the stain.
While the Foyle and the Swilly continue to flow
That stain will remain by the woods of Drumbo. [1]

[1] This was taken down verbally, and I cannot guarantee accuracy of spelling of proper names, wording or punctuation.

Like all good things, this last evening ended all too soon although the hour was late. Jack would see us off at the station on the morrow, but Dolly, knowing how unsatisfactory such protracted leave-takings always are, wisely chose this moment to bid us good-bye. Sadly then we tramped back through the dark and silent streets to spend our last night on the Shannon.

CHAPTER EIGHTEEN

FAREWELL TO IRELAND

It was on Wednesday, September 4th, that we took a last look round the little boat which had been our home for three months, and which had carried us so faithfully over four hundred and fifty miles of waterway. She looked sadly bare and forlorn now with all our belongings stripped from their accustomed places, a small empty house riding there on the broad Shannon. We lowered our luggage into the dinghy, locked the wheelhouse door for the last time, and rowed away to the shore.

Our slow journey back to Waterford might well have been a tedious anti-climax to this Irish tour, but I had been at some pains to ensure that this should not be so. Having explored the river and lake sections of the Shannon so thoroughly, I was anxious to catch at least a fleeting glimpse of the Shannon estuary. A careful study of train and bus time-tables had shown me that not only could I gratify this wish, but that we could combine it with a journey over what is probably the most fascinating of the surviving Irish narrow gauge railways - the West Clare line.

The West Clare was built under baronial guarantee between the years 1884 and 1892. Commencing at a junction with the broad gauge Limerick-Athenry line at Ennis, the county town of Clare, it runs north and west across the county to Lahinch. Thereafter it continues almost due south along the wild Atlantic seaboard of Clare to Moyasta Junction. Here the line forks into two branches, one terminating at the seaside town of Kilkee on the west coast, and the other at the port of Kilrush on the Shannon Estuary. The total length of the line is fifty-three miles, so it promised me the longest narrow gauge journey I had ever made. Calculating that the hotels of Kilkee would be crowded at this season, and having no liking for seaside resorts, I had sent a wire from Killaloe to William's Hotel at Kilrush, reserving a room for our last night on Irish soil. Once upon a time the Limerick Steamship Company operated a passenger service to Kilrush with which the West Clare trains ran in connection. This would have been a splendid way of rounding off our journey, but, sad to relate, like many other pleasant travelling facilities, this service has long ago been discontinued, and we should have to travel by bus to Limerick on the following morning in order to catch our Waterford train. I decided, however, that a journey over the West Clare would be well worth the inconvenience of the long bus journey, and I was not disappointed.

The attitude of the travelling public to-day towards road and rail travel strikes me as very curious though it may, perhaps, constitute a back-handed compliment to the railway. They will tolerate without a murmur what seemed to me to be incredible discomforts, delays and inconveniences when travelling in buses, yet the most trifling delay or discomfort on the rail will rouse them to urgent and furious protest. Though they offer a far smoother and more commodious form of transport than any bus, the narrow gauge railway obviously cannot provide as high a standard of speed and comfort as a broad gauge main line. Consequently these little enterprises have always been the butt of humour and abuse.

In this respect the West Clare line is no exception. It had not been in existence many years before it became the subject of a comic song which was, I understand, rendered with great success by the late Percy French, a noted performer on the concert platform of those days. It was called 'Are Ye Right There Michael' and is worth quoting in full.

> They may talk of Columbus' sailing,
> Across the Atlantical sea,
> But sure he never went railing,
> From Ennis as far as Kilkee,
> You run for the train in the morning,
> The excursion train starting at eight,
> You're there when the clock gives the warning,
> And there for an hour you'll wait.
> And as you're sitting in the train,
> You'll hear the guard sing this refrain:
> 'Are ye right there Michael, are ye right?
> 'Do ye think that we'll be there before the night?
> 'Ye couldn't say for sartain, ye were so late in startin,
> 'But we might now Michael, so we might'.
>
> They find out where the engine's been hiding.
> And it draws you to sweet Corofin,
> Says the guard, 'Back her down in the siding,
> There's the goods from Kilrush coming in'.
> Perhaps it comes in in two hours,
> Perhaps it breaks down on the way,
> 'If it does' says the guard, 'By the powers,
> 'We're here for the rest of the day'.
> And as you sit and curse your luck,
> The train backs down onto a truck,
> 'Are ye right there Michael, are ye right?
> 'Have ye got the parcel there for Mrs. White?
> 'Ye haven't, Oh begorra, say it's coming down to-morrow,
> 'And it might now Michael, so it might'.
>
> At Lahinch the sea shines like a jewel,
> With joy you are ready to shout,
> When the stoker cries out 'We've no fuel,
> 'And the fire's taytotally out,

'But give us a hand with that log there,
'I'll soon get ye out of a fix,
'There's a fine clamp of turf in the bog there,
'And the rest go a-gatherin' sticks'.
And while you're breaking bits off trees,
You'll hear some wise remarks like these:
'Are ye right there Michael, are ye right?
'Do you think that ye can get the fire to light?
'Oh an hour you'll require, for the turf it might be drier,
'And it might now Michael, so it might'.

Kilkee, Oh you never get near it,
You're in luck if the train brings you back,
For the permanent way is so queer, it
Spends most of its time off the track.
Uphill the old engine is toiling,
The passengers push with a will,
You're in luck when you reach Ennistymon,
For all the way home is downhill,
And as you're wobbling through the dark,
You'll hear the guard make this remark:
'Are ye right there Michael, are ye right?
'Do ye think that we'll be home before the light?
''Tis all dependin' whether, the old engine holds together,
'But we might now Michael, so we might'.

This poem © *Pigott & Co., Ltd., Dublin* inserted by special permission

This reputation of the West Clare seems to persist, for in an Irish newspaper, under the heading 'Nightmare Trip' I read a horrific account of a journey in which the train, leaving Ennis at 7.30 p.m. (two hours late) proceeded at 'a dreamy seven miles per hour' to bring 'the bored passengers and sleep-worried children' to the terminus at midnight. 'Of course', the writer concluded, 'There may be tourists who would like this sort of thing, but I don't think we should count on them'.

I suspected that these impressions of the line were somewhat exaggerated, but to be on the safe side I warned the hotel at Kilrush that we might arrive late, and we stepped out onto the platform at Ennis that evening prepared for the worst. I am, I suppose, one of those 'tourists who like this sort of thing' but I feel that even my enthusiasm might be a trifle damped by such a journey as this writer described. I need not have worried.

We consigned the bulk of our luggage direct to Limerick to await our arrival there next day, and booked a first class ticket to Kilrush. We might as well enjoy this protracted journey in the maximum of comfort and seclusion. The little train, the only one of the day, was standing in the bay, and we settled ourselves in a compartment that was a period piece in itself. The seats were covered with black American cloth well studded with buttons.

Braided arm rests (were they ever used?) were looped on the door pillars, and the captions of the ancient and faded photographs over the seat backs were hand written in painstaking copper-plate. To do justice to such an interior I should, I felt, be wearing a deer-stalker and an ulster, for it was in just such a compartment, one imagines, that Sherlock Holmes and his Watson sped down from Paddington to Devon to investigate the mystery of Silver Blaze.

IRISH NARROW GAUGE. A first class compartment on the West Clare line. 'To do justice to such an interior I should, I felt, be wearing a deerstalker and an Ulster.'

Punctually at 5.30, the train drew out. For a time we ran beside the broad gauge metals, but soon we veered away westwards and almost immediately plunged into one of the wildest tracts of country I have ever seen, country calculated to break any farmer's heart. Occasionally we sighted a solitary cabin, but for the most part we saw nothing but a wilderness of grey limestone outcrop covered with a stunted but dense scrub of thorn. At Corofin, the first important station and crossing place, the prospect improved somewhat, for there seemed to be some comparatively good pasture land between the lakes and rocks. So far we had been travelling well, certainly at no 'dreamy seven miles an hour', but now there ensued a long and laborious ascent of two and a half miles at gradients of 1 in 50 and 1 in 75 onto the summit level of the line, a boggy tract or moorland two hundred and fifty feet above sea-level. Despite this modest altitude, here, and on the long descent to Ennistymon which followed, we obtained some fine extensive views over this wild country of West Clare under a stormy sky.

At Ennistymon we made our only protracted halt. What we waited for I do not know. The fire was raked out and remade, the safety valves lifted, but still we waited. I concluded that we were waiting for an Ennis bound train to cross us, but nothing had arrived when we eventually drew out. As we did so we saw the little town clinging to the steep slopes of the gorge down which the Cullenagh River rushes to the sea.

Out train had been well filled at starting, but the majority got out at the next stop at the little seaside town of Lahinch where we passed the goods train which I had expected to see at Ennistymon. It is after leaving Lahinch that, from the scenic point of view, the most dramatic section of the line commences. It ascends steeply again for two miles, and as we panted up this long climb a truly magnificent panorama of one of the most savage, storm-swept coasts in Europe unfolded before us. We were fortunate in seeing it, not merely in clear weather, but under most dramatic conditions. Although there were dark clouds overhead, the fringe had lifted from the horizon of the western sea to leave a broad band of blue sky which, as the invisible sun sank, gradually brightened from azure to gold. Looking out towards this dazzling bar of light across the vast expanse of heaving ocean spreading without check to the Americas, it was easy to understand how tales of Hy Brasil, of magic islands in the farthest west, had fired the minds of men like Brendan. We saw the golden strand of Lahinch crooked in the elbow of Liscannor Bay, a white maelstrom of surge beating beneath the cliffs of Hags Head beyond. And as the train moved on we saw beyond the headland, the dark shape of Aran lying far out over Galway Bay.

Our next stop was at Milltown Malbay whence we could look down towards Spanish Point where, in 1588, six proud galleons of Spain's Armada were swept to destruction on this pitiless coast. So great is the fury of the Atlantic gales that stunted trees can only grow in the more sheltered places and, even so the winds have twisted and swept their branches eastward like manes of flying hair. At Quilty village, where the line is almost at sea-level, where station and post office are combined, and where we saw black upturned curraghs like stranded porpoises upon the beach, there is a wind gauge beside the line. If the velocity on this gauge reaches sixty miles per hour a warning message is sent down the line and only rolling stock which is specially weighted down with slabs of concrete is permitted to run. All traffic is suspended if the velocity reaches eighty miles per hour. Owing to the possibility of the warning not being received on account of telephone wires being blown down, it is a rule of the line that each stationmaster shall ask by phone whether the train may proceed. Failure to receive an answer is considered as a danger signal.

At each of these lonely, windswept stations along this wild coast we drew in to find the little platform crowded. But the anticipated invasion never came, and we realized that these primitive, weather-beaten people of West Clare had simply come to the station to 'meet the train'; to gaze at this one slender link of civilization and then to return to their lonely cabins until another day brings another train and with it another fleeting glimpse of strange faces and of the world beyond Clare.

After Doonbeg station we lost sight of the sea, cutting across the long narrow peninsula that guards the Shannon mouth and which terminates in Loop Head. It was fast gathering dark now, and a prospect more desolate than this great treeless expanse of marsh and bogland I have never seen.

Soon we drew into the triangular platform of Moyasta Junction, and here we changed into the single coach of the Kilrush train which was waiting at the opposite platform face, while our train went on to Kilkee. There was little delay, both trains starting out of the station simultaneously, and fortunately it was not yet too dark for me to see my last view of the Shannon. Swinging eastwards towards Kilrush, the line drew close to the shore and I could look out over the lonely saltings, through the narrows between Kileredann Point and Beal Bar, to where the dim majestic shape of Kerry Head marked the point where this great river is finally lost in the Atlantic. As we skirted the harbour of Kilrush, I caught a glimpse of Scattery Island with its ruined monastery of St. Senan and the dark finger of its round tower. Here Brendan is said to have made his first landing on his return from that momentous second voyage. But now this most interesting of railway journeys was over, and here I should like to note, for the especial benefit of the writer of 'Nightmare Trip' if he should chance to read this book, that we drew into the platform at Kilrush exactly on time.

There is little more to tell. Our hotel, which was an unknown quantity, proved to be clean and comfortable. We partook of an excellent meal followed by an equally good breakfast next morning. The bus conveyed us conveniently to the station yard at Limerick where we retrieved the rest of our luggage and entrained for Waterford. Altogether we voted our somewhat unusual choice of return route an unqualified success. I shall always remember my journey over the West Clare line. It was an experience which I should have been very sorry to miss, and one which is the more precious because I fear that before many years have passed, unless the public taste for travel changes, it may no longer be possible to repeat it.

As our steamer moved slowly away from Adelphi Wharf, most of the passengers crowded to the starboard rail, waving back to the flutter of hands on the quay. We, who had no one to wave to, stood on the port side looking down the river. And as we gazed what should appear round the bend between the woods but the familiar bluff-bowed shape of a Grand Canal boat, forging steadily up the river, the beat of her exhaust clearly audible in the evening air. As she passed by, puny beneath our sheer steel side, we waved. The man at the tiller looked up, grinned broadly and waved back. We had got our wave after all, nor could there have been any more fitting farewell.

Passage; Duncannon; Loop Head; the Irish coastline fading into the clear twilight astern; Fishguard in the early hours of the morning with the familiar line of cream and chocolate coaches standing under the lights. What were our reactions on returning to England with fresh vision? Chiefly, I am afraid, the lack of kindliness and courtesy, the sense of frenzied, purposeful, and yet somehow purposeless, hurry and bustle which left no time for the humanities. Everyone looked strained, their brows furrowed between the eyes. Partly, no doubt, the war is to blame for this, but not altogether. Here in England there is no longer 'time enough'. What, then, are my afterthoughts about Ireland when I look back now upon our visit? First and foremost I think of these very qualities which we seem to have lost; kindliness, courtesy, a greater respect for the humanities, a greater sympathy for man the individual with all his virtues, his follies and his frailties. The Irish Tourist Association publish a little book for the benefit of visitors called *Ireland of the Welcomes*. It is indeed well titled.

What does the future hold for Ireland? It would be rash indeed for me to prophesy on the strength of a mere three months' acquaintance. The present Government of the country appears to be representative of the tradesmen, the middle-class of Ireland, and in their policy they seem to be wavering between the rival claims of industry and agriculture to gain precedence in the future Irish economy. There are some Irish advocates of industrialism who prescribe a nostrum with which we are only too painfully familiar. Develop industry, they cry, not primarily to manufacture something which will bring tangible and real wealth to Ireland, but to provide employment and paper money. What to do with the product of this employment? Export! Export! they scream, but they do not say where they propose to export to in a world where the national monopolies of the great powers are preparing to do battle for shrinking markets upon a scale unparalleled.

Upon the other hand there are those who argue that Ireland should develop industries primarily to serve the needs of Ireland, and with these moderates I agree. I believe that by the wise use of modern technique, Ireland could in time become virtually self-supporting and at the same time export a substantial surplus of certain commodities. So long as this is the end in view, industry will never swell until it becomes the chronic disease of industrialism, sucking the life out of the land and its people, and turning men into machines for the sake of goods and currency becoming progressively more valueless as the monster grows.

A healthy, prosperous and populous agricultural community with an industry designed to meet its needs, this would be an ideal of the future Ireland which might set an example to the world. It is not easy of attainment. It involves many reforms including radical economic reform, but what else will prevent the young blood of Ireland from draining away from an impoverished countryside into swelling towns or overseas?

It was strange to visit a country where one heard no talk of 'Left' and 'Right' in politics. The 'Left' scarcely seems to exist for the simple reason that all collectivist doctrine is the political consequence of industrialism. If the 'export' school have their way and Ireland is industrialized, collectivism will at once gather strength, Catholicism or no Catholicism, The same problem will arise if Ireland wins back the Six Counties and with them that ugly duckling, industrialized Belfast. I am all in sympathy with those who urge the end of partition, but they should not overlook this eventuality.

We in England are too apt to regard the Irish national experiment as a piece of play-acting in questionable taste, or as a spiteful trick played by unruly children to annoy their elders and betters. With all its faults, and despite the bitterness and bloodshed which went to its making, the Free State is neither of these things. It is merely a result of our own mistakes in the past, and of the perfectly natural desire of the Irish people to lead their own lives in their own way in their own country. Such misunderstanding leads to arrogance or to patronizing contempt on the one hand and to sensitive suspicion and isolationism on the other. But we are near relations, our two islands are mutually interdependent, and the present state of our relationship is as ridiculous and futile as a family feud prolonged by custom. It will change for the better so soon as we can bring ourselves to be more tolerant, to put ourselves in the Irishman's place, and so to understand his desire for independence, and so soon as the Irishman in his turn ceases to nurse past wrongs. We each have much to give the other. We, I know, would benefit from a greater leavening of the Celtic concern for the humanities and for other than material things.

Whatever the future may hold, and whatever may be the relationship between our two countries in that future, this much I do know. That this voyage of ours over the silver waters and through the green fields of Ireland has brought to us both a precious store of memories which will remain with us always; nor shall we ever forget the kindliness and the welcome that we found there.

THE END

ITINERARY

NOTE: While I was responsible for the compilation of the Shannon and the Royal Canal itineraries, the Grand Canal Company most kindly prepared especially for me the tables relating to their canal. They are reproduced exactly as received.

ITINERARY

RIVER SHANNON NAVIGATION

MAIN LINE

Head of Lough Allen to –

Inishmagrath Island	0m 5f
Cormongan Point (left shore)	4m 4f
O'Reilly's Island	6m 3f
Rose Lodge, junction with Lough Allen Canal (not navigable) . .	8m 0f
Lough Acres	8m 5f
Drumleague Lock	10m 6f
Battlebridge Lock and junction with River Shannon	12m 3f

Battlebridge, head of present navigation, to -

Holly Park, junction with Leitrim River and line of Ballinamore and Ballyconnell Navigation (derelict). (Leitrim Quay distant 3 furlongs)	0m 5f
Junction with River Boyle Navigation	4m 5f
Carrick-on-Shannon Quays and Warehouses	5m 3f
Lough Corry	7m 0f
Jamestown Cut Junction (Jamestown Bridge and Quay distant 3 furlongs)	10m 3f
Albert Lock and end of Jamestown Cut (Drumsna distant 1 mile 5 furlongs)	12m 2f
Drumsna Railway Bridge, river enters Lough Tap	12m 6f
River enters Lough Boderg (approx.)	14m 5f
Derrycarne Narrows, river enters Lough Bofin	16m 3f
River leaves Lough Bofin (approx.)	18m 6f
Roosky Bridge, Quay and Warehouse	19m 3f
Roosky Lock	19m 6f
River enters Lough Forbes	23m 0f
River leaves Lough Forbes (approx.)	25m 1f
Tarmonbarry Bridge	27m 0f
Tarmonbarry Lock and Quay	27m 2f
Cloondara, junction with Cloondara Cut Branch, leading to Royal Canal	27m 6f
Lanesborough Bridge and Quay	34m 7f
Salisbury Lodge, River enters Lough Ree	36m 1f
Inchenagh Island (R.) (approx.)	39m 2f
Inchcleraun Island (R.) (Approx.)	43m 0f
Rindown Castle and Safe Harbour (R.)	46m 3f
Black Islands (L.) (Approx.)	46m 5f

Yew Point (R.)	49m 2f
Dead Man's Island, river leaves Lough Ree	52m 1f
Athlone Railway Bridge	53m 7f
Athlone Lock and Quay	54m 2f
Seven Churches (Clonmacnoise)	63m 7f
Shannonbridge Bridge and Quay	68m 7f
Junction with River Suck	69m 2f
Tesauren Ferry, junction with Grand Canal, main line right and left (Shannon Harbour distant 6 furlongs)	75m 2f
Banagher Bridge and quay	77m 3f
Shannon View House	79m 3f
Meelick, Victoria Lock	82m 0f
Portumna Bridge and Quay, and junction with Portumna Branch Cut. 2 furlongs in length. (Portumna distant 1¼ miles). NOTE: Headroom under Portumna Bridge is very restricted and craft larger than rowing boats or canoes must wait for bridge to be swung	90m 0f
River enters Lough Derg	91m 1f
Gortmore Point (L.)	93m 0f
Kilgarvan Quay (L. approx. 6 furlongs off course)	96m 2f
Goat Island Reef and marker (L.)	98m 5f
Illaunmore Island (L.) (Approx.)	100m 5f
Williamstown Harbour (R.)	102m 0f
Corrikeen Islands (L. Derry castle and Quay distant approx. 1 mile 6 furlongs)	102m 2f
Farrahill Point (R.), Ryans Point Reef, Riskaheen (L.) (Garrykennedy Quay approx. 1 mile 3 furlongs off course)	103m 5f
Scilly Island (R.), Head of Killaloe Bay	107m 3f
Derry Castle (L.)	110m 3f
Ballyvally, River leaves Lough Derg	112m 7f
Pier Head, junction with old Killaloe Cut (R.)	113m 5f
Killaloe Bridge, Lock and Quay (on old Cut)	114m 0f
Old Cut rejoins River, Cut not used beyond this point	114m 2f
Parteen Weir, junction with Ardnacrusha Canal	118m 2f
Ardnacrusha Lock and Power Station	125m 0f
Limerick Abbey River Lock, Quays and Warehouses	128m 0f

The following was the old line of navigation between Killaloe and Limerick prior to the opening of the Ardnacrusha Canal:
Killaloe Bridge, Lock and Quay to -

Moy's Lock	1m 0f
Cussaun Lock	1m 6f
Dorgan's Bridge, canal rejoins river	2m 0f
O'Briensbridge	5m 5f
Mona Lodge, canal leaves river	6m 6f

Erinagh Lock	9m 2f
Monaskeha Lock	9m 4f
Cloondara Lock	9m 6f
Newtown Lock	9m 7f
Gilloge Lock	11m 5f
Plassy Lock and Plassy Bridge, canal rejoins river	12m 3f
Canal leaves river	13m 4f
Park Lock	14m 0f
Limerick Lock, Junction with Abbey River branch	14m 4f
Limerick, Wellesley Bridge	14m 7f

RIVER BOYLE BRANCH

Junction with River Shannon to -

Mouth of Lough Drumharlow	0m 2f
Navigation leaves Lough Drumharlow	1m 5f
Cootehall Bridge and Quay	2m 5f
Mouth of Lough Oakport	2m 6f
Navigation leaves Lough Oakport	3m 2f
Knockvicar Bridge and Quay	4m 7f
Knockvicar Lock	5m 5f
Mouth of Lough Key	5m 6f
Navigation leaves Lough Key	9m 2f
Boathouse Ford, limit of Navigation (Boyle distant 1½ miles)	9m 6f

SCARRIFF BAY NAVIGATION

Scilly Island and Head of Killaloe Bay to -

Bushy Island (R. Mountshannon Harbour, 1 mile 2 furlongs off course)	1m 3f
Holy Island (R.)	2m 3f
Navigation enters River Scarriff.	4m 7f
Tuamgraney Quay	5m 7f
Navigation leaves River Scarriff and enters Scarriff Quay Cut (L.)	6m 2f
Scarriff Quay and Warehouse, terminus of Navigation	6m 3f

LOCKS, MAIN LINE

1. Drumleague
2. Battlebridge } Lough Allen Canal Section. Derelict
3. Albert Lock, Drumsna.
4. Roosky.

5. Tarmonbarry.

6. Athlone.

7. Meelick or Victoria Lock.

8. Ardnacrusha Double Lock.
   Fall from Lough Allen.

LOCKS, BRANCHES

1. Clarendon Lock, Knockvicar, Boyle Branch. Fall from Boyle.
2. Cloondara. This lock is situated on the Cut, 4 furlongs in length, connecting the River Shannon with the Royal Canal at the tail of Richmond Harbour Lock. Fall from Richmond Harbour.

DIMENSIONS

The maximum size of vessel which can navigate over the whole of the navigable portion of the river and its branches is as follows:

Length: 96 feet.

Beam: 19 feet.

Draught: 4 feet 6 inches (see note).

Headroom:

Abbey Bridge, Limerick at High water: 8 feet 9 inches.

Limerick to Killaloe Pierhead, approx: 13 feet.

Killaloe Pierhead to Jamestown Lock Cut: Not limited.

Jamestown Lock Cut to Battlebridge and Lough Key, approx: 15 feet.

NOTE.- There is a nominal minimum depth of water throughout the river and branches of 5 feet, but in dry seasons the level above Lanesborough may fall to 4 feet 6 inches in places.

The dimensions of the locks on the main line of navigation and branches are:

Main line: Locks 3, 4, and 5:	Length - 120 feet.	
	Width - 30 feet.	
Locks 6 and 7:	Length - 155 feet.	
	Width - 40 feet.	
Lock 8	Length - 105 feet.	
(Ardnacrusha):	Width - 19 feet 6 inches.	

Lock 8 is electrically operated and has a double lift, the combined fall being approximately 110 feet.

Branches: Locks 1 and 2 :	Length - 120 feet.	
	Width - 30 feet.	

A toll of 2s. 3d. is charged for passage through each lock and for opening each swing bridge. Unless overall height is exceptional, only Portumna Bridge need be opened. A through pass may be obtained.

Ardnacrusha Lock supersedes the locks on the old Limerick Canal section which is now disused. Ardnacrusha Power Station has altered the levels in the river and old cut at Killaloe with the result that under normal conditions the water at the head and tail of Killaloe Lock makes a level. In such circumstances either river or cut may be used at this point. The cut now rejoins the river 2 furlongs below Killaloe Bridge, and the canal section below this point is no longer used for navigation.

ROYAL CANAL

MAIN LINE

Dublin, North Wall Lift Bridge, Liffey Tidal Lock and entrance
      to Spencer Dock to -

Dublin, Spencer Dock, Sheriff Street Lift Bridge	0m 2f
Dublin, Amiens Street Loop Line Railway Lift Bridge	0m 5f
Dublin, North Strand Road Bridge and Lock No. 2	0m 6f
Dublin, Drumcondra Road Bridge and Double Lock No. 3	1m 3f
Dublin, Cross Guns, Junction with Broadstone Branch (1 f.) and head of Double Lock No. 5	1m 7f
Dublin, Mountjoy, head of Double Lock No. 7	2m 1f
H. S. Kelly's Bridge and Lock No. 9	3m 6f
Ashtown, Longford Bridge and Double Lock No. 11	4m 7f
Blanchardstown, Talbot Bridge and Double Lock No. 13	6m 2f
Granard Bridge	6m 5f
Kirkpatrick Bridge	7m 4f
Kennan Bridge	8m 0f
Clonsilla, Callahan Bridge	8m 6f
Pakenham Bridge	9m 4f
Coldblow and Lucan Station	10m 5f
Rye Water Aqueduct	12m 5f
Leixlip Station, Louisa Bridge	12m 7f
Decy Bridge and Lock No. 14	13m 7f
Pike Bridge	15m 0f
Maynooth Bridge and Duke's Harbour	16m 4f
Pond Bridge	16m 6f
Jackson's Bridge and Lock No. 15	17m 7f
Branganstown, Chamber's Bridge and Lock No. 16	19m 2f
Kilcock, Wharf, Bridge and Double Lock No. 17	20m 2f
Allen Bridge	20m 7f
McLoghlin's or Ferrans Bridge and Double Lock No. 18	22m 5f
Enfield Station and Bridge	28m 1f
Aqueduct over River Blackwater	30m 4f
Moyvalley Station and Bridge	32m 1f
Aqueduct over River Boyne	34m 6f

Blackshade Bridge	36m 1f
Hill of Down Station and Bridge	37m 5f
Ballasport Bridge	38m 4f
D'Arcy's Bridge	42m 2f
Thomastown Bridge and Killucan Bottom Lock, No. 19	43m 1f
Killucan Station, Bridge and Lock No. 23	44m 2f
Footy's Hill Bridge and head of Killucan Summit Lock No. 26	45m 0f
McNead's Bridge	46m 2f
Saunder's Bridge	52m 5f
Junction with Lough Owel Feeder (R.) (not navigable)	53m 5f
Mullingar Harbour and Scanlan's Bridge	53m 6f
Habsborough, Ballina Bridge	57m 4f
Shanonagh Bridge	59m 0f
Dolan Bridge and Coolnahay Top Lock No. 27	59m 7f
Coolnahay Bottom Lock No. 29	60m 3f
Cartron, Kildallan Bridge and Kildallan Top Lock No. 30	61m 3f
Kildallan Bottom Lock No. 34	62m 7f
Balroe Bridge and Lock No. 35	63m 5f
Ballynacarrigy Wharf, Bridge and Lock No. 36	64m 7f
Castlegaddery Top Lock No. 37	65m 7f
Castlegaddery Bottom Lock No. 39	66m 7f
Bog Bridge	68m 4f
Quinn's Bridge	69m 2f
Aqueduct over River Inny	69m 4f
Scally's Bridge	69m 6f
Abbeysrule Wharf and Webb's Bridge	70m 2f
Draper's Bridge and Lock No. 40	71m 2f
Fowlard's Bridge	74m 0f
Toome Bridge	75m 0f
Ballymahon Wharf and Longford Bridge (Ballymahon distant 1 mile)	76m 6f
Archie's Bridge	77m 2f
Mullawornia Lock No. 41	78m 2f
Pake Bridge	78m 7f
Keenagh Harbour and Island Bridge (Keenagh distant 5 furlongs)	81m 7f
Coolnahinch Bridge and Lock No. 42	82m 5f
Ards Bridge and Lock No. 43	84m 1f
Ballinamore Bridge	84m 6f
Cloonsheerin Junction, junction with the Longford Branch	86m 0f
Killashee, Agnaskea Bridge and Killashee Top Lock No. 44	86m 4f
Savage Bridge and Killashee Bottom Lock No. 45	87m 0f
Ballydrum Bridge	87m 5f
Begnagh Bridge	88m 7f
Rinn Mount Lock No. 46	90m 0f
Cloondara, Richmond Harbour Wharves and Warehouses	90m 3f

Junction with River Shannon, Cloondara Cut Branch, at the tail of
Richmond Harbour Lock No. 47 . . . . 90m 4f

LOCKS

1. Liffey (Tidal Lock)
2. North Strand Lock
3. Double, Drumcondra Road
4. Double ⌐
5. Double ⟩ Cross-Guns
6. Double |
7. Double ⌐
8. Liffey Junction
9. Kelly's Bridge
10. Pellets town
11. Double, Ashtown or Longford Bridge
12. Double, Ashbrook
13. Double, Blanchardstown or Talbot Bridge
14. Decy Bridge
15. Jackson's Bridge
16. Chamber's Bridge
17. Double, Kilcock
18. Double, McLoghlin's or Ferrans Bridge
19. ⌐
20. |
21. |
22. ⟩ Killucan
23. |
24. |
25. |
26. ⌐
     Rise from Dublin
27. ⌐
28. ⟩ Coolnahay
29. ⌐
30. ⌐
31. |
32. ⟩ Kildallan
33. |
34. ⌐
35. Balroe Bridge
36. Ballynacarrigy

37. ⎤
38. ⎬ Castlegaddery
39. ⎦
40. Draper's Bridge
41. Mullawornia
42. Coolnahinch
43. Ards Bridge
44· ⎤
45. ⎦ Killashee
46. Rinn Mount
47. Richmond Harbour
        Fall to River Shannon

LONGFORD BRANCH

Cloonsheerin Junction, junction with Royal Canal, main line to -

Aghantrah Bridge	1m 0f
Cloonturk Bridge	2m 4f
Knockanboy Bridge	3m 0f
Cartronageeragh Bridge	3m 5f
Farranyoogan Bridge	4m 3f
Longford Harbour and terminus of Canal	5m 3f
Locks Nil	

DIMENSIONS

The maximum size of vessel which can navigate over the whole of the Royal Canal system is as follows:

Length: 70 feet.

Beam: 13 feet 1 inch.

Draught: 4 feet 6 inches (theoretical).

Headroom: 10 feet.

The dimensions of the locks on this canal vary considerably. Length varies from 81 feet down to 75 feet, and breadth from 14 feet 10 inches down to 13 feet 3¾ inches. The smallest lock is No. 19, Killucan Bottom, of which the dimensions are:

Length: 75 feet.

Width: 13 feet 3¾ inches.

The deepest lock on the canal is No. 13 Double Lock, Blanchardstown, which has a combined fall of 20 feet.

GRAND CANAL

MAIN LINE

JAMES'S STREET HARBOUR, DUBLIN TO LOWTOWN

Distance from James's Street Harbour, Dublin to -

Griffith Bridge over junction with the Ringsend Branch (L.)	
Suir Road Bridge and 1st Lock (Double Lock)	0m 7f
Goldenbridge, Footbridge and 2nd Lock	1m 2f
Inchicore, Blackhorse Bridge and 3rd Lock (Double Lock) . . .	1m 7f
4th, 5th, and 6th Locks	2m 1f
Ballyfermot Bridge and 7th Lock	3m 1f
8th Lock	3m 5f
Clondalkin Bridge and 9th Lock (Double Lock)	4m 6f
Clondalkin, 10th and 11th Locks	5m 2f
Lucan Road Bridge and 12th Lock	7m 1f
Gollierstown Bridge	8m 0f
Hazelhatch Bridge	10m 0f
Aylmer's Bridge, Kearneystown	11m 1f
Lyons House (L.) and 13th Lock (Double Lock)	11m 6f
Henry Bridge	12m 4f
Ponsonby Bridge	14m 0f
Devonshire Bridge and 14th Lock	14m 4f
15th Lock	15m 7f
Sallin's Wharf, Store and Bridge	17m 7f
Soldier's Island, junction with Naas and Corbally Branch (L.) . . .	18m 3f
Leinster Aqueduct over River Liffey	19m 0f
Digby Bridge and 16th Lock	20m 3f
Landenstown Bridge and 17th Lock	21m 0f
18th Lock (last rising lock from Dublin) summit level	21m 7f
Burgh Bridge (also called Cock Bridge)	22m 5f
Bonynge Bridge, junction with the Blackwood Feeder (R.), Blackwood Bridge (on Feeder) distant 1 mile 7 furlongs	25m 1f
Robertstown, Wharf, Store and Binn's Bridge	25m 1f
Lowtown, junction with the old Barrow Line Canal (now used in conjunction with the Milltown Feeder and not for navigation (L.) . . .	26m 0f

SHANNON LINE

LOWTOWN TO SHANNON HARBOUR

Lowtown, 19th Lock (first falling Lock to Shannon) and Fenton Bridge . .	26m 0f
Lowtown, junction with the Barrow Line Canal, Jetty and Store . . .	26m 1f

Bond Bridge, Derrymullen	27m 1f
Shee Bridge, Allenwood	28m 0f
Hamilton's Bridge, Killina	30m 3f
Kilpatrick, Briquette Factory	31m 2f
Hartley Bridge, Ticknevin	32m 4f
Ticknevin, 20th Lock	33m 0f
Blundell Aqueduct (The Tunnel)	35m 7f
Downshire Bridge over junction with the Edenderry Branch Canal	
(R.) Edenderry Wharf and Store, distant 1 mile	37m 0f
Colgan's Bridge	37m 2f
George's Bridge, Killan	37m 3f
Rathmore Bridge	37m 7f
Cartland Bridge, Ballycolgan	38m 7f
Trimblestown Bridge, Ballybrittan	40m 1f
Rhode Bridge	42m 7f
Toberdaly Bridge	43m 4f
Killeen Bridge	46m 3f
Molesworth Bridge, Daingean (Philipstown), Wharf and Store	48m 0f
Chevenix Bridge, Ballycommon, and Campbell Bridge over	
junction with the Kilbeggan Canal (disused) (R.) Kilbeggan,	
distant 8 miles 3 furlongs	51m 3f
Ballycommon, 21st Lock	51m 5f
22nd Lock and Digby Bridge, Cappyroe	52m 4f
23rd Lock	52m 7f
24th Lock	54m 6f
25th Lock and Digby Bridge, Cappincur	55m 1f
26th Lock	55m 5f
Tullamore, Bury (or Whitehall) Bridge over junction with Tullamore	
Harbour (L.), Tullamore Harbour, Wharves and Stores	56m 4f
Tullamore, Kilbeggan Road Bridge	56m 6f
Tullamore, 27th Lock and Cox's Bridge	57m 0f
Tullamore, 28th Lock	57m 2f
Shra Bridge, Ballydrohead	58m 2f
29th Lock and Ballycowan Bridge	59m 3f
Ballycowan Castle and Huband Aqueduct	59m 5f
Charleville Aqueduct	60m 2f
Corcoran's Bridge, Rahan	61m 7f
Becan's Bridge, Rahan	62m 5f
Henesy's Bridge	63m 2f
30th Lock and Ballincloughin Bridge	63m 6f
31st Lock and Cornalour Bridge	64m 2f
Plunkett Bridge, Pollagh	66m 4f
Derry Bridge	69m 7f
McCartney Aqueduct, Silver River	71m 2f
Armstrong Bridge, Gallen	73m 1f

Noggus Bridge	73m 4f
32nd Lock and Glyn Bridge	74m 0f
Judges Bridge	74m 6f
33rd Lock (Double Lock) and Belmont Bridge	75m 2f
L'Estrange Bridge	76m 7f
34th Lock and Clonony Bridge	77m 4f
Shannon Harbour, Griffith Bridge	78m 3f
" " Wharves and Stores	78m 5f
35th Lock	78m 6f
36th Lock	79m 0f
Ferry and junction with River Shannon	79m 3f

BALLINASLOE LINE

RIVER SHANNON TO BALLINASLOE

Fanning Lock (37th Lock)	79m 4f
Clonfert Bridge	83m 0f
Kylmore Bridge and 38th Lock	86m 4f
Lismany Bridge	88m 4f
Poolboy Bridge	91m 7f
Dunlo Bridge	93m 0f
Ballinasloe Harbour, Wharves and Stores. Terminus of Canal . . .	93m 3f

RINGSEND BRANCH OR CIRCULAR LINE

From junction with Main Line at Griffith Bridge to -

Harberton Bridge	0m 3f
Camac Bridge, Dolphins Barn	0m 5f
Parnell Bridge	1m 0f
Robert Emmet Bridge, Harolds Cross	1m 3f
La Touch Bridge, Portobello Harbour and Portobello Lock	1m 6f
Charlemount Bridge and Lock	2m 0f
Eustace Bridge, Leeson St. and Leeson St. Lock	2m 3f
McCartney Bridge, Baggot St., and Baggot St. Lock	2m 6f
Huband Bridge and Upper Mount St. Lock	3m 0f
McKenny Bridge and Lower Mount St. Lock	3m 1f
Maquay Bridge and Grand Canal St. Lock. Entrance to Inner Basin, Ringsend Docks	3m 2f
Victoria Bridge (Swing Bridge), Ringsend Road. Entrance from Outer to Inner Basin, Ringsend Docks	3m 4f
Westmoreland Lock (Sea Lock), junction with River Liffey	3m 6f

NAAS AND CORBALLY BRANCH

From Soldiers' Island, junction with Grand Canal Main Line to -

1st Lock Naas Canal	⎤
2nd " " " and Leinster Mills	⎟
3rd " " "	⎟
4th " " "	⎬ 2m 4f
5th " " "	⎟
Naas, Wharves and Stores	⎦
Corbally Harbour and terminus of Canal	7m 7f

BARROW LINE CANAL
AND RIVER BARROW NAVIGATION

Distance from junction with Shannon Line at Lowtown to -

Littletown Bridge	0m 7f
Ballyteague Bridge	1m 6f
20th Lock, Ballyteague	2m 1f
21st " "	2m 2f
22nd Lock, Glenaree and Glenaree Bridge	5m 2f
Rathangan Bridge, Wharf and Store	7m 6f
23rd Lock (Double Lock) and Spencer Bridge	8m 2f
Wilson's Bridge	9m 5f
Umeras Bridge	11m 1f
24th Lock, Ballykelly (Double Lock) and Bridge	13m 0f
Shepard's Brook (or High) Bridge	13m 7f
Monasterevan, Wharf, Stores, Drawbridge and Aqueduct over River Barrow	14m 3f
Junction with Mountmellick Branch Canal (R.)	14m 4f
25th Lock and Moore's Bridge	14m 5f
Maryboro Road Bridge, Clougheen	15m 0f
Wooden Bridge	16m 4f
Fishertown Bridge	18m 2f
Courtwood Bridge	19m 3f
Vicarstown Bridge	21m 6f
Camac Aqueduct	22m 5f
Ballymanus Bridge	23m 0f
Milltown Bridge	25m 5f
Cardington Bridge and 26th Lock	27m 6f
Lennon's Bridge	27m 7f
Athy, 27th Lock, Wharves, Stores, and Augustus Bridge	28m 2f
28th Lock and Horse Bridge (Canal enters River Barrow) . . .	28m 4f
Ardreigh Lock	29m 3f
Tankardstown Bridge	32m 3f

Levitstown Lock	32m 6f
Manganey Bridge	34m 6f
Manganey Lock	35m 5f
Bestfield Lock	38m 2f
Carlow, Wharves and Warehouses	39m 7f
Carlow Bridge	40m 0f
Carlow Lock	40m 1f
Clogrennan Lock	42m 0f
Milford Bridge	44m 0f
Milford Lock	44m 5f
Rathvindon Lock	47m 1f
Leighlin Bridge	47m 6f
Rathellen Lock	49m 4f
Bagnalstown, Wharf and Store	50m 4f
Bagnalstown (or Lodge) Lock	50m 6f
Royal Oak Bridge	51m 4f
Fenniscourt Lock	53m 0f
Slyguff Lock	54m 4f
Upper Ballyellen Lock	56m 0f
Goresbridge, Bridge, Wharf and Store	56m 7f
Lower Ballyellen Lock	57m 4f
Ballytiglea Lock	59m 1f
Ballytiglea Bridge	60m 0f
Borris Lock	60m 6f
Ballingrane Lock	62m 2f
Clashganny Lock	63m 5f
Ballykeenan Lock (Double Lock)	64m 3f
Graigue-na-managh, Bridge, Wharf and Store	65m 7f
Graigue Lock (Tinnahinch)	66m 1f
Lower Tinnahinch Lock (Knockeen)	67m 1f
Carriglead Lock	68m 0f
St. Mullins Lock (Tidal)	69m 7f

At this point the Navigation enters the tidal section of the River Barrow not under the jurisdiction of the Grand Canal Company. The tidal portion continues as follows:

Mountgarret Bridge	77m 4f
Ringwood, junction with River Nore Navigation (derelict)	78m 6f
New Ross Bridge	81m 4f
Annagh's Castle (R.)	83m 1f
Dollar Point (L.)	88m 7f
Ballinlaw Ferry	90m 2f
Snow Hill Point (R.) and junction with River Suir (R.).	
Waterford distant 5 miles 4 furlongs, Carrick-on-Suir 24 miles	
6 furlongs	91m 6f
Dunbrody Creek (L.) and Cheek Point (R.)	93m 5f

INDEX